D0712290

Philosophy as Fiction

PHILOSOPHY AS FICTION

SELF, DECEPTION, AND

KNOWLEDGE IN PROUST

Joshua Landy

UNIVERSITY PRESS

2004

OXFORD

UNIVERSITY PRESS

Oxford   New York

Auckland   Bangkok   Buenos Aires   Cape Town   Chennai
Dar es Salaam   Delhi   Hong Kong   Istanbul   Karachi   Kolkata
Kuala Lumpur   Madrid   Melbourne   Mexico City   Mumbai   Nairobi
São Paulo   Shanghai   Taipei   Tokyo   Toronto

Copyright © 2004 by Oxford University Press, Inc.

Published by Oxford University Press, Inc.
198 Madison Avenue, New York, New York 10016

www.oup.com

Oxford is a registered trademark of Oxford University Press

Library of Congress Cataloging-in-Publication Data
Landy, Joshua, 1965–
Philosophy as fiction : self, deception, and knowledge in Proust / Joshua Landy.
p. cm.
Includes bibliographical references and index.
ISBN 0-19-516939-5
1. Proust, Marcel, 1871–1922—Criticism and interpretation.   2. Self in literature.
3. Deception in literature.   4. Knowledge, Theory of, in literature.   I. Title.
PQ2631.R63Z6577 2004
843'.912—dc22   200306085

1 3 5 7 9 8 6 4 2

Printed in the United States of America
on acid-free paper

ACKNOWLEDGMENTS

This book is the result of a failure to take two very good pieces of advice: one, hurry up and write a book based on your dissertation; two, don't, under any circumstances, produce a monograph. Having unaccountably made life harder for myself by setting aside the thesis and writing something devoted entirely to Proust, I am all the more indebted to those who have helped me along the way.

Alison Finch must take the credit, or blame, for introducing me to Proust back in 1988. In traditional Cambridge fashion, I had two weeks to read *Du côté de chez Swann*, think about it (I suppose, to be fair, that thinking was optional), and write an essay for our next tutorial. After one week, I had made it as far as page 72, but had forgotten every word I'd read. After two weeks, I had read 72 pages *twice*. The tutorial never took place, but I thank Alison for forgiving me, and for all her subsequent encouragement and assistance.

I made it through a little more of the *Recherche* while a graduate student at Princeton, in the company of André Aciman (who understands the paradoxes of jealousy, at what I hope is only a theoretical level) and Brigitte Mahuzier (whose syllabus I still treasure). I benefited too, in various ways, from the advice of my fellow students, notably Margit Dementi, Kasia Jerzak, and Richard Kaye. And my debt to Alexander Nehamas and Thomas Pavel, already considerable then, has continued to grow ever since. They remain models for me of what it is to live the scholarly life.

It is, however, at Stanford that *Philosophy as Fiction* really began to take shape, and I consider myself blessed to have fallen among such inspiring and magnanimous colleagues. Robert Harrison has been a steadfast mentor and friend, and I am also grateful to him, in his capacity as chair, for granting me a six-month leave to complete the manuscript. (An earlier leave was made possible by the Stanford Humanities Center and its thoughtful director, Keith

Baker.) Hans Ulrich Gumbrecht has aided and supported me in ways too numerous to mention—not least by means of his Pindaric advice to "sound like
myself"—as well as creating, almost single-handedly, an intellectual environment conducive to literary-philosophical investigations. Marjorie Perloff
was kind enough to offer helpful comments on the introduction. And Andrea
Nightingale, who sat patiently some years ago while I improvised an outline
of chapter 2, has done wonders, in addition, for my overall mental health. All
of these senior colleagues have gone out of their way to foster my development, far beyond the call of duty. More, they have made it a sheer delight to
be where I am.

Since coming to Stanford, I have twice taught a graduate seminar entitled
"Getting through Proust," and have been just as fortunate in my students as
I have been in my senior colleagues. I have greatly appreciated discussions
with Dustin King about the place of Marcel's project in his life, with Hervé
Picherit about the potential series of future novels, and with Heather Webb
about Albertine's lesbianism; Trina Marmarelli has served as *mot juste* con-
sultant; and Matthew Tiews has provided invaluable and extensive editorial
assistance at every stage of the process.

My colleagues "across the bay," Robert Alter, Leo Bersani, Carol Cosman,
and Karen Feldman, have been charitable enough not to hold it against me
that I teach where I do. Michael Lucey and Debarati Sanyal raised extremely
important issues when I gave a talk on the Martinville steeples at Berkeley's
French department; the discussion of "metonyphor" in chapter 1 is, I trust,
somewhat stronger as a result. From further afield, Robert Pippin, Roger
Shattuck, Jean-Yves Tadié (who confirmed a hunch about a certain piece
of toast), and Miguel Tamen have supplied excellent suggestions. And in
their different ways, Jean-Marie Apostolidès, Emma Blake, Malcolm Bowie,
Erin Carlston, Julia N. Caskey, Amir Eshel, J. Benjamin Hurlbut, Adrienne
Janus, Richard Rorty, Michael T. Saler, and Richard Terdiman have each
contributed to this project, as indeed have sundry Landys (Barry, Gertie, and
Rosalind). Above all, however, I am beholden to my friend, colleague, team
teacher, coauthor, and general partner-in-crime R. Lanier Anderson: the
reciprocal influence can be felt on almost every page.

Versions of chapter 2, chapter 3, and the coda appeared in *Philosophy and
Literature*, *New Literary History*, and the *Cambridge Companion to Proust*,
respectively. I am grateful to Johns Hopkins University Press and to Cambridge University Press for permission to reproduce those writings, and to
Denis Dutton, Nancy Easterlin, Ralph Cohen, and Richard Bales for their
generosity and sage advice. Thanks also to Meir Sternberg at *Poetics Today*
and to my infinitely gracious editor at Oxford, Elissa Morris.

CONTENTS

ABBREVIATIONS

Proust

I, II, III, IV	respective volumes of *A la recherche du temps perdu* (Pléiade, 1987–88)
BA	Introduction to *La Bible d'Amiens*
BG	*Within a Budding Grove*
BSB	*By Way of Sainte-Beuve*
C	*The Captive*
Corr.	*Correspondance* (Plon, 21 vols.)
CSB	*Contre Sainte-Beuve*
EA	*Essais et articles*
F	*The Fugitive*
GW	*The Guermantes Way*
JS	*Jean Santeuil*
MPG	*Matinée chez la Princesse de Guermantes*
PM	*Pastiches et mélanges*
S	*Swann's Way*
SG	*Sodom and Gomorrah*
TR	*Time Regained*

(*Translations from Corr., EA, and PM, as well as from* Chroniques *and the* Carnet de 1908, *are my own.*)

Nietzsche

ASC	"Attempt at a Self-Criticism" (in BT)
BGE	*Beyond Good and Evil*
BT	*The Birth of Tragedy*
DS	*David Strauss, the Confessor and the Writer*
EH	*Ecce Homo*

HI	*On the Uses and Disadvantages of History for Life*
GM	*The Genealogy of Morals*
GS	*The Gay Science*
NW	*Nietzsche's Werke* (Naumann, 1903)
TI	*Twilight of the Idols*
TL	"On Truth and Lies in a Nonmoral Sense"
WP	*The Will to Power*

Philosophy as Fiction

INTRODUCTION

Philosophy and Fiction (Nobody's Madeleine)

Houses, roads, avenues are as fugitive, alas, as the years.

—The narrator, in *Swann's Way*

That moment from long ago still adhered to me and I could still find it again, could retrace my steps to it, merely by descending to a greater depth within myself.

—The narrator, in *Time Regained*

Only at the end of the book . . . will my position be revealed. The one I put forward at the end of the first volume, in that excursus on the Bois de Boulogne . . . , is the *opposite* of my conclusion. It is just a step . . . on the way to the most objective and optimistic of conclusions. If someone were to infer from this that my attitude is a disenchanted skepticism, it would be exactly as though a spectator, having seen the end of the first act of *Parsifal* . . . , imagined Wagner to be saying that purity of heart leads nowhere. . . .

I did not want to analyze this evolution of a belief system abstractly, but rather to recreate it, to bring it to life. I am therefore obliged to depict errors, without feeling compelled to say that I consider them to be errors; too bad for

me if the reader believes I take them for the truth.

—Marcel Proust, to Jacques Rivière (February 1914)

PART 1: PHILOSOPHY

1. "Untenable, Unoriginal, and Uninteresting"

From one point of view, *In Search of Lost Time* has all the endorsement it
requires. It has long established itself as a classic, ranking alongside Joyce's
Ulysses and Beckett's *Endgame* as a tour de force of modernist craftsman-
ship. It is taught not only at universities but in some high schools besides;
it has inspired theatre, film, and even comic strip adaptations; it has been
pillaged for advice on improved quality of life; many a pilgrimage (which
doubtless has Proust turning in his grave) is made to "Combray," Cabourg,
and Caen; and lovers of Proust, as many of us know from personal experience, are regularly presented with baskets of madeleines, if not with entire
cookbooks based on the voluminous novel. From another point of view,
though, and however surprising it might sound, Proust's *Recherche* stands
today in need of rehabilitation. For what has been somewhat lost from sight,
or what has perhaps never been fully appreciated, is the profound philosophical significance of a text that is, after all, only a fiction. In addition to
constituting a brilliant reworking of the novelistic form, it also has a substantial contribution to make to philosophy; the formal innovation, which
seems at first to undermine the conceptual impact, turns out to bolster it in
intriguing and powerful ways.

   It is worth the effort to reconstruct in detail the arguments Proust makes,
based both on what his narrator says and (more interestingly) on what the
latter *fails* to say, about the operations of the mind: the types of distortion it
imposes on experience; the illusions it requires and knows how to sustain; the
dispersions to which it is subject, both simultaneous (when, say, reason com-
bats a particular desire) and sequential (when that desire gives way, in time,
to another); and the strategies it possesses, finally, for putting itself back together. Some extremely important work has already been done in this domain (one thinks, for instance, of Leo Bersani's *Marcel Proust: The Fictions
of Life and Art* and of Georges Poulet's *L'espace proustien*). But large gaps
remain, owing to the prevalence of critics who believe, and in some cases
set out to demonstrate, that Proust's philosophy is untenable, unoriginal, or
uninteresting.

   For the Otherwise-Interested, the core of the novel resides in the insight
it offers into the mind of its writer (Maar), in its treatment of homosexuality

(Sedgwick), in its Balzacian/Saint-Simonian dissection of contemporary social relations (Wolitz), or in its part-cunning, part-accidental play with language (de Man). While the Biographers—those, that is, who wish to translate every event in the novel back into an episode in Proust's life, like inverse alchemists turning gold into lead—may not always come away with usable data, while some "queer theorists" succumb to analogous alchemical enticements, and while the linguistically minded have occasionally been known to let their cynical tendencies get the better of them, still Proust's house does have many mansions, and there is much to be gleaned from looking under the multiple and miscellaneous beds. (Important archaeological discoveries have been made, for example, by Elisabeth Ladenson in *Proust's Lesbianism* and by Antoine Compagnon in *Proust entre deux siècles*.) We should merely be careful to check *all* of the square footage, and to start, if possible, at the front of the house.

We should also avoid the temptation to reduce Proust's position to that of an illustrious philosophical predecessor.[1] When, for example, Gilles Deleuze nonchalantly notes that "Proust is a Platonist" (165), he is doing him something of an injustice.[2] It is true that symphonies and sculptures sometimes appear, in Proust, to fall from a bona fide Beyond (the world of Forms, perhaps). But "appear" is the operative word. We do not read that musical motifs are actually Platonic Ideas, but instead that Swann, the half-hearted aesthete with a palpable "ignorance of music" (S 294–95), "*regarded* musical motifs as actual ideas, from another world" (S 496; translation modified, emphasis added). Similarly, we do not read that the pleasure Swann derives from Vinteuil's sonata is the pleasure of gaining entry into the *au-delà*, but merely that it is "*akin* . . . to the pleasure which he would have derived . . . from entering into contact with a world for which we men were not made" (S 336, again my emphasis).[3] Proust's narrator—to whom, following convention, I shall habitually refer as "Marcel"—has something very different to say when he speaks in his own voice on the subject: "art," he writes, "exteriorises in the colours of the spectrum the intimate composition of those worlds which we call individuals" (C 343). Far from giving access to a single, transcendent realm shared, at moments of ecstasy, by all human beings indiscriminately, compositions and paintings provide a passport to many, infinitely many universes, each consisting in the perspective of the relevant creator. About this view, which is fully endorsed by Proust,[4] there is nothing particularly Platonic.

Nor, for the same reason, is there anything particularly Schopenhauerian or Schellingian about it, however much Anne Henry, who feels that "Vinteuil's score is written by Schopenhauer" (1981: 8), may insist on the connection. Since, on the Proustian approach, an artwork conveys nothing more nor less than the perspective of its maker, what we perceive in it is not the gleam of Platonic Ideas, not the "teleological fulfillment of nature which makes use of the creator's person in order to become visible to itself" (ibid. 279), and not the metaphysical Will either.[5] The sole and only reference to "la Volonté en soi" in the *Recherche* is couched in negative terms (I:524/BG 146), and elsewhere *volonté* tends to designate a faculty within the individual, indeed a faculty far too practical—"toiling incessantly . . . to ensure that the self may never lack what is needed" (BG 614)—to be what Schopenhauer has in mind. It is true that Marcel's views on love often have a pessimistic flavor: just as *The World as Will and Representation* states that "the nature of man consists in the fact that his will strives, is satisfied, strives anew, and so on and on," and that "the non-appearance of satisfaction is suffering; the empty longing for a new desire is languor, boredom" (I:52), so Marcel laments that "there can be no peace of mind in love, since what one has obtained is never anything but a new starting-point for further desires" (BG 213) and that "my life with Albertine was on the one hand, when I was not jealous, nothing but boredom, and on the other hand, when I was jealous, nothing but pain" (C 530). But whereas for Schopenhauer the appropriate response is clear-sighted resignation, for Marcel (and for Proust)[6] it is self-deception. (I return to the topic of necessary illusions in chapter 2.) As Duncan Large convincingly speculates (24), Proust ends up in a position very similar to Nietzsche's simply by reacting in the same way against Schopenhauer, while knowing almost nothing of Nietzsche's work.

"To Schopenhauerian principles," writes Henry, "Proust accords . . . an axiomatic immunity"; "Proust . . . follows Schopenhauer's descriptions step by step" (2000: 56, 1981: 49). Such emphatic statements, and even the more moderate claims of Samuel Beckett (19, 91–93), should come as a bit of a surprise. For Proust is no Western Buddhist—"this subjective idealism," he complains at one point, "is a little boring" (EA 332)—and neither is his character, at least not for long. The beautiful picture Marcel inherits from Bergotte, all that talk of the "vain dream of life" and the "inexhaustible torrent of fair forms," is already abandoned by the time he reaches college, where "the metaphysicians to whom I was actually to become attached . . . would resemble him in nothing" (S 134). What is more, Bergotte himself, whose "language had in it something down-to-earth . . . which disappointed those who expected to hear him speak only of the 'eternal torrent of forms'" (BG 171), appears less than fully committed to his own theory. Not only, then, does Proust find subjective idealism unfounded and dull, but he also implicitly accuses its advocates of hypocrisy. Chief among them Schopenhauer, notorious for the lavishness of his meals: "I knew, of course, that idealism, even subjective idealism, did not prevent great philosophers from still having hearty appetites," says Marcel (GW 273), with a knowing wink in the direction of Frankfurt.

If, such evidence notwithstanding, Henry continues to view Proust's novel as "the most literal translation" of *The World as Will and Representa-*

tion (1989: 24), it is because her motivation is polemical, her aim to correct (indeed to abolish) "the previous hermeneutic tradition which contented itself with admiring [the *Recherche* as] the product of brilliant intentions" (1981: 45). In her opinion, Proust's writings not only accord on every single point and down to the finest detail with a given philosophical system but are even *generated* from that system (96), each character or event representing one of its aspects, in a vast and slavishly accurate allegory. Proust's sole contribution consists in fictionalizing the ideas he has lifted "faithfully" (53) and "point by point" (68) from previous thinkers. As Henry puts it, "his stroke of genius was that he managed to extract a coherent novelistic situation from a system of aesthetics, scrupulously transforming its every illustrative clause into a dramatic structure" (1981: 258); "the originality of the *Recherche* resides in the ingenious exploitation of these [Schopenhauerian] propositions" (2000: 61).[7]

Henry's spirit of polemicism is shared, mutatis mutandis, by Jonathan Dancy, whose stated ambition, in the sardonically titled "New Truths in Proust?," is to prove that all of Proust's insights can be subsumed under, and indeed surpassed by, David Hume's "momentary theory" of selfhood. (In chapter 3, I shall set out Proust's complicated response to Hume, and explain its cogency.) And Henry's idea that the *Recherche* does no more than dramatize arguments and propositions is shared by Richard Chessick, who sees it as "an artistic illustration of [Henri] Bergson's philosophy" (19).[8] To be sure, when it comes to Bergson (as opposed to Plato or Schopenhauer), one can fully understand why scholars like Chessick (and Curtius) would wish to press the connection. Proust heard Bergson speak at the Collège de France in 1900 and had read and annotated *Matière et mémoire* by 1911.[9] Like Proust, Bergson holds that our memories remain stored within us indefinitely, albeit unconsciously, and are in principle all available at once: as Roger Shattuck points out (144), the famous early line from the *Recherche*, "when a man is asleep, he has in a circle around him the chain of the hours, the sequence of the years, the order of the heavenly bodies" (S 4), is strikingly reminiscent of Bergson's claim that "a human being who *dreamed* his life ... would probably thus keep constantly in sight the infinite multitude of details of his past history."[10] And though Proust himself vehemently denies it, Bergson shares with him a belief that some of the memories return unbidden—"involuntarily" (Proust), "spontaneously" (Bergson)—in a procedure during which "a multitude of events contiguous to the memory trace immediately attach themselves to the [present] perception."[11]

Still, matters are not so straightforward when it comes to temporality. On the one hand, Proust would probably agree with Bergson that the conscious mind distorts reality by taking "snapshots" of it (*Creative Evolution* 306), artificially arresting the movement brought about by duration. "Although we know that the years pass," writes Marcel, "the manner in which—by means of a sort of snapshot—we take cognisance of this moving universe whirled along by Time, has the contrary effect of immobilising it" (TR 402). On the other hand, the narrator is referring here to changes that take place over long periods ("years"), not to a flux that happens in the moment, that indeed vitiates the very notion of a "moment." If "we always see as young the men and women whom we have known young" (ibid.), the problem is not that we took a mental photograph of them long ago, but rather that we have not taken another more recently; our freeze-frames are just *outdated*, not *inaccurate*. Whereas for Bergson time merely *appears* (erroneously) to consist in a succession of isolated instants, for Proust time really *is* a succession of isolated instants. And an important corollary, which I will discuss at length in chapter 3, is that the Self really *is* an accumulation of discrete states.[12]

In short, there *are* "new truths in Proust." His novel is not just a fictionalized *Creative Evolution*, a dramatized *World as Will and Representation*, a storybook *System of Transcendental Idealism*, or a *Phaedrus* with a little less dialogue. There are indeed echoes of Bergson, of Leibniz, and, we now know thanks to Anne Henry's painstaking research, of one Gabriel Séailles in the *Recherche*. But Proust is, to repeat, closer to Nietzsche—whose work he barely knew—than to any other philosopher, and Alexander Nehamas and (more recently) Duncan Large have helped immeasurably to make Proust's actual commitments perceptible. What we might wish to add to Nehamas's account is the fact that Proust sometimes goes *beyond* the Nietzschean schema, in ways I specify in chapter 3; and what we might want to subtract from Large's is the notion that Proust ultimately fails to create a workable position.

Large is not alone in his view. Instead a fairly sizeable group of scholars (whom, with due apologies to Eliot Ness, we might dub *The Untenables*) have assigned themselves the mission of putting Proust in the dock, no matter what the charges. For Vincent Descombes, the perspectivist understanding of art I described above cannot hold, because (in the view of Wittgensteinians like himself) prelinguistic mental contents do not exist; for Martha Nussbaum, the inaccessibility of other minds is an intolerable, almost immoral doctrine, which she ascribes to Proust's personal foibles; for Duncan Large, the *Recherche* represents an abortive bid on Proust's part to fashion his own life; and for David Ellison, it is "a work that presents itself, *stricto sensu*, as unreadable" (1984: 176).[13] I shall address the criticisms of Ellison, Large, and Nussbaum in the remainder of this introduction, and those of Descombes and Paul de Man (Ellison's deconstructionist precursor) in chapter 1. It is one of the primary aims of my book to show that if we employ the principle of charity rather than the hermeneutics of suspicion, we can in fact extract a consistent, powerful, and original philosophical system from *A la recherche du temps perdu*.

2. A Philosophy of Mind in the Moralist Tradition

If we wish, then, to start at the front of the many-roomed house that is Proust's novel, we need to think philosophically and literarily more than sociologically and linguistically. Proust himself clearly thought of his novel as dealing primarily with philosophical issues. While titles of the individual volumes occasionally gesture in the direction of class structure (*Le côté des Guermantes*) or identity politics (*Sodome et Gomorrhe*), the unifying header, *A la recherche du temps perdu*, presents the work as a reflection on broader questions. So, too, most of the other possibilities Proust entertained, such as *Les intermittences du coeur*, *Les intermittences du passé*, *Les stalactites du passé*, *L'espérance du passé*, *Le visiteur du passé*, *Le voyageur dans le passé*, *Les reflets du passé*, *Les reflets du temps*, and *Les miroirs du rêve* (Corr. 11:151, 12:231), display a preoccupation with temporality (lost time, sedimented time, time regained) and with subjectivity. What is more, the former is easily subsumable under the latter: time here means memory, and memory is of course subject to the vicissitudes of human consciousness, flowing freely when unbidden, ebbing as soon as summoned. In fact, all of the novel's major motifs—time, love, art, interpretation, knowledge, personal identity—are but special cases or illustrations of *a general theory about minds and their relations with the world*, about the illusions they entertain, the types of fragmentation they experience, the subtle consistencies they manifest, and (above all) the range of faculties they deploy.

In as much as he is fascinated by the interplay of such faculties, and in as much as he borrows terminology from La Rochefoucauld and company, we could call Proust a *philosopher of mind in the moralist tradition*.[14] "I attempt in my novels to place myself within their school," he writes (EA 282), referring to the seventeenth-century French *moralistes*; and sure enough, some of the maxims in the *Recherche*, whether reducing virtue to hidden vice ("nobility is often no more than the inner aspect which our egotistical feelings assume when we have not yet named and classified them" [BG 87]) or parsing self-esteem into vanity, conceit and concern with appearances ("I was extremely sensitive to the opinion of others. Not that this kind of unconfessed self-esteem [*amour-propre*] has anything to do with vanity or conceit" [BG 590–91]), could easily have been written by La Rochefoucauld. For the most part, however, the influence is more discreet and less direct, taking the form of a vocabulary for, and an interest in the quirks and paradoxes associated with, the mechanics of deliberation and action.

First paradox: *all significant cognition depends more on intuition than on intellect*. Those objective facts that intellect is able to cull are not "what is most important to our hearts or to our minds," since objective facts are, by definition, external to "the domain of what is for each one of us the sole real-

ity, [namely,] the domain of his own sensibility" (TR 284). The only type of
knowledge we care about, the only kind that can transform our life, is knowledge of subjective "truths," and such knowledge is granted by intuition.[15]
Hence, for reasons set out in chapter 1, our intuition not only precedes but
also *supersedes* the workings of our intelligence. And there is, in addition, a
corollary: *it is rational not to be too rational.* "It is life that, little by little, case
by case, enables us to observe that what is most important to our hearts or
to our minds is taught us not by reasoning but by other powers," contends
Marcel. "And then it is the intelligence itself which, acknowledging their
superiority, abdicates to them through reasoning" (F 569).[16] Or, as the *Contre
Sainte-Beuve* would have it, "if intellect ranks only second in the hierarchy
of virtues, intellect alone is able to proclaim that the first place must be given
to instinct" (BSB 21).

Conversely, the second paradox: *in certain contexts, intellect keeps us ignorant.* Although the intellect manages perfectly well under ordinary circumstances—identifying an acquaintance after a gap of many years (BG 550–51,
TR 337), deciphering an impressionist painting (BG 569), mapping a complicated piece of music (C 501–2)—it is easily corrupted by desire (SG 705,
F 824); when an emotional investment is at stake, it does not so much reason
as *rationalize*, constructing endless "pretexts" (TR 275) for doing what we
already wanted to do and believing what we had already decided to believe.
Inexhaustibly creative (C 21), maintaining close contacts to (perhaps being
synonymous with?) the imaginative faculty, intellect roams unconstrained,
has an answer for everything, and produces systems of perfect internal coherence, arguments that are so palpably *valid* it is hard to remember that
they may not be *sound.* "The ideas formed by the pure intelligence have no
more than a logical, a possible truth," Marcel reminds us. "Not that the ideas
which we form for ourselves cannot be correct in logic; that they may well be,
but we cannot know whether they are true" (TR 275).[17]

Thus we are wrong in conceiving of the intellect as "a means, of no importance in itself, of trying to attain to certain external verities" (BG 199):
the way it functions, the very feature that guarantees its success in reaching
some of those "external verities," is the same feature that prevents it from
ever gaining an accurate assessment of *inner* verities, whether they concern
our bodily condition (TR 352), our feelings (F 564), or our needs (BG 614).
Data does not travel to consciousness through a pure, clear conduit "of no
importance in itself," but rather through a *machine*, an apparatus that processes the raw material, sometimes beyond recognition. What is more, we
are *happy* that intellect prevents us from learning the (objective) truth. For
as the third paradox states, *intellect is essential to love.* At least, intellect is essential to the *continuation* of love, once jealousy has set in. From the moment
that intuition, which had previously spent its time telling us how attractive
the other person is, begins telling us how untrustworthy she is, and how little

she differs in herself from her peers,[18] the only thing that can save us from its relentless, nagging skepticism is the "on the whole optimistic" intelligence (BG 278). Chapter 2 will explain how both of these paradoxes operate.

As for the *birth* of love, that—less surprisingly—falls within the purview of sensibility and imagination, working in tandem. While sensibility intuits that a given person is a token of one's affectional "type" (Albertine, for example, belongs to the class "elusive women"), imagination "makes us extract from a woman so special a notion of individuality that she appears to us unique in herself and predestined and necessary for us" (F 677). What is perhaps more surprising is that the overvaluation, which necessarily carries with it such enduring and devastating consequences for our emotional life, is, for all that, devoutly to be wished: "whatever the inevitable disappointments that it must bring in its train, this movement toward what we have only glimpsed, what we have been free to dwell upon and imagine at our leisure, this movement is the only one that is wholesome for the senses, that whets the appetite" (BG 620). Love, which gives us not only pleasure but also insight into who we are, subsists on illusion.

Most remarkable of all is the role imagination has to play in personhood, so remarkable that it is worthy of being considered a fourth paradox: *in order to become who we are, we must believe we are something else.* For reasons I will spell out in detail in chapter 3, self-fashioning involves a delicate mixture of clear-sightedness and creativity, and can even involve a simultaneous awareness of the illusion under which we are laboring. (Fifth paradox: *I know it is false, but I believe it anyway.*) If, then, readers of the *Recherche* can rightly say that there is philosophy in the fiction, they should be careful to add that there is, in addition, *fiction in the philosophy*. Indeed, it is precisely because it recognizes the crucial importance of fantasy in the process of self-fashioning, while at the same time tackling traditional philosophical questions with traditional philosophical arguments, that the *Recherche* constitutes such a paradigm case of a literary philosophy—not just a philosophy *in* literature but a philosophy *of* literature, a painstaking presentation of the role fiction has to play in the formation of a successful human life.

3. Intellect and Intuition

Imagination, then, occupies a commanding position in the Proustian geography of the mind. An equally strategic site is held by the will: just as the heart, in Pascal's schema, "has reasons of which reason knows nothing" (146), so here the conative faculty seems to command its own type of understanding, a preternatural awareness of how the needs of the organism as a whole can best be served. It knows when we should follow our instinct, ignoring the dismissive claims intellect makes about the value of pleasures that are assured (BG 614–15), and it knows when we should follow our intellect, ignoring the urgent demands of instinct that we make life as painful for ourselves as possible (for which antithetical impulses, see chapter 2). Still, both imagination and *volonté* are remote outcrops in the landscape compared to the imposing masses of intellect (also known as reason) and intuition (also known, here, as instinct, sensibility, and unconscious mind).[19] So imposing are they, in fact, that one could almost call the novel as a whole an extended meditation on the interplay between the intuition and the intellect, on their conjunctions, collisions, and occasional collusions.

The previous section showed how intellect and intuition can function autonomously, giving us, respectively, knowledge of the world and knowledge of oneself, and further how they can come into conflict, conjuring up optimistic and pessimistic "hypotheses" (again respectively) about the inner lives of other people. Now from time to time, intellect and intuition may also go hand in hand. Famously, they conspire to bring about the phenomenon of involuntary memory: it is only because "voluntary memory, the memory of the intellect" (S 59) has intervened, discarding from our mnemonic record anything it cannot use "for its own rational purposes" (TR 260), that involuntary memory, housed in *sensibilité* (SG 590), can do its work. Hence

> what best reminds us of a person is precisely what we had forgotten (*because it was of no importance*, and we therefore left it in full possession of its strength). That is why the better part of our memories exists outside us, in a blatter of rain, in the smell of an unaired room or of the first crackling brushwood fire in a cold grate: wherever, in short, we happen upon what our mind [*notre intelligence*], *having no use for it*, had rejected. . . . Outside us? Within us, rather, but hidden from our eyes in an oblivion more or less prolonged. *It is thanks to this oblivion alone* that we can from time to time recover the person that we were, place ourselves in relation to things as he was placed, suffer anew because we are no longer ourselves but he, and because he loved what now leaves us indifferent. (BG 300–301; my emphasis)

Actually, intellect controls the process at both ends, first sealing the memory in an "airtight compartment" (S 190) where its vitality is safe from the degradations of habit, and then, once the sensory image has drifted from the dark warehouse of recollections into the light of consciousness, inspecting it, subjecting it to analysis—"developing" it, as Proust's narrator would say (TR 299)—so as to bring out its nature and significance. The production of art is an analogous process: starting with impressions (subjective appropriations of sensory input), the artist then transforms these into "équivalents d'intelligence" (IV:621/TR 525). The detour via intuition allows the artist to convey to others something of his or her "world," his or her true (intuitive, perspectival) self, as opposed to that everyday, social, conversational self of which the intellect takes indolent charge.[20] For in Proust the true self is not only hidden, as with the *moralistes*, but also too individual to be captured in direct language. What is more, since the true self is hidden even from its *owner*, artistic expression is the only route to authentic introspection, the only avenue along which "we are free to advance . . . towards a goal of truth" (BG 664). Art "alone expresses for others *and renders visible to ourselves* that life of ours which cannot effectually observe itself," concludes Marcel (TR 300; my emphasis).

The emphasis on art as royal road to subjective insight should, however, put us on notice, cautioning us not to overlook the artistry of the *Recherche*. The novel's literary aspects may, first of all, reinforce the philosophical framework in subtle ways. And indeed, in perfect conformity with the theory of style I briefly sketched above, Marcel's deepest nature is designed to be partially invisible to him but at the same time visible to *us*, thanks to his inadvertent use of imagery. As I shall explain in chapter 1, the persistence of metonymic metaphors—metaphors chosen on the basis of spatial propinquity, rather than that of conceptual appropriateness—reveals something about him that he does not know about himself, namely that he continues at an unconscious level to be susceptible to the myth of aura, to the fantasy that every place has a distinct and unitary essence. Similarly, the juxtaposition within the same text of two types of maxim, one set holding good for all of humanity, the other only for Marcel, confirms the disjunction between subjective and objective types of "truth." (I explore maxims in detail below, and examine a wide range of formal devices, together with their appropriateness to the picture of selfhood and epistemology, in the coda.)

Secondly, however, we should be ready for the literary and philosophical elements to part company. The *Recherche*, which was initially conceived as a pair of independent texts, "the story of a morning" and a separate "essay,"[21] remains at the mercy of their mutual interference. Theory threatens to submerge narrative, as when plot is put on hold, in the final volume, for a fifty-page excursus on aesthetics; and while many Proust scholars (including Luc Fraisse, Justin O'Brien, and Alain de Botton) may turn a blind eye to it, fiction takes its revenge by periodically undermining the (surface-level) philosophy. Of the various statements Marcel makes, some must be discarded, as conveying nothing more than the perspective of a fictional character (so that studies which merely synthesize collections of such statements cannot be accurate representations of the novel), and yet at the same time *some* must be preserved and taken entirely seriously (so that suspicious hermeneuts are misguided in claiming, as they frequently do, that the *Recherche* seeks only to show the impossibility of all stable belief). What is needed, therefore, is an account that combines the literary-critical circumspection of a Malcolm Bowie or a Gérard Genette with a careful—and charitable—attention to the detail of philosophical views both stated and implied. It is this need that the present study, within the limits of its capabilities, endeavors to fill.

PART 2: LITERATURE

1. Biography

The Madeleine Proust Never Ate   While the philosophical program underlying the *Recherche* rewards patient reconstruction, as I have argued above, it would nonetheless be rash to attempt such reconstruction merely on the basis of Marcel's explicit assertions. For one thing, Proust cannot possibly hold all of the views in question, since they do not always cohere internally: Proust cannot mean *both* what Marcel says at the end of the first volume *and* what Marcel says at the end of the last volume, the two statements—lost time cannot be regained, lost time can be regained—standing in direct conflict.[22] Nor, further, do Marcel's views always correspond to Marcel's *practice*, or to the events he so carefully describes (Marcel's apparently universal theories of love, for example, often apply only to himself). Finally, there may be aspects of Proust's project that simply outstrip the character, leaving him incapable of formulating them, much less of putting them into effect. In short, if we really wish to understand what Proust is trying to say and to do in and with his novel, we must strenuously resist the temptation to take Marcel as his entirely reliable mouthpiece.

The temptation is admittedly great. Proust agrees with much, indeed perhaps most, of what his narrator says over the course of the *Recherche*. And just as the beliefs frequently overlap, so too do Marcel's *experiences* bear marked similarities to those of Proust. Both are nervous, sickly aspiring writers, yoked to the mother's apron strings, fascinated by society life; both travel to Venice; both translate Ruskin; and so on and so on. But the novel is not simply a glorified autobiography, and it *matters* that it be not. To take a famous example, we cannot say with any great conviction that Proust ever had an epiphanic encounter with a madeleine. In an earlier draft of the novel, known as *Contre Sainte-Beuve*, what the narrator dips in tea to such ecstatic effect is not a madeleine but instead a humble piece of toast (BSB 17). When, therefore, we hear it said—as we so often do—that "the taste of a madeleine brought to life a lost era of his childhood," we should understand the "his" as pertaining to Marcel, and not to Proust: here of all places, we need to be careful with our pronouns.[23]

Proust's two main English-language biographers, George Painter and Ronald Hayman, are at least somewhat careful with theirs, refusing to attribute the madeleine experience to the author. Yet all they do is repeat the misattribution at a higher level, insisting that while no madeleine ever made much impact on Proust's weltanschauung, a piece of toast did affect it, indeed transformed it definitively, "on or about 1 January 1909" (Painter 2: 129). This piece of toast was responsible for Proust's "seminal moment of insight" (Hayman 300), "one of the most momentous events of his life" (Painter 2:129); the lightly fictionalized madeleine version involves, accordingly, little more than a change in ingredients.[24] Out of the baking tray, into the oven: scrupulously avoiding an identification of Proust with his narrator in the *Recherche*, Hayman and Painter replace it with an identification of Proust with his narrator in the *Contre Sainte-Beuve*, as though the latter were anything less of a fiction.[25] When we look for the documentary evidence they have to support the claim that a momentous, proto-madeleine incident actually occurred in January 1909, we find that they adduce not a letter from Proust to a friend, not eyewitness testimony from Céline Cottin, not a reported conversation à la Gide, but simply the *Contre Sainte-Beuve* passage itself (Painter 2:393n129, Hayman 522n31). That is, in order to prove that a scene from a novel is based on biographical fact, they cite—an earlier version of the same novel!

Is it really true, then, that a piece of toast changed Proust's life on or around New Year's Day 1909? Might it not have been a danish pastry, or a *pain aux raisins*? Might it, indeed, not be the case that there never was an enchanted encounter with baked goods, and that Proust made the whole thing up, lock, stock, and biscuit? Let us not forget that Proust had written about involuntary memory long before 1909. Take the following passage from the 1895–96 manuscript *Jean Santeuil*, in which a storm at Réveillon makes the eponymous protagonist think of Brittany:

> to go there [back to Penmarch] was no longer necessary [cf. TR
> 270–71], for the desire roused in him by the wind and the memory of
> Penmarch would not find satisfaction in the self-regarding pleasure he
> once had had at Penmarch, but in the reality of poetry made from the
> sense of his own existence [TR 304], felt in the recovered moments
> of Penmarch. . . . He found indeed that he was no longer gulping life
> down with a sense of anguish at seeing it disappear beneath a surface
> pleasure, but that he was tasting it with an assured confidence, know-
> ing that a day would come when he would find again the reality con-
> tained in these few minutes—provided only that he did not try to—in
> the sharp reminder of the howling wind, in the smell of firewood
> burning [C 24–25], in the sight of a drooping sky, sunlit but with a
> threat of rain, above the line of roofs. For that reality is something
> of which we are not conscious in the passing moment, connecting it
> as we do with some self-regarding project [TR 259]. It is something

which in the sharp return of disinterested memory sets us floating between the present and the past in an element common to both [TR 263–64], which in the present has recalled the past to us, an essence which deeply thrills us, in so far as it is ourself [S 60].[26]

In suspending Jean's goal-oriented relationship to the world, involuntary memory allows him to perceive a deep continuity between two experiences, an "essence" which, being that of his own inner nature, will go on to form the basis of his literary production; almost everything the *Recherche* has to say on the subject is, in other words, already here. That being the case, there is absolutely no need to view the *pain grillé* episode in *Contre Sainte-Beuve*—written a full decade after *Jean Santeuil*—as the faithful transcription of a transformative moment, when it could just as well represent one more effort on Proust's part to make literary capital out of a long-familiar mental state. Proust may never have been spectacularly affected by a piece of toast, and almost certainly never was spectacularly affected by a madeleine. (Jean-Yves Tadié, who excerpts much of the *Jean Santeuil* passage above in his 1996 biography [348; cf. 1971: 28], maintains a decorous, *boulangerie-* and *pâtis-serie*-free silence in his account of the year 1909.)

Nor did Proust, unlike his narrator (GW 472–73), suddenly remember Doncières, a site that will not be found on any map of France; to say, as Gaëtan Picon does, "Proust maintains that the pleasures he remembers from Doncières are pleasures that were experienced at the time" (1995: 116; my translation), is to make a truly perplexing type of statement. No less perplexing are some of the remarks Richard Rorty makes about the *Recherche* in his deservedly influential book *Contingency, Irony, and Solidarity*. "Proust," writes Rorty, "dreaded being . . . turned into a thing by the eye of the other (by, for example, St. Loup's 'hard look,' Charlus's 'enigmatic stare')" (102). "Proust," Rorty goes on, "put the events of his own life in his own order, made a pattern out of all the little things—Gilberte among the hawthorns, the color of the windows in the Guermantes's chapel, the sound of the name 'Guermantes,' the two walks, the shifting spires" (105). Picon and Rorty are making inadvertently eccentric claims when they place the mortal Marcel Proust on the same ontological level as imaginary entities such as Doncières, Saint-Loup, and Gilberte. It is as though they spoke of Sir Arthur Conan Doyle dreading Moriarty, Vladimir Nabokov vividly recalling the time that he went out for a drive with Dolores Haze, and J. R. R. Tolkien making a pattern out of the events of his life on Middle Earth.

What I am saying here may sound like a minor distinction, one that changes little in the way we read the novel. But it is, in fact, a vital moment in several lines of interpretation. First of all, it underwrites a large number of what one might term uncharitable readings, according to which the novel is little more than an attempt at self-therapy on the part of its author. Thus the entire discussion of involuntary memory can, according to David Ellison, be written off as a fantasmatic answer to Proust's personal problems. As Ellison has it (150), "the *objet herméneutique* is in fact the esthetic fictionalization of the fearsome energies emanating from . . . the Oedipal triangle. To eat the madeleine, for example, is to consume and interiorize maternal substance."[27] And the skeptical attitude toward other minds can also be written off, according to Richard Chessick, as the idiosyncratic attitude of a lonely and guilty son: Proust's "continual emphasis on how we are irremediably alone," he writes, "is his way of expressing his longing for his mother" (32).[28] In each case, we are spared the necessity to take seriously one of the central motifs in the novel—involuntary memory, monadic isolation—since we can dismiss it as a peccadillo of an eccentric living a "dissolute life" (Chessick 31).

Even a number of charitable readings rely on the identification of Proust with his narrator. To return to Richard Rorty, his more general thesis—that the *Recherche* constitutes a glorious act of self-fashioning on the part of its author—stands or falls on whether the narrator is Proust in all but (nonexistent) name. Ostensibly, Proust becomes an exemplary ironist by "putting the events of his own life in his own order"; ostensibly, "Proust became who he was by reacting against and redescribing people—real live people whom he had met in the flesh" (100). But seeing Gilberte among the hawthorns is not an event in Proust's own life, and Robert de Saint-Loup is not a real live person. At best he is a (fictional) composite of *two* real live people, Bertrand de Salignac-Fénélon and Edmond de Polignac (see II:1383n1, 1428n1)[29]—and that is a conservative estimate. In a general remark on the subject, Proust potentially raises the number to eight or ten. "Dear friend, there are no keys [*clefs*] to the characters in this book; or else there are eight or ten for each," he writes to Jacques de Lacretelle in 1918 (EA 260). And in a passage that strongly brings Saint-Loup to mind, Marcel sets it at sixty: "beneath the name of every character of his invention he [the creative writer] can put sixty names of characters that he has seen, one of whom has posed for the grimaces, another for the monocle, another for the fits of temper, another for the swaggering movement of his arm, etc." (TR 305; cf. TR 510–11). For Marcel, "this is one reason for the futility of those critical essays which try to guess who it is that an author is talking about" (TR 316–17). Marcel's warning (is it also Proust's?) has, however, gone unheeded, so that even today we continue to read "futile" critical essays pinning down once and for all "who it is that Proust is talking about" when he "talks about" Albertine.

In short, the character Robert de Saint-Loup is made up of two, or eight or ten, or sixty people combined; and he is doubtless more besides, incorporating additional features emerging from Proust's strictly literary impulses. After all, Robert is based as much on the Henri de Réveillon of *Jean Santeuil* as on Bertrand de Fénélon; in George Painter's paradoxical formulation, "Proust created the character before he met the original" (1:205). It is hard, then, to see how Saint-Loup (let alone Vinteuil, say, who has even vaguer moorings in the real world) is supposed to function as a redescription of any particular individual of Proust's acquaintance. And it is hard to see, by extension, how events in which Saint-Loup figures are supposed to count as events in Proust's personal history. But if the *Recherche* is not a record of that history, how can it be said to redeem it by redescribing it? If I take the various protagonists of my life story and give them different names, force them to exchange certain traits with one another, and add in some auxiliary details purely from my overactive imagination (the inner monologue of a dying man,[30] for instance, hardly seems like something Proust has personally witnessed), might it not be more accurate to call the result a fiction loosely inspired by my life than to term it my life redescribed? Yes, many of the episodes in the novel have echoes in Proust's own experience; but this is only to say that Proust, like other artists, fashioned something beautiful out of that experience—not that he fashioned himself in the process. *Marcel* may be fashioning himself in *his* autobiography, but Marcel's autobiography is Proust's *novel*, and Proust is not Marcel.

Ils and elles   Matters become even more complicated when it comes to Albertine Simonet, a character Rorty mercifully omits from his list of elements in Proust's "own life." In her case, the "redescription" is radical: not only is she composed of multiple real-world entities, but at least one of these entities, who shares her passion for motor cars and her untimely death, is of a different biological sex. Now critics like Justin O'Brien do not see a problem here.[31] Proust, they argue, is transparently writing about his love affair with Alfred Agostinelli, changing only the name. After all, if we are to believe Gide, Proust admitted as much in explicit terms: "he says he regrets that 'indecision' which made him transpose anything graceful, tender, and charming his homosexual memories suggested to him into 'the budding grove' ['*à l'ombre des jeunes filles*'], in order to feed the heterosexual part of his book, with the result that the grotesque and the abject are all that is left for *Sodom*" (694; my translation). That is, in order to placate a conservative reading public, Proust "transposed" all his more pleasant homosexual experiences onto female characters, so that the "jeunes filles en fleurs" at Balbec—Albertine included—are thinly veiled reproductions of young boys.[32]

There are, however, a number of problems with the O'Brien-Gide line. For one thing, it cannot be the case that *all* female objects of desire are merely "transpositions" of male love interests. When biographers give sources for Gilberte and the Duchesse de Guermantes, they tend to mention Marie Bénardaky and the Comtesse de Greffulhe (Tadié 1996: 386); few, if any, go in search of an elusive *Gilbert*, let alone an elusive *Orian*.[33] For another thing, it is not even straightforwardly the case that Albertine can be identified with Agostinelli. To be sure, by the time she has been reduced to the "grey captive" (C 225) of Paris, she has acquired many an Agostinellian trait. But before her "incarceration," while she is still the colorful bird of Balbec, she owes her (fictional) existence to a number of other people, many of them women. As Painter puts it (2:208), "until the last episode of the story, she is based primarily on female originals. In the first holiday at Balbec Albertine's chief model is Marie Finaly, in her visits to the Narrator's home she resembles Louisa de Mornand and Marie Nordlinger, and during the second visit to Balbec she is the young girl of Cabourg in 1908 and 1909. . . . Albertine becomes Agostinelli for the first time in the Agony at Sunrise and the captivity in Paris."[34]

This means, quite fascinatingly, that the oft-cited comment reported by Gide turns out to be seriously misleading. The "gracious, tender, and charming" facets of Albertine in Balbec do not, after all, represent cherished memories of Agostinelli, with gender altered to protect the innocent; Proust has not, after all, distributed his stock of "souvenirs homosexuels" to his characters in the manner suggested, with tender grace going to girls and grotesque abjection to boys. First of all, it cannot be that every happy moment with Albertine is a transposed happy moment with Alfred, since many recall Proust's experiences with *women* (something Proust did not want to admit, perhaps, to Gide). And conversely, it cannot be that all "abject" aspects of interpersonal relations are allotted to Sodom and Gomorrah, since Odette and Rachel torture Swann and Robert every bit as much as Morel tortures Charlus.

The most we can say, then, is that a portion of Albertine's life, namely the period from late *Sodome et Gomorrhe* onward, finds analogies in the biography of Alfred Agostinelli. And that, in fact, is probably more than we *should* say, for the late-phase Albertine is not just Agostinelli in a dress.[35] As Proust was no doubt well aware, gender transpositions involve an author in additional adjustments; a man cannot enter a turn-of-the-century novel as a woman, after undergoing a virtual sex-change operation on his way into the fictional world, and still act and be perceived in exactly the same manner. It is true, as O'Brien alleges (1949: 942; cf. Maurois 231), that Albertine's comportment is unconventional by prewar standards: she cohabits with Marcel in Paris, and even commits the apparently egregious crime of lighting a cigarette in a train carriage.[36] Albertine's irregular behavior does not, however, prove—as Justin O'Brien thinks it does—that she is "really" a man. In fact it reinforces her femininity, precisely because everyone around her *knows* her behavior is irregular.[37]

Before the cohabitation, Albertine worries that it will appear "drôle" (III:508/SG 715); during the cohabitation, Marcel routinely pretends that Albertine is his cousin (see, e.g., C 290), while his mother finds it "odd, if not shocking, that a girl should be living alone with [him]" (C 6); and the cohabitation ends, according to Andrée, primarily because of Albertine's concern as to what people will think (F 821). Marcel is fully aware that the reader will raise an eyebrow at Albertine's activities, and is quite ready to offer an explanation. "That at one time Albertine should have come to see me at midnight, and that she should now be living with me," he writes, "might perhaps have been improbable of anyone else, but not of Albertine, fatherless and motherless, leading so free a life that at first I had taken her, at Balbec, for the mistress of a racing cyclist" (C 54). O'Brien and his followers would have us think that since Albertine's conduct is more typical of a real-life man than of a real-life woman, she must actually be a man. But we can turn matters around and say that since the *response* to Albertine's conduct (whose anomalies, as we have seen, are explicitly accounted for by Marcel) is more typical of real-life responses to women than of real-life responses to men, she must actually be a woman. In terms of *bienséances*, things operate in Proust's fictional world more or less as they would in the real world of the early twentieth century: Marcel can stay with Robert without arousing suspicion (GW 97), because he is male; Albertine cannot stay with Marcel without arousing suspicion, because she is female.

And then, we must surely take into account the fact that Proust has Marcel provide a full description of Albertine's naked body, something which seems a little curious if Proust's intention is to leave it *sous-entendu* that Albertine is a man in disguise. "Her two little uplifted breasts were so round that they seemed not so much to be an integral part of her body as to have ripened there like fruit; and her belly (concealing the place where a man's is disfigured as though by an iron clamp left sticking in a statue that has been taken down from its niche) was closed, at the junction of her thighs, by two valves with a curve as languid, as reposeful, as cloistral as that of the horizon after the sun has set" (C 97). Albertine's breasts are, as it happens, of considerable interest to Marcel. He fantasmatically projects them onto the mountain range outside the window as he sits by her bed (BG 700); he mentions them when he lists the mental "snapshots" he has taken of her over the years (F 659); and he receives from them, as they lubriciously rub up against those of Andrée in the "danse des seins" (SG 264), the first clue to Albertine's "guilty" desires.

Now it is the "guilty" desires of Albertine that definitively clinch her status as a female character, required by the internal logic of the narrative. Albertine *has* to be a woman, and indeed a woman who loves women, *so that Marcel can suffer from the kind of jealousy only a heterosexual man could experience.* Within the world of the *Recherche*, a homosexual man is never troubled by his lover's heterosexual affairs—thus Charlus, who is insanely (and murderously) jealous of Morel, enjoys joking with him about his various female conquests, and even wishes him to marry[38]—whereas a heterosexual man finds his lover's homosexual affairs immeasurably threatening, because strictly unimaginable. "That other kind of jealousy, provoked by Saint-Loup or by any young man, was nothing," explains Marcel. "But here the rival was not of the same kind as myself . . . , I could not compete on the same ground, give Albertine the same pleasures, *nor indeed conceive of them exactly.*"[39] Even when he knows what lesbianism looks like, having paid two laundry maids to have sex in front of him (F 742), Marcel is none the wiser: "one wants to know not only what she has done, but what she felt while she was doing it, what she thought of what she was doing" (F 709; cf. 735).

This is the most important point in the whole discussion around the gender of Proust's characters. What Marcel seeks here, and what he seeks relentlessly in various other contexts throughout the novel, is a way to move beyond his own subjectivity and to enter the consciousness of another human being. When in love, he contends, "one does not think of oneself, but only of escaping from oneself [*sortir de soi*]" (S 222). What he learns, of course, is that love (or again friendship) will not allow us to do so—"man is the creature who cannot escape from himself [*sortir de soi*], who knows other people only in himself" (F 607)—and that we are left, at most, with the in-direct route of aesthetic contemplation: "through art alone are we able to emerge from ourselves [*sortir de nous*]" (TR 299).[40] Now Proust, who appears to agree with Marcel about the predicament of insular subjectivity, forever locked out of other minds, finds in female homosexuality, considered from the point of view of a heterosexual male, a maximally dramatic way of pre-senting it. Albertine has to be a woman, and Marcel a heterosexual man, be-cause her bisexuality has to be something he cannot understand, something that fills him with unparalleled dread by representing, in an excruciatingly vivid synecdoche, the breadth of the gulf that separates her consciousness from his.[41]

Once again, then, the distinction between Proust and Marcel turns out to be a distinction that *matters.* In hastily assuming that Proust is essentially writing an autobiography, and that female characters like Gilberte and Alber-tine are really men in makeup, critics have neglected to consider the strictly *literary* reasons why Proust might have chosen a heterosexual protagonist for his novel. To be sure, it is *conceivable* that Proust set out with the intention of producing a sanitized portrait of Agostinelli (i.e., one acceptable to a largely homophobic French reading public), and later made the changes imposed on him by its incorporation in a particular literary universe. It is, however, more *plausible*, given Proust's specific literary project, to imagine him set-ting out to produce a female love interest for a heterosexual character—just as he had done, repeatedly, from "Avant la nuit" (1893) through *Jean San-teuil* (1895–96)[42] to *Un amour de Swann* (1913)—and simply borrowing his fond memories of Agostinelli in order to flesh out the former. Of course, we should remain wary of attempts to "straighten" Proust, who remains a writer keenly interested in, and often making an apologia for, homosexual relations. But there may actually be something uncharitable in the reverse attempt to "queer" Marcel, the implicit assumption appearing to be that a homosexual author is only capable of constructing, or only has the right to construct, homosexual protagonists.[43]

Proust and Marcel   Extending outward from the case of Agostinelli, we can posit as a general working hypothesis that the most fruitful way to approach Proust's novel is as a piece of literature penned by a man who has doubts about the power of his imagination. Proust, I am suggesting, wishes to be a novelist, not an autobiographer; it is just that his capacity for ex nihilo creation happens, in his own opinion, to be somewhat limited. "Everything is fictional, at the cost of great effort, for I have no imagination," says a voice in the *Carnet de 1908* (69), a voice I am tempted to hear as belonging to Proust himself (in the *Carnet*, it is not always easy to determine which of the notations are fragments of the novel-in-progress and which reflect Proust's process and plans). Proust, that is, strives hard to fabricate a pure fiction, and seems to take pride in the fact that "everything has been invented by me in accordance with the requirements of my theme [*ma démonstration*]."[44] If we are able, nevertheless, to detect elements of reality behind the "demonstration," it is because he has simply not had the energy to do any better: "through excess of fatigue," he writes, "for purely material details, I spare myself the trouble of making things up for my hero and take some real traits from myself."[45]

We should, I think, take his word for it. For the longer Proust worked, the less autobiographical his output became (Tadié 1971: 24, Genette 1980: 249, Schmid 62). Between *Contre Sainte-Beuve* and the *Recherche*, he removed the narrator's younger brother, leaving Marcel an only child (again, one wonders whether Rorty would countenance the idea of a tale of a *fils unique* "redeeming" the life of a *frère aîné*); between "Impressions de route en automobile" (1907) and the steeples passage in the novel, he replaced Agostinelli with an anonymous coachman and Caen with the fictional Martinville (see chapter 1 here for a fuller discussion); and between typescript and printed page, he routinely eliminated the word "Marcel," amending the text at *Swann* 50, *Sodom* 234, and *Captive* 145.[46] Only two mentions of the name remain, and the first, far from establishing an identity between author and narrator, makes it, if anything, even less likely. "Then she would find her tongue," it runs, referring to Albertine waking from a nap, "and say 'My—' or 'My darling—' followed by my Christian name, which, if we give the narrator the same name as the author of this book, would be 'My Marcel' or 'My darling Marcel'" (C 91).

This little passage, discreetly buried in the fifth volume of the novel, is truly an extraordinary literary event, a dazzling flash of Proustian brilliance. For in fictional worlds, epistemological access only works in one direction: narrators are allowed to know things about characters (their future for example), but not vice versa; and authors are allowed to know things about narrators, but not the other way around (Lejeune 16). Here, by contrast, it appears—quite scandalously—as though the narrator knows what his maker is called. (Molly Bloom's "O Jamesy let me up out of this," in James Joyce's *Ulysses* [769], is the only contemporary parallel of which I am aware.) To put it less paradoxically, Proust's sentence mixes together two voices, two implicit first-person pronouns. Whereas the "I" behind "my Christian name" belongs to Marcel, the "I" behind "if we give" pertains to Proust. And so it effects a demarcation between author and narrator both in content and in form, content explicitly noting that their names need not be alike, form showing that their voices (and intentions) collide and conflict within the very texture of the prose.[47] Ironically, then, the very statement that seems to seal the equivalence between Proust and Marcel actually drives them further apart.[48]

The "darling Marcel" passage may be virtually unprecedented in the tradition of serious prose fiction, but it does have a precedent in the *Recherche* itself. Early in *Sodom and Gomorrah*, in a self-reflexive interlude reminiscent of Diderot's *Jacques le fataliste* but with added Proustian intricacy, a "reader" suddenly arises and berates the "author" for what may, or may not, be the latter's own failing: "it is a pity that, young as you were (or as your hero was, if he isn't you), you had already so feeble a memory" (SG 69). Just as the "darling Marcel" case involves the juxtaposition of two distinct first-person pronouns, so the "young as you were" sentence brings together a pair of only apparently identical second-person pronouns, the first ("young as *you* were") applying to Marcel, the second ("*your* hero") referring to a version of Proust. Amusingly enough, the "reader," having made the appropriate qualification, immediately relapses into his or her earlier mistake—"*you* already had so feeble a memory"—as though Proust were light-heartedly reminding us how great the temptation will always be to read the fiction as an autobiography.

Fascinatingly, the very same paradoxical pronoun-play reappears in Proust's essay on Flaubert—in a context, that is, which would normally dictate a more straightforward (nonironic) mode of communication. Here, while discussing the early episodes of the *Recherche*, Proust writes that "some crumbs of 'madeleine,' dipped in herb tea, remind me (or at least remind the narrator, who is not always me) of a whole period of my life" (EA 295). For a third time, we see the now familiar pattern of I-Marcel ("remind *me*") giving way to I-Proust ("not always *me*"), only to reassert itself ("*my* life") once the necessary caveat has been put in place. Proust must surely have known that many readers would overlook the caveat and take the fact that he habitually uses the first person when describing the novel—in essays, correspondence, and dedications alike—as a telltale sign that the novel is his own life history. "In his letters, he speaks so nonchalantly of his Narrator in the first person

singular as to make a rigid textualist shudder," writes one of those readers,
Michael Maar (2001: 137). But the use of the first person singular need not,
by itself, suffuse a textualist with existential dread. Coupled with the present
tense ("a madeleine *reminds* me"), it suggests only the *compte rendu* of a first-
person fiction; as Muller points out (161–62), the synopsis of an autobiography would necessarily command the imperfect or past historic ("a madeleine
reminded me"). What is more, a synopsis of Proust's autobiography would, to
say it once again, make no mention of madeleines at all.[49]

In the 1913 "interview" coinciding with the appearance of *Du côté de
chez Swann*, Proust makes matters still more explicit. "Already, in this first
volume, you will see the character who narrates, who says 'I' (*and who is not
me*) suddenly finding again years, gardens, and people he has forgotten, in the
taste of a mouthful of tea into which he has dipped a piece of madeleine," he
writes (EA 254; my emphasis; cf. *Letters* 227). Elsewhere too, he refers to the
narrator in the third person ("my little boy, in my book" [Corr. 17:356]) and
at times indeed by name ("Man of letters near Cabourg . . . Marcel goes to
see him" [*Carnet* 61]). But even the Flaubert essay, with its unusual phras-
ing, should really not confuse us. Proust is merely rehearsing an invented
narrative here, not giving us the facts about himself. That is what allows him
to make statements of the peculiar form we have been discussing, arrogat-
ing the events of the narrative to himself at the very moment in which he is
disclaiming them, simultaneously closing (in appearance) and holding open
(in reality) the gap between author and character. If he uses the first person,
it is perhaps as a deliberate warning: wherever we see the word "I"—which is
to say, throughout the *Recherche*—we are to keep in the back of our minds, at
all times, the knowledge that this "I" and Proust's "I" are not, or at least not
always, one and the same.[50]

2. Axioms

The "Laws" of Love   I hope to have shown how surprising a claim Richard
Rorty's turns out to be, that Gilberte among the hawthorns, Robert de Saint-
Loup's "hard look," and the sound of the name "Guermantes" constitute
"the events of [Proust's] own life." Proust was acquainted with no one by
the name of Gilberte Swann, or even anyone quite like her (a red-haired,[51]
self-hating half-Jew, married to a bisexual man, and on intimate terms with
a famous novelist)—let alone anyone quite like Albertine Simonet (a woman
with whom he has had a sexual relationship). And while he must at some
point have come across the proper noun "Guermantes," he never met a
single person answering to it: the very reason that he used it in his novel
is that no living members of the family remained (see the 1909 letter to
Georges de Lauris, Corr. 9:102).[52] Proust is unlikely, therefore, to share his
character's spellbound prostration before "that amaranthine colour of the

closing syllable of [the Guermantes] name" (GW 280), "its glowing amber envelope" (GW 30), "the amber light which glowed from the resounding syllable 'antes'" (S 242), "the amber hue of [the] sonorous syllable" (S 247; cf. TR 19). The Guermantes clan is not a part of Proust's experience, and even the orange (or amaranthine) coloring of the syllable [ãt] may belong to Marcel and Marcel alone. Proust, that is, may well have decided to invent for his protagonist a system of color attribution à la Rimbaud,[53] just as he has invented for him a system of metaphors (which I will explore in chapter 1), a sexual preference (heterosexual), and a particular dispositional "type" of love object.

The distinction, to repeat, is one that counts, because it means that Proust's novel is neither the tortured confession of a closet homosexual (O'Brien) nor an abject form of talking cure (Ellison), nor yet a heroic act of self-fashioning on the part of its author (Rorty), though the last suggestion is ingenious and, as we shall see, ultimately runs parallel to the truth. But there is a further important consequence. Once we recognize that Proust's life story is not the same as Marcel's life story, so that statements of the form "I did *x*" are not directly attributable to Proust, we are free to raise the question whether statements of the form "it is true that *y*" are more reliable. Just as it is rash to assume that any given fact of Marcel's life is also a fact of Proust's, so it is rash to assume that the latter concurs with any given opinion held by the former; in other words, *we cannot always take Marcel's philosophy as the philosophy of Proust.*[54]

Most readers have, of course, done exactly that. A well-intentioned compilation entitled *The Maxims of Marcel Proust*, edited by Justin O'Brien in 1948, consists in a set of general pronouncements severed from their context and unabashedly presented as the novelist's wit and wisdom, as though *A la recherche du temps perdu* had been written by La Rochefoucauld.[55] More recently, Alain de Botton has collated various excerpts into his best-selling self-help guide *How Proust Can Change Your Life*. If Proust can "change your life," however, it is in part, as I shall argue below, by means of the very *inconsistency* of the philosophy he has Marcel articulate, and by means of the discrepancy, at some junctures, between Marcel's outlook—even where consistent—and his own.

It is instructive to consider the elaborate network of statements on the subject of love. They have been much discussed, whether in abstract terms (Bales, Girard, Maurois, May) or with specific reference to homosexuality (Sedgwick). In almost all cases, they are presented as Proust's own views— indeed, there are even those who take Proust to task for "his" cynicism, accusing him of extrapolating from his personal neuroses (Chessick 32) to a universal portrait of love that falls far short of the truth (de Souza 100)[56]— and taken to constitute a fairly monolithic set. To be fair, they do, at times, give the appearance of forming an intricate genus-species structure whose precision would be the envy of a nineteenth-century German natural scientist. Thus the laws of homosexual love are a subset of the laws of love more generally;[57] the laws of love fall under the laws of the imagination (GW 317); the laws of the imagination belong in the category "lois psychologiques" (GW 304–5, BG 117); these in turn are a branch of "human natural history" (F 880); and human laws reside within the laws of nature as a whole (BG 644, GW 382). Because everything lines up so neatly, with all phenomena ruled by "increasingly higher laws" (SG 3), Marcel is at liberty to draw analogies not only between homosexuality and other types of love but also between these and snobbery and even war, within the space of a single paragraph:

> In the case of M. de Charlus, which on the whole, with slight discrepancies due to the identity of sex, accords very well with the general laws of love, for all that he belonged to a family more ancient than the Capets, that he was rich and vainly sought after by fashionable society while Morel was nobody, he would have got nowhere by saying to Morel, as he had once said to me: "I am a prince, I want to help you"—it was still Morel who had the upper hand so long as he refused to surrender. And for him to persist in this refusal, it was perhaps enough that he should feel himself to be loved. The horror that grand people have for the snobs who move heaven and earth to make their acquaintance is felt also by the virile man for the invert, by a woman for every man who is too much in love with her. M. de Charlus possessed, and would have offered Morel a share in, immense advantages. But it is possible that all this might have hurled itself in vain against a determined will. And in that case, M. de Charlus would have suffered the same fate as the Germans—in whose ranks in fact his ancestry placed him—who in the war at that moment taking its course were indeed, as the Baron was a little too fond of repeating, victorious on every front. But of what use were their victories, since after every one they found the Allies yet more firmly resolved to refuse them the one thing that they, the Germans, wanted: peace and reconciliation? (TR 188–89)

And yet a number of maxims threaten to introduce a dash of Gallic idiosyncrasy into the admirable Germanic regimentation. I shall focus on three, all of which have on one occasion or another been attributed to Proust (see, respectively, de Botton 165–67, O'Brien 1948: 110–11, and Beckett 55), starting with what I shall call the first postulate: that *all love springs from anxiety*. "One can feel an attraction toward a particular person. But to release that fount of sorrow, that sense of the irreparable, those agonies which prepare the way for love, there must be," declares Marcel with his usual firmness, "the risk of an impossibility" (BG 561–62). Marcel has similar things to say elsewhere (e.g., BG 513, 597), and indeed so familiar is the territory that few would dispute the quintessentially Proustian flavor of the precept. Perhaps, however, the few would be in the right. For when it comes to the Duchesse de Guermantes, Marcel's attraction derives not from her remoteness but, quite the contrary, from her warmth. "This smile fell upon me," he writes. "And at once I fell in love with her, for if it is sometimes enough to make us love a woman that she should look on us with contempt, as I supposed Mlle Swann to have done, and that we should think that she can never be ours, sometimes, too, it is enough that she should look on us kindly, as Mme de Guermantes was doing, and that we should think of her as almost ours already" (S 250–51; cf. C 180). The Duchesse, one of the only three sustained infatuations recounted in the novel, forms an immediate counterexample to the general law. And if that law does not even hold good for Marcel's loves, what hope is there of it applying to humanity at large? Marcel appears to appreciate the restriction himself, for some of his later statements on the subject show increased caution, arguing merely that love is "more often than not" (C 115)—or even just "as often as not" (C 79–80)—the fruit of distress, anxiety being indispensable only "at a certain stage in life" (F 682).

Let us proceed to the second postulate, which states that *each of us seeks a partner who will make us unhappy*. Marcel considers that "desire, reaching out always towards what is most opposite to oneself, forces one to love what will make one suffer" (F 825), and again he has other remarks to make in similar vein (e.g., BG 647). Good Proustian pessimism? Yes and no. For just as the first postulate fails to account for the Duchesse de Guermantes, so Mme Elstir escapes the clutches of the second.[58] In the painter's studio, Marcel discovers that "a certain ideal type illustrated by certain lines, certain arabesques which reappeared incessantly throughout his work . . . was the most intimate part of [Elstir] himself; and so he had never been able to look at it with detachment, to extract emotion from it, until the day on which he encountered it, realised outside himself, in the body of a woman, the body of the woman who had in due course become Mme Elstir" (BG 586–87). In short, the painter "had adored in Mme Elstir the archetype of that rather heavy beauty which he had pursued and caressed in his paintings" (TR 116). What looked like an unconditional rule thus turns out to be a regularity of Marcel's world alone, merely a "type" of woman liable to stimulate his interest and, ultimately, spur his productivity (TR 439–40). Elstir's type, responsible for the choice of a wife who does not seem to have caused undue suffering, follows an entirely different pattern. And so, for that matter, does Charlus's type, which Marcel is so far from sharing that he needs to make a special mental effort merely to discern it at all.[59] (Incidentally, any one of these cases would suffice to defeat the equally famous, but entirely incompatible, postulate that women are "interchangeable instruments of a pleasure that is always the same" [S 222; cf. BG 676].)

Third postulate: *everyone remains jealous, even after love has faded.* "Jealousy is thus endless, for even if the beloved, by dying for instance, can no longer provoke it by her actions, it may happen that memories subsequent to any event suddenly materialize and behave in our minds as though they too were events, memories which hitherto we had never explored, which had seemed to us unimportant, and to which our own reflexion upon them is sufficient, without any external factors, to give a new and terrible meaning" (C 107). This is the famous *jalousie de l'escalier* (III:594/C 106) which Beckett mentions in his study of Proust (55). Once again, however, an exception emerges, and from a most unlikely source at that: it is none other than Charles Swann, whom most critics consider to be "a mere variant of the narrating I" (Spitzer 413), "his double" (Rousset 146), "a tragic doppelgänger" (Macksey 109) whose story stands as an "archetype of all Proustian loves" (Genette 1980: 46). Far from agreeing with Rousset (ibid.) that Swann has "the same way of loving and suffering," Marcel explicitly describes himself as "differing in this respect . . . from Swann who, when he was no longer jealous, ceased to feel any curiosity as to what Odette might have done with Forcheville" (F 743).[60] Jealousy may be endless for *Marcel*, who dwells obsessively on Albertine's past long after she has disappeared from his life, but for Swann it has a definite limit. The third postulate is thus no more categorical than the first or second. Just like love, jealousy varies from one person to the next; it is "one of those intermittent maladies the cause of which is . . . always identical in the same patient, [but] sometimes entirely different in another" (C 28).

Objective and Subjective Laws   To be sure, there are similarities among various of the love affairs depicted in the *Recherche* (between, say, Marcel with Gilberte and Marcel with Albertine). But the similarities are not always due to the fact that everyone always loves in exactly the same way. Rather, this first rationale, which I shall term the *universal-essential*, is just one of four proposed explanations for the recurrences (cf. Finch 171, Wassenaar 195). On a second, *universal-genealogical* approach, the mechanism of desire is held in common with humanity at large, but the objects it generates vary from person to person. All of us, that is, are shaped by events in our early childhood, but by different events, and hence with different results. Thus Marcel is tempted by the notion that his interest in the elusive Albertine could derive, in part, from the periodic elusiveness of Maman: "this terrible need of a person was something I had learned to know at Combray in the case of my mother" (SG 179; cf. S 260–61).[61] Do events in the *Recherche* then conform to the idea, "well-known in psychoanalytic circles" (Genette 1972: 58–59), according to which one maternal surrogate leads to the next in an endless metonymic chain?[62] There is some debate on the issue, with Shattuck (109), Terdiman (1976: 177), and Bersani (1965: 114) arrayed on one side, and Deleuze (69–70), Poulet (1952: 407), and May (66) on the other.

It seems to me, however, that the universal-genealogical explanation need not really detain us for too long. For in Marcel's opinion (quite the opposite of Freud's), romantic love occupies "a deeper layer of the heart" than does filial affection (C 108); it is therefore entirely possible for Swann, ever the counterexample, to develop an anxiety-pattern without having suffered a childhood trauma akin to that of the *baiser de Maman*. "To him that anguish came through love," writes Marcel, "but when, as had befallen me, it possesses one's soul before love has yet entered into one's life, then it must drift, awaiting love's coming, vague and free" (S 40).

Two accounts remain. On the *individual-genealogical*, our desire is again determined by our history, but not necessarily by our ancient history, each of us being affected by memories from disparate stages of life; nor does the process operate in the predictable, straightforwardly causal manner that Freud sometimes suggests. What is responsible for our present emotion is not an earlier, identical emotion (say, anxiety) but the mere reappearance of familiar epiphenomena. Having once known pleasure during a heat wave, one is forever gripped by passion when temperatures rise to unusual heights; having once loved a woman with brown hair and from the lower middle classes, one can henceforth never be interested in any other kind.[63] Incidental properties become catalysts for, or even essential prerequisites of, future attachments, as "a first love . . . paves the way for subsequent loves" (C 120). And since "self-plagiarism" of the romantic kind affects not only Marcel but also Swann (BG 133–34) and Charlus (SG 41), we can consider it—unlike the *universal*-genealogical effect—a genuine regularity of the Proustian world.

The most important motor driving consistency of behavior is, however, the *individual-essential*. Here, what gives our several liaisons an *air de famille* is quite simply that "they are . . . a product of our temperament" (BG 647), that a deeply hidden agency has, unbeknownst to us and often as it were in spite of us, been doing the work of selection. Second wives resemble first wives not because all attraction is fundamentally alike (universal-essential), nor because all attraction springs from an early trauma (universal-genealogical), nor again because each second wife just happens to remind her husband of her predecessor (individual-genealogical). No, the reason is that there is such a thing as an affective "type"; my successive partners may have nothing in common physically, but there is something about their (perceived) nature, something I intuit about the potential interaction, which makes them alluring to me.[64]

> I might have been able to feel that same exclusive love for another woman [than Albertine] but not for *any* other woman. For Albertine, plump and dark, did not resemble Gilberte, slim and fair, and yet . . . there was a look in the eyes of both whose meaning was difficult to grasp [cf. BG 217, 282, 510]. They were women of a sort that would

not attract the attention of men who for their part would go mad
about other women who "meant nothing" to me. A man has almost
always the same way of catching cold, of falling ill; that is to say, he
requires for it to happen a particular combination of circumstances;
it is natural that when he falls in love he should love a certain type of
woman. (F 677)

When it comes to Marcel, the primary individual-essential law of love,
a "law" which we glimpsed while exploring the novel's lesbianism and to
which we shall return in chapter 1, states that *love is a desire to exit the prison
of subjectivity and to enter another world.* "The belief that a person has a share
in an unknown life to which his or her love may win us admission is, of all
the prerequisites of love, the one which it values most highly," writes Marcel
(S 139), speaking only for himself. A woman he finds appealing—and who
may very well "mean nothing" to, say, an Elstir or (a fortiori) a Charlus—will
therefore always and necessarily convey a mystique, a "prestige" (IV:132),
a sense that she belongs to and can open up an entire cosmos of interwoven
experiences. If Marcel invariably ends up with women who cause him pain,
it is perhaps simply as an unintended consequence of his inexorable yearning
for the radically different: "desire, *reaching out always towards what is most
opposite to oneself,* forces one to love what will make one suffer" (F 825; my
emphasis). He will always prefer an Albertine, dangerously divergent, to an
Andrée who is "too like myself" (BG 714).

What lures Marcel on is not, however, merely the inner universe of the
woman herself, that distant solar system inferable from certain movements
and never visible to the naked eye. For there are also the accessory realms to
which she appears to be a conduit, whether these be (a) geographical sites,
(b) art worlds, or (c) mythical kingdoms peopled by demigods. "In the people
whom we love," writes Marcel in a culminating retrospective on his romantic
life, "there is, immanent [to them], a certain dream which we cannot always
clearly discern but which we pursue. It was my belief [*croyance*] in Bergotte
and in Swann which had made me love Gilberte, my belief in Gilbert the Bad
which had made me love Mme de Guermantes. And what a vast expanse of
sea had been hidden away in my love . . . for Albertine!" (TR 216).

In other words, Marcel's imagination links the Duchesse de Guermantes with Gilbert le Mauvais and Geneviève de Brabant, half-historical,
half-legendary figures from his magic lantern and from the Saint-Hilaire
tapestries and stained glass windows.[65] It also links Albertine (and the rest
of the *petite bande*) with Balbec, just as it ties Mlle de Stermaria to Brittany,
Gilberte to the Tansonville hawthorns, and Roussainville peasant girls to the
côté de Méséglise:[66] in each instance, "it seemed to me that the beauty of the
trees was hers also, and that her kisses would reveal to me the spirit of those
horizons" (S 220). And it connects Gilberte to Bergotte, the writer for whose

novels Marcel has developed a quasi-sacramental reverence in the gardens of Combray;[67] Gilberte gains "prestige" by being on intimate terms with Bergotte, just as Albertine will gain prestige by being on intimate terms with Elstir (BG 578). But even without knowing artists personally, a woman may rise dramatically in Marcel's estimation by corresponding somehow with their aesthetic, by fitting within their vision. "On the days when I did not go down to Mme de Guermantes," notes Marcel, "I would take up an album of Elstir's work, one of Bergotte's books, or Vinteuil's sonata. . . . I found myself suddenly and for an instant capable of passionate feelings for this wearisome girl. She had at that moment the appearance of a work by Elstir or Bergotte" (C 65–66).[68] For both types of connection are (apparent) routes to increased acquaintance, one direct and one indirect, with the mental "world" of a creative genius.

All in all, then, there are four explanations for why "Albertine might be said to echo something of the old original Gilberte" (BG 647), for why Marcel is, as he would put it, so "faithful to himself" in being so unfaithful to specific love objects (cf. C 93, TR 317). Perhaps it is because all loves are based on anxiety (the universal-essential explanation); perhaps because people always carry their childhood traumas, like that of the *drame du coucher*, over into their adult life (universal-genealogical); perhaps because Marcel's later loves are shaped by his adventures with Gilberte (individual-genealogical); or perhaps because Marcel is hardwired to seek out women behind whose shifty gaze he dimly guesses at an alluring secret life. Marcel himself hesitates as to which account to pick. "Thus already they were acting upon me, those influences which recur in the course of our successive love-affairs," he writes with confident firmness, before adding more cautiously "or which at least have recurred in the course of mine. Perhaps they are inseparable from love; [or] perhaps everything that formed a distinctive feature of our first love comes to attach itself to those that follow, by virtue of recollection, suggestion, habit, and, through the successive periods of our life, gives to its different aspects a general character" (BG 562). Ultimately the answer is that it is probably a mixture of three of them. The individual-genealogical complements and strengthens the individual-essential—"what we call experience is merely the revelation to our own eyes of a trait in our character which naturally reappears, *and reappears all the more markedly because we have already once brought it to light*, so that the spontaneous impulse which guided us on the first occasion finds itself reinforced by all the suggestions of memory" (F 586; my emphasis)—and both are accompanied by the universal-essential, by features of love that are fundamentally inescapable.

As a result, when we look at Marcel's superficially homogeneous repertoire of maxims, we are forced to divide it into two groups. Some of the statements (those that describe the universal-essential features of love) live up to their implicit promise of including the whole world within their ambit. Others, however—those that describe individual-essential properties—apply only to the set of people like Marcel, a set which at times contains but a single member. There are two kinds of laws, objective and subjective, corresponding to the objective and subjective types of "truth" Marcel discusses at C 468.[69] The subjective laws still count as laws, because they denote regularities, constants of Marcel's attitude and conduct; yet these laws are by no means binding on the rest of humanity. Even when Marcel appears to be, and perhaps thinks he is, speaking for the entire world, he is very often speaking only for himself.[70] And at such moments, to say it once more, he is certainly not speaking for Proust.

Lower- and Higher-Order Laws   It might be asked: why? Why, if Marcel himself understands in principle the difference between subjective and objective laws, does he nonetheless act so often as though his own quirks, such as staircase jealousy, were ubiquitous features of human life? Why acknowledge that "as soon as one gets close to other people, other lives, ready-made labels and classifications appear unduly crude" (C 398–99; cf. Shattuck 106) and yet still persist in applying labels to everything in sight, like a shelf-stocker with dementia? The answer is that there is something in the nature of his character which drives him to do so. It is, so to speak, a *higher-order law* of Marcel's personality that he is invariably delighted "when, beneath the particular instance, [he is] afforded a glimpse of the general law" (GW 151) and that, in consequence, he looks for laws everywhere he goes. His desire for everything to conform to articulable patterns makes him see regularities where none can possibly be there, as when—in what must surely be, on Proust's ironic part, a reductio ad absurdum of the tendency—he attempts, like the discoverer of an unfamiliar solar system, to explain the erratic behavior of the *petite bande* as governed by a series of as yet unknown but in principle derivable rules. "How many observations," he wonders, "must one accumulate of the movements, to all appearance irregular, of these unknown worlds . . . before deducing the incontrovertible laws . . . of that passionate astronomy!" (BG 561).

Marcel should know better. For the inexplicable (and a fortiori unclassifiable) does happen, even in the *Recherche*; there is room for the miracle, "that wind of fortune which favours us at times" (F 761). The principle of irony itself, one of the most powerful laws operating in the Proustian fictional universe, is periodically susceptible of suspension. Under ordinary circumstances one can expect the exact opposite of any desired outcome to take place;[71] yet there are occasions (which is perhaps crueler still, since it means that one cannot even count on consistency in despair, and abandon all hope) on which the regulations are suddenly abrogated and all at once one finds oneself, for example, allowed to sleep in the same room as Maman (S 48), or back in the affections of the Swanns (BG 99).[72] Marcel should know (or learn) better, but he does not. The rage for generalization is a deep and ineradicable element of his individual being. It enables him to imagine that the world is predictable and therefore controllable (Large 138, Genette 1980: 124); to protect himself from painful discoveries (in the context of the half-hearted self-analysis that I treat in chapter 2, Marcel produces a strikingly vacuous maxim—"watching someone sleep without moving becomes tiring"—in order to explain, or rather to avoid explaining, his actions); and to feel the stab of pain less keenly. Just so, writing takes "our individual suffering" and transposes it into "a general form which will in some measure enable us to escape from its embrace, which will turn all mankind into sharers in our pain, and which is even able to yield us a certain joy" (TR 313).[73]

Maxims and Hypotheses   We have seen that several of the apparently objective and universally valid laws of love turn out to have exceptions, because, as Marcel is periodically aware, no two people love in exactly the same way. Accordingly, the innumerable adages strewn across the pages of *A la recherche du temps perdu* frequently designate "truths" valid for Marcel alone, or at best for Marcel and one or two fellow-sufferers. Things are, however, even more complicated, for a number of the maxims are not even subjective "truths," but only *hypotheses* (Bowie 1987: 47, Shattuck 86)—mere conjectures that Marcel, confusingly, insists on presenting as absolute facts. In one variant, the *pseudo-certitude*, the narrator offers as his own the opinion of the character (that is, Marcel puts in writing an opinion he used to espouse but has since discarded); this is a rare, *self-directed* form of free indirect speech, or, if you prefer, a curious phenomenon of "deliberate unreliability," in which a narrator expressly sets out to voice convictions he no longer (officially) holds. (I discuss this first variant in chapter 1.)

In a second variant, the *provisional conclusion*, the narrator offers his own opinion, "true" at the time of writing, but which gives way, as the narrator subsequently evolves, to another that supersedes it.[74] (We are asked to imagine that the fictional narrator Marcel writes his manuscript over a period of time, just as the real-life author Proust takes some years to write his.) Not that the narrator explicitly takes up an earlier view, reassesses it, finds it wanting, and offers a replacement; no, in general he simply presents his "truths" one after the other, as though there were no conflict among them. Thus what looks, in the very first section of the novel, like a belief in reincarnation turns out to be no more than a colorful way of talking about the discrete phases of a single earthly life, leaving poetic fame as the sole viable path to immortality—until, that is, even the notion of living forever in the collective consciousness of successive generations is rejected as excessively optimistic.[75] Like the pseudo-certitudes, such provisional conclusions serve the project of turning our reading into an experiential process: Proust, we recall, "did not want to analyze this evolution of a belief system abstractly, but rather to recreate it, to bring it to life." Appreciating the novel becomes not just a matter of digesting a set of illuminating doctrines, as it would be with a philosophical treatise, but also in part a matter of being seduced by *delusions* along the way,[76] being forced to *wait* for the truth and, in some instances, to derive it ourselves from a mass of heterogeneous indications.

The maxim with which our whole discussion of unreliability began—Marcel's sweeping statement at the end of *Swann's Way* to the effect that "houses, roads, avenues are as fugitive, alas, as the years"—provides a perfect example, since, as anyone who has finished the *Recherche* knows, it is just waiting to be replaced, in the last volume, by remarks about the extratemporal self which has the power to recall Lost Time (TR 263) and about the capacity of involuntary memory to suspend the "ineluctable law" (clearly not as ineluctable as all that!) "which ordains that we can only imagine what is absent" (ibid.). A similarly misguided early conviction, that sensory impressions cannot form the basis of literature, underlies a sentence from the preamble to the Martinville Steeples episode, a sentence I discuss in chapter 1. But provisional certitudes do not always take so long (nearly the entire length of the novel) to be corrected. Early in *Sodom and Gomorrah*, speaking of homosexual men like Charlus and Jupien, Marcel claims that "their happiness is somehow far more extraordinary, selective, profoundly necessary than that of the normal lover" (SG 37); the retraction follows within five pages. "Contrary to what I had imagined in the courtyard," he now avers (42), "these [apparently] exceptional creatures with whom we commiserate are a vast crowd."

Indeed, when it comes to homosexuality, Marcel is fully capable of expressing antithetical views in the very same breath (cf. Tadié 1971: 420). Is it a vice (TR 112), regrettable and blameworthy? A sickness (SG 34–35, TR 215), baleful but innocent? Just a "taste" which merely "passes for an unnatural one" (TR 483), neither destructive nor desirable? Or, finally, something positively beautiful, a veritable blessing (SG 38)?[77] Is it to be castigated, pitied, studied, or valued? Marcel seems unable to decide, and changes his mind within the space of a single sentence: "This scene was not, however, positively comic; it was stamped with a *strangeness*, or if you like a *naturalness*, the *beauty* of which steadily increased" (SG 6); "One may say that for him [Charlus] the evolution of his *malady* or the revolution of his *vice* had reached the extreme point at which the tiny original personality of the individual, the specific qualities he has inherited from his ancestors, are entirely eclipsed by the transit across them of some generic *defect* or *malady* which is their satellite" (TR 107; my emphasis throughout). Just as Marcel continues, to the bitter end, to entertain a pair of conflicting "hypotheses" concerning Albertine's fidelity (I return to the Albertine dilemma in chapters 2 and 3), so he keeps alive various options in relation to "*le charlisme*." After all, "there is no idea that does not carry in itself its possible refutation, no word that does not imply its opposite" (F 814); there is always a countermaxim, always a competing hypothesis.[78] What we stand to gain from these stabs in the dark is, then, not so much insight into the workings of same-sex desire (queer-theoretical approaches to Proust tend to cherry-pick tendentiously among the claims) as insight into the essence of Marcel's disposition. It is, we should say, *a higher-order law of Marcel's mind* that it cannot come to a definitive judgment about the *hommes-femmes*.[79]

In short, many of the maxims are less eloquent on the subject of humanity at large than on the subject of Marcel. They show us, first, his unchanging and unitary core, in the individual-essential "laws" of love to which he adheres (that attraction derives from anxiety, that it attaches to those who will hurt us, that jealousy is endless) and in the higher-order regularities, such as his propensity to view each new circumstance as the manifestation of a universal axiom. They show us, second, an area of his mind that is unchanging but divided, unchangingly divided into conflicting hypotheses (as, say, about homosexuality). And they show us, finally, that evicted attitudes never quite pack their bags, that they continue to be endorsed by several of his soul's inhabitants (hence perhaps the present tense for ostensibly abandoned positions) even as the number of repudiators steadily rises. Now given that the "objective truths" in the *Recherche* very often have to do with selfhood, with the uniqueness of perspective and with the synchronic and diachronic divisions to which we are all subject—ideas which chapter 3 will set out in detail—we should probably see the "subjective truths" as forming, together, an extended *example* with which Proust is illustrating his account. Perhaps it is a peculiarity of individualist philosophies, which are after all general theories of the specific, that they seem to require such filling in: just like Nietzsche, Proust offers us a case study to accompany his grand conceptual vision.

It might be asked, though: how are we to distinguish objective from subjective truths? How are we to steer a middle course between O'Brien's Scylla (all maxims taken seriously) and Tadié's Charybdis (all maxims dismissed as "fictional"),[80] without lapsing into an arbitrariness of our own? The answer is twofold. First of all, unless we really wish to ironize every last aphorism—and how many of us can genuinely sustain such an interpretation?[81]—we should proceed on the assumption that Marcel speaks for Proust *until and unless there is reason to think otherwise*.[82] "Reason" here means *internal contradiction*, a discrepancy either between one maxim and another (as we saw in the case of the epigraphs on time regained) or between a given maxim and the events depicted in the narrative (as we saw in the case of the laws of love). By discarding the offending aphorisms, synthesizing what is left, and appending a metaprinciple explaining the deployment of ironized statements, we should be able to reach a coherent Proustian position. There is precedent for such an approach, since it is also the way many people read Plato's dialogues: Socrates speaks for Plato, such readers surmise, unless there is reason to think differently, and the combination of (1) a set of unironized statements with (2) a hypothesis about Platonic irony will yield a plausible overall understanding of the texts.

With Proust, mind you, we are in a better position than with Plato, for here—and I come now to the second part of the answer—we have at our disposal a large number of nonfictional writings, in the form of articles and letters (letters whose authenticity, unlike in Plato's case, is not in doubt), confirming a number of the theses advanced by Marcel. (If, at various junctures in this book, I follow quotations from the *Recherche* with references to EA and the correspondence, it is in part to indicate Proust's assent to a claim made by his narrator.) The most important example may well be the letter to Antoine Bibesco of November 1912, later recycled into the interview Proust gave Elie-Joseph Bois for *Le temps* (EA 253–55). Here, Proust states quite clearly (1) that he must not be confused with his narrator; (2) that he is, however, just as firm a believer in involuntary memory as is Marcel; and (3) that we should take entirely seriously the idea that human beings are individuated according to the subjective way in which each experiences the world, a "vision" that remains constant across a lifetime and emerges only in style. "Style is in no way an embellishment, as certain people think, it is not even a question of technique; it is, like color with certain painters, a quality of vision, a revelation of a private universe which each one of us sees and which is not seen by others. The pleasure an artist gives us is to make us know an additional universe." (Similar indications may be found in the essay on Flaubert and the preface to Paul Morand's *Tendres stocks*, at EA 288 and 311, respectively.) It seems to me that we have no reason, given this testimony and in the absence of any real counterevidence within the *Recherche*, to put into question the famous statements on style made in the context of Vinteuil's *septuor* (C 343) and of the *matinée Guermantes* (TR 299).[83] They remain standing, even when several of their surrounding claims, as I am about to suggest, fall by the wayside.

3. Aesthetics

Récit and Oeuvre   In the previous section, I focused on the laws of love in order to show that many of the apparently universal theories produced in the course of the *Recherche* are in fact local, or provisional, or subjective. I chose the laws of love as a sample set because they offer the clearest instance of the general trend. The most *important* case, however, is that of the aesthetic principles, the rules for creation Marcel sets out at the end of the novel, when he is about to embark on his own (unnamed) literary project. Now just as we should not take the statements Marcel makes about love as a key to Proust's theory of desire, so, I want to argue, *we should not take the statements Marcel makes about writing in the final volume as a key to Proust's literary project.* Although the issue is clearly crucial, we rarely find it broached, since almost all critics—including many of those who draw a line between Proust and Marcel—assume that the novel Marcel ends up writing is none other than the *Recherche* itself. For such readers, matters take on a pleasingly circular structure: Marcel, it is said, undergoes various experiences that finally enable him to write a book in which a character undergoes various experiences that finally enable him to write a book, and so on (Nehamas 1985: 168). On reaching the conclusion of *Le temps retrouvé*, we can simply return to the very first page, which we now see as forming a seamless, *Finnegans Wake*–like continuation, wrapping around from end to beginning.[84] We can now read "Longtemps je me suis couché de bonne heure" not merely as the sincere introduction to a memoir but also as the artful opening gambit of a literary craftsman. "In the final pages, we see the character and the narrator come together," as Jean Rousset puts it in *Forme et signification*; "The narrator . . . will soon be able to start constructing the work which is coming to a close, and first of all to write *Combray*. . . . This novel is conceived in such a way that its end engenders its beginning" (144; my translation).

Rousset is far from alone in his assessment. Narrator and hero, agrees Louis Martin-Chauffier, "tend toward a meeting, tend toward the day when the hero's trajectory . . . leads to that table at which the narrator . . . invites him to sit down next to him, so that together they may write the words 'The End'" (56). "Marcel and the Narrator move slowly toward one another," concurs Roger Shattuck, using the same metaphor of intersection, "until they finally meet in the closing pages. That reunited *I* . . . produces a whole which is the book itself" (38). Even those who put the circular structure into question usually take it for granted that the novel entices us to experience the (fraudulent) circularity, "the convergence of author and narrator at the end of the novel" (Paul de Man 16), so that "we pretend that at the end of the narrative Marcel is on the point of setting out to write the novel—the narrative itself" (Richard Terdiman 1976: 173). Similarly, while Gérard Genette distinguishes between Marcel's novel and Proust's novel on the basis of their ostensible composition time (1980: 223), "the rest," he continues, "is already known to us by the very novel that concludes here" (226). And thereafter, with a few notable exceptions—Roland Barthes (1986a: 283, 1972: 121), Antoine Compagnon (1989: 301–2), Pierre-Louis Rey and Brian Rogers (IV: 1174–75)—a review of Proust scholarship rapidly acquires the sound of a litany. "The novel the narrator undertakes to write has just been finished by the reader" (Fránk 23); "the future work of art is now actually the plot of the novel we are reading" (Bales 73);[85] "it is, we suppose, the book we have just been reading" (May 15); "'As of tomorrow' Marcel intends to retreat to the solitude of his office and to start writing, writing that *Recherche* which the reader already knows" (Warning 16).[86]

Marcel's novel can, however, not be equivalent to the *Recherche*. There is a straightforward logical reason why not: if we were dealing with a single work, then it would end up the case that Marcel had, at one and the same moment, both written and not written it. For when Marcel arrives at the *matinée Guermantes*, he has drafted large quantities of his autobiography but has produced not so much as a word of his future novel, and indeed considers himself entirely incapable of ever devising one. He has jotted down the idea at least for "a story about Swann and his inability to do without Odette" (C 493)—otherwise known as *Swann in Love*—during the period of Albertine's "captivity" in Paris;[87] as Muller points out (44), Marcel requires no madeleine in order to recount Swann's story, it being based on third-party testimony rather than on Marcel's retrospection. And during the period following the madeleine episode, which restores Marcel's own earlier life to consciousness, he has begun to record that earlier life, too, so that at least some of his recollections have been committed to paper by the time he steps off the train in Paris.

That Marcel has been busy not just thinking about but setting down his past is evident from a number of clues. For one thing, he must have written "Place Names: The Name" some time before the final revelation of *Time Regained*, since the former is recounted by a man who lacks, "today" (I:414), the power to invest the world with belief, who nostalgically laments "the happy days of my credulous youth" (S 602), and who decries "the contradiction of seeking in reality for the pictures that are stored in one's memory" (S 606; translations modified).[88] (As I mentioned above, Proust is quite categorical that the "disenchanted skepticism" of the Bois de Boulogne visit is "the *opposite* of my conclusion.") For another thing, certain segments of the story are clearly told by a subject living in the prewar period. The scene we have just been discussing is one example, according to Gérard Genette (1980: 225); another is *The Captive*, in which Marcel speculates as to what might happen "should a war ever come" (C 313).

Finally, there is an intriguing moment, during the climactic visit to the Guermantes residence at the end of the novel, in which Marcel all of a sudden remembers something *new* about Combray, something we did not read about in the early pages of *A la recherche du temps perdu*. "A level ray of the setting sun recalled to me instantaneously an episode in my early childhood to which I had never since that time given a thought: my aunt Léonie had a fever which Doctor Percepied feared might be typhoid and for a week I was made to sleep in Eulalie's little room looking out on the Place de l'Eglise, which had . . . a muslin curtain that was always buzzing with a sunshine to which I was not accustomed" (TR 276). Given that the memory is important enough to include here, surely it is important enough to include in its proper place, which is to say in the second chapter of *Combray*, following the madeleine episode. If Marcel has not written this chapter by the time he recalls his sun-filled week spent in Eulalie's bedroom, then he is bound to incorporate the latter within its pages. But as we know, Marcel will say nothing of the unusual week when he comes to draw up *Combray*—or rather, since this is undoubtedly the more plausible scenario, Marcel *has said* nothing about it. *Combray*, as an early volume of Marcel's memoirs, is already signed and sealed before the day of the fateful *matinée*.

The overall chronology must, in fact, be something like this:

- Swann's life with Odette (before Marcel's birth).
- *Drame du coucher* (presumably predates other Combray memories, which feature Marcel reading on his own, rather than being read to by Maman).
- Events depicted in the sequence from *Combray II* to *La prisonnière* (more or less in order of narration), with the exception of Marcel's visit to the Bois de Boulogne.
- Writing (or at least drafting) of *Un amour de Swann*.
- Events depicted in the sequence from *La prisonnière* to *Le temps retrouvé*, up to and including the return to Tansonville.
- Long years spent in and out of sanatoria. The period of early bedtimes, by which point the visit to Tansonville is no more than a distant memory, begins here.
- The madeleine episode, during a stay at home, perhaps between visits to sanatoria.[89]
- Writing of (more of) the memoir, including childhood experiences rescued from oblivion by the madeleine.[90] All of *Combray II*, and at least part of *La prisonnière* (some of which is prewar material).
- Visit to the Bois de Boulogne, "this year" (very likely still prewar).
- Visits to Paris in 1914 and 1916.
- Climactic *matinée* at the Guermantes salon (postwar); a new memory of Combray (Eulalie's bedroom).
- Full draft of the memoir, including the opening, an account of the *matinée* itself, transitions, and revisions (especially prolepses).[91]
- Shift to sleeping during the day. A fall downstairs on return from an outing.[92]
- Seclusion (with the exception of some *légères amours*).
- Beginning of the *novel*. Sketches shown around to uncomprehending friends.
- Continued sporadic work on the memoir: the latest events narrated are (a) a meeting with the now-senile Odette, three years after the *matinée*; (b) receipt of a letter from the late Baron de Charlus, some time around 1926.[93]

The book we have in our hands cannot, therefore, be the novel Marcel is about to write, for two simple reasons: one, he is not about to write it because he has already written it, and two, what he has already written is not a novel, but only (from his point of view) a memoir. This is why he can tell Albertine, in spite of the fact that he has been busy drafting *Un amour de Swann*, "I'm not a novelist" (C 510); this is why he considers, in spite of the fact that he has been producing manuscripts for several years, that "literature had played no part in my life" (TR 304) and that "I was embarking upon my labour of construction . . . without knowing anything of my trade" (TR 521). Marcel clearly classes his memoir alongside the articles, translations, and even Martinville prose poem in the category of minor efforts, compositions he has hatched while nevertheless feeling that, when it comes to the masterpiece of which he has always dreamed, he is still irremediably blocked. The two projects are rigorously distinct.

What is more, the two projects are kept apart by a fairly robust linguistic barrier (decisive evidence, it seems to me, though to my knowledge it has never before been mentioned). With but a single exception (I:515), Marcel habitually refers to the text at hand as "ce *récit*" (or the more neutral "cet ouvrage"), whereas he almost always refers to the future/inchoate work as "mon *livre*" or "mon *oeuvre*" (with its associated forms "oeuvre d'art," "oeuvre littéraire": the nuance speaks for itself). To be sure, there are occasional deviations from the norm—one misplaced "récit" (IV:620), one inapposite "livre" (I:515), a couple of misplaced "ouvrages" (I:569, IV:618)—but they are surely outweighed by the relentless barrage of *livres*—

> a life, in short, can be realised within the confines of a book [*un livre*]! How happy would he be, I thought, the man who had the power to write such a book [*un tel livre*]! What a task awaited him! . . . for this writer . . . would have to prepare his book [*son livre*] with meticulous care. . . . In long books [*livres*] of this kind there are parts which there has been time only to sketch, parts which, because of the very amplitude of the architect's plan, will no doubt never be completed. . . . But to return to my own case, I thought more modestly of my book [*mon livre*] and it would be inaccurate even to say that I thought of those who would read it as "my" readers. For it seemed to me that they would not be "my" readers but the readers of their own selves, my book [*mon livre*] being merely a sort of magnifying glass like those which the optician at Combray used to offer his customers—it would be my book [*mon livre*], but with its help I would furnish them with the means of reading what lay inside themselves. . . . I should construct my book [*mon livre*], I dare not say ambitiously like a cathedral, but quite simply like a dress. (TR 507–9)

—and the equally relentless barrage of *oeuvres*:

> I felt that I no longer possessed the strength to carry out my obligations
> to people or my duties to my thoughts and my work [*mon oeuvre*], still
> less to satisfy both of these claims. . . . I was indifferent to the verdict
> which might be passed on my work [*mon oeuvre*] by the best minds of
> my age, and this not because I relegated to some future after my death
> the admiration which it seemed to me that my work [*mon oeuvre*] ought
> to receive. . . . The truth was that, if I thought of my work [*mon oeuvre*]
> and not of the letters which I ought to answer, this was not because I
> attached to these two things . . . very different degrees of importance.
> The organisation of my memory, of the preoccupations that filled my
> mind, was indeed linked to my work [*mon oeuvre*], but perhaps simply
> because, while the letters which I received were forgotten a moment
> later, the idea of my work [*mon oeuvre*] was inside my head, always
> the same, perpetually in process of becoming. But even my work had
> become for me a tiresome obligation. . . . In me . . . , the powers of the
> writer were no longer equal to the egotistical demands of the work
> [*l'oeuvre*]. Since the day of the staircase, nothing in the world, no happi-
> ness, whether it came from friendship or the progress of my book [*mon*
> *oeuvre*] or the hope of fame, reached me except as a sunshine unclouded
> but so pale that it no longer had the virtue to warm me. (TR 521–22)

Once we notice the fact that Marcel is thinking differently about (1) the
récit he has (largely) completed and (2) the *oeuvre* he has (largely) yet to undertake, something very interesting comes into focus, namely that Marcel
occasionally refers to both texts more or less in the same breath, *but using
the past tense for one and (effectively) a future tense for the other.* In speaking,
for example, of the "important truths, worthy of being used as the cement
which would hold part of my work [*mon oeuvre*] together" (TR 407), Marcel
notes that some of them will be derived from the lives of characters "the portrayal of [whom] was attempted in the first pages of this work [*ce récit*]" (TR
410). Marcel even goes so far as to suggest that what he will do in the novel
is going to *depart from* what he has done in the memoir. "Many errors" (he
says) "there are, as the reader will have seen that various episodes in the story
[*ce récit*] had proved to me, by which our senses falsify for us the real nature
of the world. *Some of these, however, it would be possible for me to avoid* by the
efforts which I should make [in the *oeuvre*] to give a more exact transcription
of things. In the case of sounds, for instance, I should be able to refrain from
altering their place of origin, from detaching them from their cause, beside
which our intelligence only succeeds in locating them after they have reached
our ears" (TR 526–27; my emphasis).[94]

In another case, Marcel worries that he will not perhaps have time, when he begins his novel, to "represent some of my characters as existing not outside but within ourselves," a technique "the needfulness of which, if one is to depict reality, has been made manifest in the course of my narrative [*ce récit*]" (TR 527,8). How can such a worry even be conceivable, if the *récit* and the *oeuvre* are identical? If the two texts are one and the same, then either Marcel has written both or he has written neither. If he has written neither, then he cannot know what has been (or rather what will be) "made manifest" in the *récit*. If he has written both, then he must know what is contained within the *oeuvre*; he must have precise information as to how people are going to be (are already) represented there, and must at the very least be aware of his ability to complete it. (Notice that the narrator of the *récit* is eternally confident of returning to certain motifs, no matter at what distance across the text; the man about to create the *oeuvre*, by contrast, fears being struck dead in the middle of the next sentence.[95] If, as the standard hypothesis suggests, the *oeuvre*-inventor metamorphoses effortlessly into the *récit*-narrator, then why does he not carry over with him his intimations of mortality?)

There is also a puzzle that works in the opposite direction. I have said that the *récit* cannot be Marcel's *oeuvre* because he has already nearly finished the *récit*; but conversely, the *oeuvre* is also unlikely to be the *récit* because Marcel has already begun the *oeuvre*. Critics who talk of the circular structure of the *Recherche*[96] are often simply overlooking the fact that Marcel has, by the end of *Time Regained*, actually produced several pages of text—long enough to include passages of what looks like "pedantic investigation of detail"— which he circulates among his uncomprehending friends. "Before very long I was able to show a few sketches. No one understood anything of them. . . . Those passages in which I was trying to arrive at general laws were described as so much pedantic investigation of detail" (TR 520). Thus the last page does not, in the end, close quite so neatly and seamlessly upon the first.[97] And we are also left wondering why Marcel's habit of the knowing backward glance has deserted him at this precise moment. Why does he not refer, here as elsewhere (e.g., C 233), to events "which we have already observed in the course of this narrative"? Why be so vague about the "sketches," rather than explaining that they are totally familiar to us, in the form of the half-remembered rooms and the *drame du coucher*? Why, in other words, does Proust allow Marcel to start but not to complete his *oeuvre*, if he really wishes us to take it for the *Recherche*?

Proust's Project and Marcel's Project   We have just seen that it is somewhat incautious to attribute the *Recherche*, without further ado, to Marcel as a novel he is just about to write. It is Proust's novel, and it is Marcel's autobiography, but it is not Marcel's novel. We are dealing, in fact, with three separate texts:

1. Marcel's memoir (*récit*), an autobiography;
2. Marcel's future novel (*oeuvre*), a fictionalized autobiography;
3. Proust's novel, a fiction (with some autobiographical borrowings).

For the sake of clarity, though in full awareness of how awkward and arbitrary the attribution is, I am going to give titles to the first two. We now have

1. *My Life; or, The History of a Vocation*, a memoir by Marcel;
2. *The Magic Lantern*, a novel by Marcel; and
3. *A la recherche du temps perdu*, a novel by Proust.

Using the above nomenclature, we can say that Marcel is left having more or less completed *My Life*, and having begun work on *The Magic Lantern*, by the time the *Recherche* draws to a close. But it is not merely the (imaginary) titles, nor the respective states of (in)completion, that set the three tomes apart. Though Marcel's novel shares much of its content with his memoir, it is nonetheless distinct in *style*. For while *The Magic Lantern* contains (to repeat) as few optical and auditory illusions as possible, *My Life*, for its part, is positively bursting with them. When describing, for example, Robert de Saint-Loup's watch, Marcel states in his *récit* that "[its] tick changed place every moment" (GW 92); when describing Albertine's face, Marcel tells us that she has a mole on her chin (BG 578), then that she has a mole on her cheek (BG 618), and finally—the truth, this time—that she has a mole on her upper lip (BG 624–25); and when describing a street scene, Marcel writes that "a woman with no pretence to fashion . . . came past, too brightly dressed in a sack overcoat of goatskin; but no, it was not a woman, it was a chauffeur" (C 175). (I discuss the "optical illusions" further in chapter 1.) In *The Magic Lantern*, Marcel will presumably content himself with stating the location of the watch ("cause" of the ticking), with situating Albertine's mole on her lip from the outset, and with calling a chauffeur a chauffeur, rather than rechristening him a frumpily dressed woman.[98]

Surprisingly perhaps, *My Life* and the *Recherche* are also discrete entities. True, the two are superficially indistinguishable: Proust's novel reiterates every last syntagm, from "Longtemps je me suis couché de bonne heure" to "dans le Temps," of Marcel's lengthy memoir. But *My Life* carries Marcel's signature, the *Recherche* that of Proust, and the nuance is decisive. It turns the identical set of phrases into a pair of nonidentical books, if we understand by "book" not just a series of marks on a page but a system of meanings, expressions, and effects.[99] In Jorge Luis Borges's short story "Pierre Menard, Author of the *Quixote*," the eponymous twentieth-century French poet rewrites the seventeenth-century classic *Don Quixote* word for word. Yet because of the passage of time (including the fact that there already exists one *Don Quixote!* [42]), the Menard version becomes a whole new work: "The archaic style of Menard—quite foreign, after all—suffers from a certain affectation. Not so that of his forerunner, who handles with ease the current Spanish of his time" (43).

If there is a disparity between Menard's *Quixote* and Cervantes's *Quixote*, this is because *the attribution of an author crucially co-determines the meaning of a text* (Nehamas 1981). That is why we can change our minds about the gist of a document when we make new discoveries about its author—consider those who take "A Modest Proposal" seriously, and only later learn what Swift was up to—and that is why we can disagree over interpretations with those who take certain manuscripts to have been authored by God, say, rather than a human being, or the Earl of Shaftesbury, say, rather than William Shakespeare. When an atheist reads in the Gospel of Matthew (21:1–9) that Jesus entered Jerusalem riding two animals at once, she is likely to construe it as a clumsy mistake on the part of the Gospel's author, who clearly wishes to give the impression that Jesus has fulfilled all Old Testament prophecies but who has misunderstood Zachariah 9:9; when, on the other hand, a literalist believer reads the passage, he will probably understand it as a kind of miracle. (In the Gospel of Thomas, Jesus says "It is impossible for a man to mount two horses" [47]—but what is impossible for a man is presumably trivial for the son of God.)

In very much the same way, Proust's "Longtemps . . . dans le Temps" document (*A la recherche du temps perdu*) differs in import and impact from Marcel's "Longtemps . . . dans le Temps" document (*My Life*). It is pointless, for example, to wonder about the significance of individual proper nouns as long as we are treating the text as Marcel's autobiography. Marcel calls Combray's physician "Dr. Percepied" because that is his name; with Proust as our postulated author, however, we may begin to speculate as to how we should take Dr. Pierce-Foot, French cousin to Oedipus (or perhaps to that famous surgeon of club feet, Charles Bovary). Similarly, we may legitimately ask why the main aristocratic family in the novel needs to be called "Guermantes," given that Proust himself may have had no particular fascination with the "golden" syllable [àt], any more than he had a fascination with madeleines.[100] We are at liberty to *interpret* the choice of a madeleine, rather than a piece of toast (or a storm in Brittany), as trigger for the most famous involuntary memory.[101] And we can admire the artistry with which, as Gérard Genette brilliantly observes (1972: 42), Proust places a flowering plant in the Guermantes' courtyard just so that Marcel can "discover" it and use it as an image for the miraculous encounter between Charlus and Jupien. In all such cases, elements of Marcel's reality, dutifully reported in *My Life*, are, in the *Recherche*, artistic choices made by Proust.

Now just as *The Magic Lantern* and the *Recherche* depart from *My Life*, so too does the *Recherche* diverge from *The Magic Lantern*. The reason is that the *Recherche*, as we saw above in the context of the Agostinelli debate, includes thoroughly fabricated elements. Two sentences from *Le temps retrouvé* make the contrast particularly salient.

[a] "In this book in which there is not a single incident which is not fictitious, not a single character who is a real person in disguise, in which everything has been invented by me in accordance with the requirements of my theme, I owe it to the credit of my country to say that only the millionaire cousins of Françoise who came out of retirement to help their niece when she was left without support, only they are real people who exist." (TR 225)[102]

[b] "And I understood that all these materials for a work of literature were simply my past life; I understood that they had come to me, in frivolous pleasures, in indolence, in tenderness, in unhappiness, and that I had stored them up without divining the purpose for which they were destined or even their continued existence any more than a seed does when it forms within itself a reserve of all the nutritious substances from which it will feed a plant." (TR 304)

Sentence [a] is of a highly unusual type. Most statements in the *Recherche*, even if they are ultimately endorsed by Proust, belong in the first instance to Marcel: thus when a voice proclaims that "there is a psychology in time, in which the calculations of a plane psychology would no longer be accurate" (F 751), it is technically Marcel speaking, though Proust, as we know from independent evidence (EA 253, *Letters* 226), happens to agree with him; and when a voice says "I tasted the madeleine soaked in tea" (C 513), Marcel is speaking for himself alone, unsupported by his inventor. Sentence [a], by contrast, cannot belong to Marcel at all. For whoever has produced it clearly considers the Larivière family to be the only real people in the book, which means that from this person's point of view, Gilberte, Albertine, Robert, Charlus, Oriane de Guermantes, Mme Verdurin, Swann, Maman, and even Marcel himself—all living, breathing entities as far as Marcel is concerned— are nothing more than fictional characters, spawned for "the requirements of my theme." Someone else has to be talking here, someone at a higher ontological level than Marcel, and it is reasonable to assume that this someone is (a figure for) the author.

Let us say, then, that sentence [a] represents Proust's assessment of his present work (the *Recherche*) and sentence [b] a description by Marcel of his future work (*The Magic Lantern*). The contrast between the two is dramatic, and would probably look quite surprising to anyone who believed that both cases involve Proust discussing his own literary production. Proust sets out to construct a world maximally remote from our own, all but two of its countless characters springing fully armed from his head; Marcel, quite the reverse, sets out to devise a book virtually devoid of invention (on his view, "A man born ... without imagination might, in spite of this deficiency, be able to write admirable novels" [TR 307]).[103]

Of course, the self-assessment of Proust (or his delegate) is a touch exaggerated, and conversely *The Magic Lantern* will include *some* stylization of the episodes reported (otherwise it would hardly be a "work of literature"), yet the warning is nonetheless apt. Proust's novel is not the same as the novel Marcel promises to write, because Proust's novel is to a considerable degree a work of fantasy. Proust never ate a madeleine that brought back lost memories; Proust was never privy to the thoughts of a dying writer; Proust never visited towns named "Balbec" or "Combray"; Proust never heard a *septuor*[104] by Vinteuil; and so on, and so on. There is no room in Marcel's aesthetics for such pure inventions, no room for a piece of fiction.[105] The upshot is that *we cannot determine Proust's project merely by contemplating Marcel's theories.* If Marcel were really a paragon of perfection, then Proust, who does not follow his admonitions in all respects, would come up short, showing marked deficiencies as a creative writer. Marcel's project, to be materialized in *The Magic Lantern*, and Proust's project, materialized in the *Recherche*, are palpably distinct.[106]

From the beginning, Proust scholarship seems to have overlooked this possibility, in spite of going through substantial variations over the years. At first, critics drew upon the aesthetic principles in *Le temps retrouvé* as a way of understanding the novel as a whole, on the assumption that they represented Proust's honest and accurate self-appraisal. Later, with the advent of a hermeneutics of suspicion, critics found (and in some cases invented) discrepancies between theory and practice in order to blame Proust for failing to deliver on his grandiose promises, still taken to be sincere but no longer taken to be apposite.[107] Most recently, critics have begun to take the suspicious hermeneutic from the other end: rather than castigating Proust for not writing the work he promises, they applaud him for writing—all unawares—a *better* work. In Gérard Genette's words, "what has been said of Courbet could also be said of Proust, that his vision is more modern than his theory" (1966: 53); in those of Vincent Descombes, "the Proustian novel is bolder than Proust the theorist ... the formulations of Proust the theorist do not do justice to the intuitions of Proust the novelist" (6, 233).[108] Perhaps they feel that the ultimate vindication, for a man who denies the ability of artists to understand at a conscious level what they are doing,[109] would be to create a masterpiece whose greatness entirely escapes him.

There is something very reasonable, plausible, and indeed charitable about the Genette-Descombes view. After all, Proust's hope for *Contre Sainte-Beuve* was that "when people have finished the book, they will see (I'd

like to think) that the whole novel is nothing other than the practical application of the artistic principles stated in that last part, a sort of preface, if you
like, placed at the end" (Corr. 9:155). Proust may have preserved the same
self-interpreting strategy for *A la recherche du temps perdu*, and then changed
his position somewhere along the way (Nathan; qtd. in Jauss 256), gradually
separating himself from Marcel and his *principes d'art*. Consider the fact that
the most flagrantly self-reflexive moments, including sentence [a] above, are
later additions (Muller 169), and that *Contre Sainte-Beuve* leaves its narrator
on the threshold (perhaps) of a future work, rather than having him draft a
number of potentially unrelated "sketches."[110] The degree to which Proust
was aware of the progressive distance between himself and his erstwhile
mouthpiece can of course never be established, but I would like to propose
the possibility that Proust knew exactly what he was doing. He famously
pronounced himself happy with the manuscript in spring 1922 (Tadié 1996:
892), meaning that although a number of minor corrections remained to be
made (including the miraculous reappearance of dead characters, like the
twice-resurrected Cottard [C 321, 371; TR 116, 148]), he considered the
essential elements to be in place. My submission is that Proust realized the
aesthetic treatise no longer fully captured the essence of his achievement, but
consciously decided to leave it just as it was, as another index of the distance
Marcel would have to travel if he were ever to catch up with his author, and,
by consequence, as an index of the distance we too have to travel if we are to
understand the nature of what Proust is offering us.

Training through Fiction   From the assumption that Proust deliberately left
an ironic gap between his narrator's blueprint for the ultimate artwork and
his own literary masterpiece, a number of intriguing hypotheses follow. As a
first corollary, we find ourselves at liberty to credit Proust with a full understanding (or at least intuition, as would be in keeping with Proust's perspective on the creative process) of his own accomplishment. We do not have to
say that Proust fails to practice what he preaches, or is unable to live up to
his own theories: these are not his theories, and the preacher is not he. We
also do not have to say, with Duncan Large,[111] that the *Recherche* constitutes
an abortive attempt at self-fashioning on the part of Proust, since we can see
that it is rather a successful (or at least preliminary) effort at self-fashioning
on the part of a fictional character, Marcel.

   Second, we find ourselves forced to recognize the tacit injunction to follow the lead of the implied author, rather than that of his narrator. If we
wish to emulate Proust, that is, we must not do what Marcel speaks of doing,
namely produce a lightly touched-up ("redescribed") autobiography, but
instead do what Proust himself has done, which is to say invent a world full
of interesting characters, improbable events (the meeting of Charlus and
Jupien, the "inversion" of almost every character by novel's end . . .), and

impossible insights. What we write should be a *Recherche*, not a *Magic Lantern*. Only a work of imagination, after all, can convey our deepest essence, the way we see the world. Style, as Marcel puts it, "is the revelation, which by direct and conscious methods would be impossible, of the qualitative difference, the uniqueness of the fashion in which the world appears to each one of us, a difference which, if there were no art, would remain for ever the secret of every individual" (TR 299).[112]

It is, however, not indifferent that Proust has chosen to write a novel in the first person, a novel whose protagonist manages, against multiple obstacles (spelled out in detail in chapter 3), to impose a measure of order on his life. And that brings me to my third point: by means of a single narrative, Proust is actually presenting us with two separate objects of imitation. While the *Recherche* is an example of how to make art, *My Life* (to return to the fanciful nomenclature introduced earlier) is an example of how to make a Self. The sequence of words from "Longtemps" to "dans le Temps" does not serve the function of constructing an impressive or consoling or coherent narrative of Proust's existence, since it is only a novel; but it does serve just that function for *Marcel*, since from his point of view it is a *memoir*. On that basis, it also offers a formal model for how we, too, could do the same thing with our own lives, using the same set of strategies, both small- and large-scale, for corralling the chaotic mass of material that is our personal history into a pleasing overall shape.[113] (My coda will lay out the strategies concerned.) More or less unwittingly, Marcel does an effective job of aesthetic self-fashioning in this, his memoir (*My Life*), and we can only imagine that he will do an even better job in his coming effort (*The Magic Lantern*), a work which consists in the same autobiography with increased stylization. Indeed, there are strong intimations that such an enterprise will never be concluded. What Proust achieves, in giving us Marcel's first version and his set of transformation rules for the second, is actually to give us the basis for a potentially infinite series of texts, book 1 (*My Life*), book 2 (*The Magic Lantern*), . . . book *n* (the latest treatment, still and always incomplete).[114]

One might well wonder, given that the task can never be brought to a satisfying close, why anyone would ever embark upon it. And I venture to suggest—as my fourth point—that Proust is implicitly raising the very same question. He is inviting us, that is, to consider the ultimate fruitlessness of committing our fashioned and continually refashioned self to paper; he is inviting us to take Marcel's memoir as a model for how we should *think* about our lives, not how we should *write* about them (consider that Proust himself left no autobiography behind, only a work of fiction). We should live our lives in the way Marcel narrates his, which is to say *as though* they were about to be memorialized in prose at any moment. Our ideal should be life *as* literature, not life *in* literature. And at the same time, while we live our literary lives, telling ourselves carefully composed autobiographies, we need to take a certain ironic distance from those stories, acknowledging them for the local, ephemeral, partly artificial constructs that they are. My fifth and final point, then, is that Proust's novel, with its simultaneous promptings to empathize with and to stand back from its narrator, trains us in this too. We learn, in a manner I discuss further in chapters 2 and 3, to be lucid in our illusions.

Once we see that Proust's ambition is primarily to train, rather than to teach, we can finally understand why it is not important that Marcel's every last aphorism ring true. Indeed, we can understand why it is vital that many of them ring *false*. To be sure, we must take a subset of the philosophical statements at face value—some of them, after all, explain the purpose of our training—but we must also maintain a degree of suspicion vis-à-vis the rest, however convincing they may sound, precisely so that we may hone our capacity for self-detachment. Furthermore, to the extent that a number of the views conflict with one another while nonetheless plausibly belonging, on a long-term basis, to a single clearly defined character, we are invited to consider our own inevitable theoretical inconsistencies as raw material for the creation of an aesthetically unified persona. Marcel, with his hard-nosed cynicism sharing office space with ineradicable tendencies to *croyance* (in, say, the magic of the Guermantes name, or the immortality of the soul), becomes the paradigmatic philosophical self-fashioner,[115] namely one who achieves unity not only in spite of but *out of* conflicting philosophical systems. The implied author of *A la recherche du temps perdu* is not a neurotic prone to putting his daily affirmations in print, nor a man who needs to speak in code of his socially unacceptable desires, nor yet a glorious literary failure. He is, instead, an artist who wishes to offer himself as an exemplar of creativity, his character as a model of philosophical self-fashioning, and his massive novel as a training ground for lucid self-delusion.

I

Perspective (Marcel's Steeples)

It was certainly not impressions of this kind that could restore the hope I had lost of succeeding one day in becoming
an author and poet, for each of them was associated with
some material object devoid of intellectual value and suggesting no abstract truth.

—*Swann's Way*

It is natural for human beings to consider their epistemological situation
cause for despondency. Caught, as Blaise Pascal would say, between the infinitely large and the infinitely small, unable to speak with greater certainty
about elementary particles than about the vast reaches of space, we are also
condemned, so it seems, to irremediable ignorance concerning the contents
of other minds, all the more so as we cannot even fathom the contents of our
own minds, or indeed the very kind of thing a mind *is* in the first place. Faced
with such a predicament, some counsel humility, while others (like Pascal
himself) propose religious faith. Rare are those who invite us to celebrate
the obstacle, to love the limit, to become a fan of finitude. Yet such is exactly
the consolation that Proust has to offer, just as Friedrich Nietzsche, the
brother-in-arms Proust never recognized, had offered it some thirty years
previously. For if Proust's protagonist is anything to go by, the human adventure is a matter of repeatedly bumping up, in increasing frustration, against
the variably colored, translucent "barrier" between mind and world (S 115,
TR 420), only to realize that the glass itself—our individual perspective—is
far more interesting than any aspect of external reality, however accurately
grasped, could hope to be.

This is Proust's "Copernican turn," his revolution in the way we approach
cognition. It accounts, as is plain, for the overall structure of *A la recherche
du temps perdu*, an immense Bildungsroman in which the protagonist succes-

sively abandons the search for essences in one domain after another (nature, society, friendship, love) and concludes, in each case, that its essence is either nonexistent or unavailable, the only accessible essence—accessible, at least, outside of aesthetic contemplation—being that of his own mind's index of refraction. What is perhaps less evident is that Proust's Copernican turn also accounts for a curious section of *Swann's Way*, a section, in fact, in which the ratio between notoriety and justification reaches its zenith; which is to say, almost all readers of Proust know that they are supposed to take it seriously, yet very few are quite sure why. The passage in question concerns Marcel's very first piece of creative writing, his *petit poème en prose* (I:447/BG 35) dedicated to the steeples at Martinville.

> *Alone, rising from the level of the plain, and seemingly lost in that expanse of open country, the twin steeples of Martinville rose towards the sky. Presently we saw three: springing into position in front of them with a bold leap, a third, dilatory steeple, that of Vieuxvicq, had come to join them. The minutes passed, we were travelling fast, and yet the three steeples were still a long way ahead of us, like three birds perched upon the plain, mo-tionless and conspicuous in the sunlight. Then the steeple of Vieuxvicq drew aside, took its proper distance, and the steeples of Martinville remained alone, gilded by the light of the setting sun which, even at that distance, I could see playing and smiling upon their sloping sides. We had been so long in approaching them that I was thinking of the time that must still elapse before we could reach them when, of a sudden, the carriage turned a corner and set us down at their feet; and they had flung themselves so abruptly in our path that we had barely time to stop before being dashed against the porch. We resumed our journey. We had left Martinville some little time, and the village, after accompanying us for a few seconds, had already disappeared, when, lingering alone on the horizon to watch our flight, its steeples and that of Vieuxvicq waved once again their sun-bathed pinnacles in token of farewell. Sometimes one would withdraw, so that the other two might watch us for a moment still; then the road changed direc-tion, they veered in the evening light like three golden pivots, and vanished from my sight. But a little later, when we were already close to Combray, the sun having set meanwhile, I caught sight of them for the last time, far away, and seeming no more now than three flowers painted upon the sky above the low line of the fields. They made me think, too, of three maidens in a legend, abandoned in a solitary place over which night had begun to fall; and as we drew away from them at a gallop, I could see them timidly seeking their way, and after some awkward, stumbling movements of their noble silhouettes, drawing close to one another, gliding one behind another, forming now against the still rosy sky no more than a single dusky shape, charming and resigned, and so vanishing in the night. (S 255–56)*

Although it might, at first glance, seem an innocuous (if not insipid) piece of juvenilia, and although it flagrantly fails to deliver on the promises made for it by Marcel, the "little prose poem," when considered in context, actually betrays a set of crucial insights into the constraints placed on our acquaintance with external objects, the respective roles played by intuition and intellect in information-gathering, and the primacy of self-knowledge over other types of cognition. In addition, it *fills in* the theory, by revealing, through its imagery—and, at a higher level, through the larger mechanisms that subtend image-production—just what kind of distortion Marcel's individual perspective imposes on the world before his eyes. This meager and apparently blunt shred of metal turns out, on closer inspection, to be the key that unlocks the epistemology (and to some extent also the axiology) of the *Recherche*.

1. The Martinville Enigma

If one thing is clear from the Martinville steeples episode, it is that we are supposed to consider it significant. After all, the *petit poème en prose* is the one and only piece of creative writing by Marcel that we are ever given to read, and indeed, quite conceivably, the one and only such effort that he publishes in his entire life. Of course, he has dashed off some pages of his great masterwork by the time the novel ends, but as yet they count simply as "sketches" that he hands around to his uncomprehending friends (TR 520) and that may, given the delicate state of his health, never amount to a finished project (TR 507–8). As for the youthful manuscript approximating to *Les plaisirs et les jours* (TR 521/IV:618)—which is perhaps the same abandoned novel Marcel mentions at S 132—it remains stashed in a drawer, along presumably with the text we are reading, Marcel's memoir (or "récit"), and with any independent "paperies [*paperoles*]" there may be (TR 319, 609). All that he has in print, other than the Martinville steeples passage, falls under the heading of nonfiction, whether it be the set of "very slight articles" (TR 405) he produces in subsequent years or the translation of Ruskin's *Sesame and Lilies* which he deems a mere "travail" (IV:224/F 874). In between the prose poem and the masterwork, there is—nothing at all.

One might say, then, that the Martinville steeples passage constitutes the sole piece of evidence that Marcel has any talent whatsoever as a creative writer; and one might add, more specifically, that it constitutes the sole indication that he is capable of writing the particular type of book he describes. For if the *oeuvre* is to contain (among other elements, but centrally) a set of sensory impressions "translated" into language (see TR 273 and 290–91), then it would be reasonable to wonder, in light of the ratio of translated to untranslated impressions, as to its overall feasibility. At Montjouvain, the play of light on a pond, appearing to smile just as the light on the steeples will (S 256), elicits nothing more than a barely articulate expression of enthusiasm—"zut, zut, zut, zut" (I:153/S 219)—which Marcel is too indolent to investigate further. At Hudimesnil (BG 404–8), Marcel does try a little harder to penetrate the secret of the trees before him, using a technique of self-distraction which will work perfectly on the madeleine (S 62), but soon gives up, falling back on human company[2] and on the suspicion that he may be experiencing a déjà vu, or at best an involuntary memory, rather than a sensory impression; failing, that is, to realize that the unknown quantity he seeks is not a memory of a specific previous encounter with similar trees but an essence or "spiritual meaning" pertaining to all such trees in general (TR 273). Even at Tansonville, finally, where Marcel does everything right (self-distraction included), nothing comes of all his effort: "I returned to the hawthorns, and stood before them as one stands before those masterpieces which, one imagines, one will be better able to 'take in' when one has looked away for a moment at something else; but in vain did I make a screen with my hands, the better to concentrate upon the flowers, the feeling they aroused in me remained obscure and vague, struggling and failing to free itself, to float across and become one with them" (S 194).

It is no wonder that Marcel repeatedly refers back to the Martinville steeples, whether to mention the experience itself—set alongside the madeleine episode as one of the most important "foundation-stones for the construction of a true life," one of the crucial steps toward "the invisible vocation of which this book is the history"—or to narrate the progress of the written account: produced in the first volume, shown to the diplomat Norpois in the second, revised and sent to the *Figaro* in the third, anxiously awaited in the fifth, published and circulated in the sixth.[3] Not just a privileged moment among others, Martinville is a privileged moment that generates writing, since it is clear that what lies "behind" it (unlike what lies behind the madeleine) is more than a bygone era, and since its mystery (unlike those sensed at Montjouvain, at Hudimesnil, at Tansonville, and on the train) appears to be eventually unlocked, its oracular speech decoded.

Yet here, precisely, is where the problem lies. As readers, we are by no means convinced that we are hearing the voice of an oracle (although some critics are so taken with the beauty of the passage that they do not notice the scandal of its failure to live up to its billing).[4] What Marcel promises us, in a relentlessly extended metaphor of surface and depth, of core and husk, is an exact transcription of "what lay *behind* [the surface of] the steeples of Martinville" (255), "the mystery which lay *behind* them" (257), the secret lurking "*behind* that mobility, that luminosity" (254) or hidden *within* them ("caché en elles" [S 178]). Having sensed the existence of such a quality on numerous other walks along the Guermantes Way, having intuited "the mystery that lay hidden *in* a shape or a perfume" (253) and sought "to perceive what lay hidden *beneath* them" (252), here he is finally able, he claims, to lift the "lid" and extract the "treasure" (252). We expect, there-fore, something rather dramatic by way of a revelation, something on the order of what Marcel's grandmother might see—what *she* finds "beneath the surface" of half-lit steeples is "grandeur,"[5] an abstract quality, perhaps even that "tallness" which serves as a prime example of a Platonic Form (see *Parmenides* 131d–32b)—or at least an insight comparable to that delivered by the Guermantes's courtyard, when all of a sudden every last mystery of the Baron de Charlus's behavior finds a perfect explanation in his hitherto concealed homosexuality.[6]

We are, however, in for a disappointment. What "reality" lies hidden "be-neath the surface" of the Martinville steeples? What transformative knowl-edge, what Platonic essence, does Marcel detect in their depths? Nothing in the passage gives the slightest indication of any such discovery. In order to make any headway at all, we are obliged to resort to a type of arithmeti-cal calculation. For we fortunately possess not one but two accounts of the excursion, not just the prose poem itself but also, right before it, the history of its genesis, the very same scene described in a down-to-earth, factual way, more or less as Marcel would doubtless have phrased it had he never had the epiphany.[7] Now if we start from the prose poem and then subtract the narrative, what we are left with is presumably the epiphanic inspiration, the "thought . . . which had not existed for me a moment earlier" (255). Given prose poem, take away prose, and what remains should, by rights, be equal to poetry. So let us consider the two renditions side by side.

NARRATIVE	"PROSE POEM"
Our speeding carriage makes the Martinville steeples, lit up by the setting sun, appear to move.	The Martinville steeples [appear to] rise from the plain.
The distant Vieuxvicq steeple seems right next to them.	The Vieuxvicq steeple [apparently] moves to join them.
	We travel fast, but the three steeples [appear to] stand still.
	The three steeples look like birds on the plain.
	The Vieuxvicq steeple [apparently] moves away again, leaving the Martinville steeples alone in the smiling light of sunset.
The Martinville steeples seem far away, but all of a sudden we stop right in front of them.	The Martinville steeples seem far away, but all of a sudden they [appear to] throw themselves in front of us.
While waiting for the doctor, I get down to talk to my parents.	

We resume our journey, leaving Martinville.	We resume our journey, leaving Martinville.
	The village [apparently] accompanies us.
I turn my head to see the steeples for the last time.	The three steeples, still lit up, [appear to] wave goodbye.
	The road turns, and the three steeples [appear to] veer out of sight, like three golden pivots.
When the sun has set, they become visible again.	When the sun has set, they become visible again.
	They look like three flowers painted on the sky.
	They also evoke three young girls of a legend.
They fall out of sight, become visible one last time, then disappear.	As we gallop away, I see them [appear to] huddle together and eventually disappear.

It may perhaps come as little surprise that the "poetic" rendition diverges from the "prosaic" in having collapsed a two-part experience into a single seamless whole, eliding the narrator's descent from his elevated post on the front seat and the pause, of indeterminate length, while Dr. Percepied makes his house call. And it is only slightly more interesting that the poem plays with the order of events, relegating the steeples' swerve from the very beginning to a position toward the end (the point at which they are compared to "golden pivots"). By far the most significant change, however, is neither what has been moved nor what has been removed, but instead what has been *appended*. A cursory glance at the above table is sufficient to expose the difference in semantic density, the poem making nearly double the number of statements concerning the steeples. More specifically, the poem brings two fresh features into the description, a series of images and a set of personifications (notice that I have inserted the terms "appear to" or "apparently" no fewer than seven times in my synopsis). The steeples resemble birds, pivots, flowers, and girls; they are capable of autonomous movement ("timidly seeking their way, . . . drawing close to one another"), equipped with distinguishing character traits (Vieuxvicq is "bold" and also disdainful, "taking its proper distance" from the other two) and endowed with agency—to the point, indeed, of bearing responsibility for their "actions" (Vieuxvicq being censured as "dilatory"). It is these two addenda, I will argue, that constitute the very heart of the insight newly introduced into Marcel's (dim) awareness.[8] Together they notify a part of him that there is a distinction between the steeples considered objectively and the steeples as *he* sees them, and that what is left over when the first is subtracted from the second is something he did not know he had—namely, a perspective.

2. Optical Illusions and Pre-Predications

What Marcel learns, in other words, is that "in all perception there exists a barrier as a result of which there is never absolute contact between reality and our intelligence" (TR 420; cf. S 115); separating the world from the conscious mind stands the preconscious perspective of the perceiver. Now this perspective itself breaks down into two aspects, the universal (one shared, or potentially shared, by any member of the human race) and the individual (one that varies from person to person). In the next section, I shall explain how the imagery (of flowers, birds, and girls) proceeds from and testifies to Marcel's individual perspective, and how this makes the Proustian view a sophisticated (and unwitting) refinement of Nietzschean perspectivism. For now, I shall focus on the personifications, which are largely a product of the mental constitution he holds in common with everyone else: to be sure, the steeples do not really move at all, let alone huddle together and drift apart, but from the point of view of someone—anyone—set in a certain location and traveling at a certain speed, they *appear* to do so, just as the sun "comes up" and "goes down" for all of us (give or take the occasional peculiarly hardened scientist). What I see depends on where I am situated with respect to the relevant object, and is exactly the same as what you would see in my place.

Viewed in this light, the two accounts of the Martinville episode diverge dramatically (cf. Milly 132–34). Whereas the first is careful to present optical illusions as illusions, clearly indicating the mechanism of mystification, the second simply lists them as though they were facts:

> Narrative: "At a bend in the road I experienced, suddenly, the special pleasure which was unlike any other, on catching sight of the twin steeples of Martinville, bathed in the setting sun and constantly *appearing to change* their position *with the movement of the carriage and the windings of the road. . . .*"
> Prose poem: "*then the road changed direction, they veered* in the evening light like three golden pivots, and vanished from my sight. . . ."[9]

Even where the prose poem *does* allude to the movement of the carriage, we notice, it merely juxtaposes the allusion with an animistic description of the steeples' (seeming) displacement, as though the two types of motion simply happened to occur at the same time, rather than one being the cause of the other. The final sentence, similarly, opts to preface the main clause, "I could see them timidly seeking their way," with the subordinate "as we drew away from them at a gallop" (256), rather than the less misleading "*because* we drew away from them at a gallop."

We should therefore understand the pair of passages as conveying (1) the event as it is belatedly processed by the faculty of reason, with optical illusions revealed for what they are and assigned clear causes, and (2) the event as it is initially experienced, filtered through a standard human subjectivity at a particular set of spatiotemporal positions. Borrowing Marcel's *moraliste* terminology, we might say that the narrative is composed by *intellect* and the prose poem by *intuition*, the latter being a faculty for immediate insight, placing us directly in touch with objects of cognition. As a result, the prose poem is very close to impressionist paintings produced by the fictional Elstir, whose ambition was "to reproduce things not as he knew them to be but according to the optical illusions of which our first sight of them [*notre vision première*] is composed" (BG 570; cf. GW 574).[10] Whereas the narrative version presents what Marcel *knows* about the carriage ride, what he has worked out post hoc, the impressionist paragraph gives only what he *registered* at the time, the initial optical illusion.

In a related way, Proust's narrator will often begin a sentence with a descriptive phrase or set of phrases, and only proceed at the very end to identify what is being described.[11] "A little tap on the windowpane, as though something had struck it, followed by a plentiful light falling sound, as of grains of sand being sprinkled from a window overhead, gradually spreading, intensifying, acquiring a regular rhythm, becoming fluid, sonorous, musical, immeasurable, universal: it was the rain" (S 140–41). Now whereas the optical illusion merely renders an effect on the senses, this technique—call it "pre-predication"—also conveys an effect upon *mood*. From "sonorous" to "musical," and from "immeasurable" to "universal," the nuance is discreet but distinct: Marcel is registering no longer a fact of perception but the way heavy rain makes us *feel*, the subjective (but shared) impression of majesty and harmony it generates about itself. The opening line of the Martinville steeples prose poem is just such a pre-predication. We know right away that *something* is "alone, rising from the level of the plain, and seemingly lost in that expanse of open country" but we do not yet know *what* is alone, rising, and lost; so that what we have, for the time it takes us to reach the noun, is a vague intimation of disorientation, remoteness, and solitude (cf. Spitzer 462).

With its very first two words, then, the composition announces its intent, immediately drawing on both impressionistic devices. "Alone," the pre-predication, registers an effect on the heart before indicating its cause; "rising" registers a trompe l'oeil effect on the senses, hinting (albeit *pianissimo*) at the extended personification that will govern the poem as a whole. We may barely notice, so long has the metaphor been dead, but "s'élevant" (literally "raising itself") implicitly attributes agency to the subject of the elevation, just as "s'abaissa," in a line Proust cites from Flaubert's *Sentimental Education*, attributes agency to the subject of the lowering.[12] Already, Marcel is indicating his refusal to reproduce the world as it is, which is to say as he consciously *knows* it to be, and his desire instead to reproduce the world as it confusedly appears to our *vision première*; taking a leaf out of Elstir's book, he is endeavoring to "remove what he already knew from what he had just felt" (GW 574).[13] And in doing so, Marcel is revealing a part of what lies "hidden behind the steeples" (S 255), or at least behind the imprint they have made on his imagination. The new truth is in fact a truth about the human mind, not about the steeples: it is about the primacy of intuition, and the qualitative difference between the pictures it offers (delineated in the prose poem) and the corrected pictures subsequently generated by intellect.

3. "Metaphor" as Indicator of Perspective

So far, I have discussed only one aspect of the "poetry" in Marcel's prose poem, and the more mundane aspect at that. To be sure, the optical illusions and pre-predications do testify to the "barrier . . . between reality and our intelligence," but only insofar as the barrier is held in common by every human being. All of us, that is, would perceive the steeples as moving, and all of us would (it is implied) be struck by their lofty isolation;[14] but not all of us would compare the steeples to birds, pivots, flowers, and girls. These images (which Marcel would loosely term "metaphors") are the character's alone, and they carry the burden of indicating the second, unique aspect of his perspective, the part he shares with nobody else.[15] They are what turn "*the* steeples" (S 254) into "*my* steeples" (S 255; cf. Chabot 33). They speak as eloquently about Marcel as the comparison of a steeple to a nail planted in a bleeding sky informs on the bellicose narrator of Céline's *Voyage au bout de la nuit*.[16] Now, whereas the optical illusion has been a staple of Martinville scholarship since Curtius and Spitzer (see Curtius's chapter "Perspectives," and Spitzer 465), the individual aspect—which is ultimately far more important to Proust's portrait of the mind—has received relatively short shrift.[17] It will be my focus, therefore, in the remainder of this chapter. I will attempt to explain (a) how imagery can serve to disclose a point of view on reality, (b) what Marcel's metaphors specifically say about *his* point of view, and (c) whether we can defend the theory against a number of critical objections.

How, first of all, can imagery convey perspective? The answer is that perspective, just like metaphor, is a matter of combination.[18] What I do when I train my consciousness on the world is to organize the latter's objects into classes, and I do so by isolating key features which certain of them have in common. Thus, for example, I may connect scallops with salmon on the grounds that they are members of the marine kingdom, and cinnamon with cilantro on the basis of their appurtenance to the plant realm. So far, we are dealing with standard taxonomical procedures, and our account is more or less in accord with Kant's universalizing picture of the way experience takes shape in the human mind.[19] What, however, if I decide that scallops are just as similar to cilantro plants as they are to salmon, because a crucial feature of scallops and cilantro alike is to be utterly revolting when consumed? At this point, although I may have reasons for making the connections I do, and although I may even perhaps be able to make you understand them, I am nonetheless moving away from shared structures and into a more private domain of association. Based on my own idiosyncratic passions and attachments, I focus on a particular feature f (say, unpalatability) of object A (the scallop), which then brings it into conceptual proximity with object B (the cilantro). To take a more Proustian example, if I am fascinated by the way in which people are more attracted to those who flee them than to those who pursue them, I may well end up comparing romantic love to Franco-German relations in the early years of the century, rather than to a red, red rose.[20]

Here we are departing from Kant and moving closer to Nietzsche, for whom the mind organizes experience not under a uniform set of transcendentally necessary "categories" but under a unique perspective dictated by the individual's interests, needs and values.[21] In Proustian terms, everything is filtered through "that little disk of the eye's pupil, through which we look at the world and on which our desire is engraved" (BSB 161; cf. SG 534). We are still dealing with an overarching system that gives shape to the mass of conceptual material by combining it according to reliable rules, so that each separate association makes an implicit claim upon the entire network, but here the rules are almost certain to vary from one human being to the next.

One corollary is that if we wish to learn something about the inner "world" of another individual—that aspect of her perspective which is not held in common with the rest of humanity—we can do so only by studying the combinations that she typically (and unconsciously) produces among the elements of any given domain.[22] Thus, in conversation with Albertine, Marcel senses that her "words themselves did not enlighten me unless they were interpreted," which is to say unless they are understood as "the involuntary, sometimes perilous contact of two ideas which [she had] not expressed" (C 109); thus, too, he and his author immediately sense the originality of a novel by the fact that "the relations between things [a]re so different from those that connected them for me" (GW 444, EA 311); and thus, finally, he intuits behind the arrangements of musical notes "that essential quality of another person's sensations into which love for another person does not allow us to penetrate" (C 206).[23]

We have seen that associations between pairs of ideas, concepts, or even musical notes are, on Marcel's theory, always governed by invariant rules. I would go further and venture that the local rules are also indicative of *higher-order* laws of perspective. If the former determine which concept (e.g., cilantro) will reliably find itself linked to which other concept (e.g., scallop) in my mind, the latter represent the more general principles behind all such connections, which is to say the *types* of category my mind is wont to impose upon experience, the joints at which it tends to carve up the world. It may well be, in fact, that the local rules can periodically be suspended, as when my palate learns to appreciate the delicacy of seafood, with the higher-order laws nonetheless remaining firmly in place. (One imagines the editors of Borges's celebrated "Chinese encyclopedia" continuing to group animals under rubrics like "embalmed," "trained," "chimerical," "trembling as though mad," and "resembling flies when seen from a distance" even when a particular animal turns out not, say, to resemble a fly when seen from a distance, or not to tremble as though mad: the encyclopedia's second edition may well require changes in content, but its overall form will be unaffected.)[24] As a result, the higher-order laws—to which I shall return later in this chapter—probably serve as the more accurate guide to the deep structure of my personality.

4. Perspective and Viewpoint

We may dispute some of Marcel's observations on the nature of music, but we have, I think, no reason not to take the idea about "metaphor" seriously— unless, of course, we are hardened Wittgensteinians, too linguistically turned to believe in any preverbal inhabitants of the mind. One such Wittgensteinian is Vincent Descombes, according to whom Marcel's theory "appeals to entities whose status is impossible" (220). There is no such animal, maintains Descombes, as an original and arcane outlook (a "private language"); I do not see things differently from you, but merely from a different *standpoint*. If you were to come to where I am, you would see them exactly the way I do.

Descombes's line of reasoning merits at least a brief examination, because it sets out to demonstrate not only that Marcel is *wrong* to believe what he believes but that he is *obviously* wrong: that the novel, in other words, itself proves exactly the opposite of what Marcel is trying to put forward. And although there is at present little evidence to adjudicate in general between the austere Wittgensteinian view and its more permissive rivals, we can at least show that Descombes is a little hasty in attributing his own skepticism to the text. For one thing, he offers no real substantiation for his overall claim about the "myth of interiority" (203, 220).[25] For another, when he seeks to back up the more specific idea about emplacement, his choice of example can at times be somewhat misleading.

Take the scene in which Marcel suddenly becomes aware that Rachel, the actress for whom his friend Robert de Saint-Loup is sacrificing money, worldly reputation, and sleep, is the very same Rachel he himself used to be offered for one *louis* in a brothel (BG 206, GW 211). Since the two-bit prostitute Marcel knows differs radically, as hardly needs stating, from the glamorous actress Robert knows, it would be tempting (writes Descombes) to label these as "Rachel seen from two different perspectives." That, however, would be an error, Descombes continues, for one of the two "perspectives" is *correct* and the other is *incorrect*. To be sure, Proust has Marcel explicitly state that neither opinion should be privileged—"the little tart Rachel, the real Rachel, *if it can be said that Rachel the tart was more real than the other*" (GW 214; my emphasis)—but only, continues Descombes, because he has painted himself into a theoretical corner. "Optical perspectivism obliges Proust[26] to take these two descriptions of Rachel—*tart* and *woman of great price*—as equally well founded, when the whole point of this section of the narrative is to expose the illusion a lover lives in" (269).

Marcel's practice, in other words, belies his theory: in defiance of endless declarations about all perspectives being of uniform validity, the narrative itself presents a stark contrast between perfect accuracy on the one hand and outright (and transparent) delusion on the other. Instead of presenting "Rachel seen from two different perspectives," the scene shows us merely "the real Rachel" and "the false Rachel." And in spite of all the assertions about perspectives being inaccessible to others, Marcel is here able to share Robert's delusion—perhaps precisely because it is a delusion, and nothing more subtle or complicated than that—as he watches Rachel on stage. "Marcel realizes that he now sees her as Robert does, since he occupies the same vantage point," argues Descombes; "the narrator can actually share Robert's perspective" (268).[27]

Are "vantage point" and "perspective" really equivalent, however? The *Rachel poule* episode does not prove that they are, as it really has nothing to say about the latter. Far from being an anecdote designed to convey or confirm theories about individual perspective, it presents itself quite clearly as a case of interchangeable attitude. Rather, that is, than suggesting that Marcel considers Rachel a two-bit prostitute because of the way his mind works, or that Robert worships her because of intrinsic mental properties of his own, it straightforwardly accounts for the divergence in sentiment by noting that one first met her in a brothel and the other in a theater.[28] Like an optical illusion, the "amorous chimera" from which Robert suffers (TR 313) is a potentially universal (and therefore universally comprehensible) fallacy: just as anyone can climb onto a carriage and witness steeples appearing to move, so all of us are liable to adopt a different outlook on person X depending on which aspect of X's character first meets our attention.

For we are dealing here primarily with genuinely existing features of Rachel's personality, and only secondarily with the subjective contribution of her two observers. Descombes may be justified in pointing out that she is hardly a "woman of great price," but it is misleading to conclude that Marcel is on the mark and Robert off target:[29] to claim that Rachel is "really" a prostitute is, it seems to me, to give in to a certain recent bias according to which a person's most vicious trait is exclusively allowed to define her identity. Marcel's own view runs counter to such bias. Speaking of the type of girl who begins by showing "the purity of a virgin" and then goes on to show "more boldness," he asks "in herself was she one more than the other? Perhaps not, but capable of yielding to any number of different possibilities in the headlong current of life" (C 78). Just so, Rachel is "in herself" no more a "tart" than a "woman of great price," both being, in a sense, facets or potentialities of her complex being (she has, after all, enough talent as an actress to rise to the top of her profession). All that the episode proves is that people display various sides of themselves at various times and in various situations, and that those who meet them are accordingly susceptible to misjudgments, taking the part for the whole.

Thus the episode is very much about *point de vue*, a term Marcel rarely uses to designate an individual perspective—in the classic statements on the subject, he prefers expressions like "vision," "qualitative essence of sensations," "way of seeing," "temperament," "world," or "universe"—and far more often to designate aspects of experience accessible by all (the *Recherche* is packed with topics considered "from a physical point of view," "from a spiritual point of view," "from a practical point of view," "from an intellectual point of view," "from an aesthetic point of view," "from a moral point of view," "from a social point of view," or "from a historical point of view"). Marcel's comments on Robert leave the issue of individual perspective open.

Descombes is mistaken, therefore, in alleging that the novel's examples undermine its own claims, revealing an (unconscious) awareness on Proust's part that the theory of perspective is false, with the result that Marcel is not just wrong but obviously wrong. If Wittgensteinians wish to dismiss the *Recherche*, they must do so by making the unargued-for claim that the mind is as bare and spare as the house Wittgenstein built himself in Vienna; they can gain no support from the text itself. On the contrary, Proust's novel clearly presents the deepest mental states of an individual not as simple and standard but as sophisticated and obscure. Where we are dealing with genuine instances of individual perspective, there is no easy access, but merely three degrees of minimal acquaintance. We may, in the first case, know nothing at all of another person's perspective; or we may become aware of its existence, usually thanks to the pain caused by her escaping our cognitive appropriation (think of Albertine, the perennial "fugitive" from Marcel's understanding); or, finally, we may gain the odd glimpse at its nature, based on clues (speech patterns, dress styles, etc.) that we have to interpret. What we cannot do is *adopt* it in any meaningful sense. Thus heterosexuals can train themselves, as Marcel does, to detect the more overt signs of homosexuality, but they can never aspire to the uncanny mutual awareness Marcel considers unique to members of the "race" (SG 15).

The only exception to the rule—to return to a point made in the previous section—is art. "All the residuum of reality which we are obliged to keep to ourselves, which cannot be transmitted in talk, even from friend to friend, from master to disciple, from lover to mistress, that ineffable something which differentiates qualitatively what each of us has felt and what he is obliged to leave behind at the threshold of the phrases in which he can communicate with others only by limiting himself to externals, common to all and of no interest—are brought out by art," Marcel famously states (C 343). And once again, the events of the narrative turn out to be perfectly in harmony with his idea.[30] Marcel, who used to shun as unpoetic "that sordid moment when the knives are left littering the tablecloth" (BG 372), now lingers at the table. "Since I had seen such things depicted in water-colours by Elstir, I sought to find again in reality . . . the broken gestures of the knives still lying across one another," he explains. "I tried to find beauty there where I had never imagined before that it could exist, in the most ordinary things, in the profundities of 'still life'" (BG 612–13). Similarly, having once seen canvases in which land and sea become interchangeable, he is in a position, on the second Balbec visit, to generate the same spectacle for himself, to witness the mast of a fishing boat becoming (what else?) a steeple:

> my eyes, trained by Elstir to retain precisely those elements that once I
> had deliberately rejected, would now gaze for hours at what in the for-
> mer year they had been incapable of seeing. . . . there were days now
> when . . . the sea itself seemed almost rural. On the days, few and far
> between, of really fine weather, the heat had traced upon the waters,
> as though across fields, a dusty white track at the end of which the
> pointed mast of a fishing-boat stood up like a village steeple. A tug, of
> which only the funnel was visible, smoked in the distance like a fac-
> tory. (SG 247–48; cf. Descombes 255)[31]

Marcel has clearly internalized a way of looking at the world, expanded his range of conceptual possibilities, added a new device to his cognitive toolbox. He can, when he so chooses, see the world through the eyes of Elstir.

Judging by Proust's 1895 article on Chardin and Rembrandt, we are dealing here with a case of unanimity between author and character. When you have absorbed a number of still-life paintings by Chardin, Proust writes, "you will be a Chardin" in your own right, "you for whom, as for him, metal and pottery will come to life and fruit will talk" (EA 70). You too, in other words, will start to see apparently dull objects as though they were beings endowed with life, energy, and agency. In Proust's view as in that of Marcel, art possesses the unique capacity to transmit its creator's perspective in a way that allows us, to a certain extent, to make it our own. To be sure, we do not simply surrender our own perspective and replace it with another's, do not literally "become the man himself."[32] Art merely grants us the opportunity to "see the universe through the eyes of another, of a hundred others" (C 343), and not through our own transformed eyes: we will always remain aware of the disjunction between what is innate and what is borrowed vision (as we saw above, Marcel "*sought* to find again . . . the broken gestures of the knives," "*tried* to find beauty there where I had never imagined before that it could exist"; it does not come naturally).[33] But even if an artist's world is only ever on loan, to borrow it is to increase the size of the universe. "Thanks to art, instead of seeing one world only, our own, we see that world multiply itself and we have at our disposal as many worlds as there are original artists, worlds more different one from the other than those which revolve in infinite space" (TR 299).

5. Marcel's Perspective

What, then, about the Martinville steeples passage? If Marcel's own literary output is to live up to his claims for aesthetic production in general, then the *poème en prose* should convey something about his deepest mental states; it should convey not only the objective side of his perspective (via the optical illusions and pre-predications) but also its subjective side, via the series of images. With the spirit of Descombes staring intently over our shoulder, we need now to ascertain whether the images concerned really tell us anything about the mind of their creator, whether they really offer us anything more than the impression of a vivid but ultimately unruly imagination. In a sense, the theory stands or falls on this example, the one clear instance of artistry that we ever witness emerging from the pen of the narrator. It should be possible for us to recast Marcel's metaphors as a set of propositions about his inner world, even though, as the same theory demands, propositions can only go so far in making Marcel's character tangible to us: just as, in life, the fullest description of a stranger will always fall short of the knowledge we derive from acquaintance, so here we should expect to end up with a photo-fit drawing of Marcel that is no substitute for his voice, his style itself.

It can at least be asserted that the terms of comparison Marcel selects for the steeples are far from being arbitrary. If we set aside the rather prosaic pivots, presumably invoked merely on the basis of physical similarity, and temporarily postpone discussion of the birds (to which I shall return in the next section), we are left with flowers and girls, two of the most frequently recurring leitmotifs of the novel as a whole. Indeed, flowers and girls may well be particularly prominent in Marcel's mind at the time of the visit to Martinville, since they have been the object of his attention on almost every afternoon expedition from Combray. When not gazing longingly at "some girl from the fields" around Roussainville (S 213–14), he is intently studying the obscene gesture of Gilberte (S 197–99); when not pressing a bank of hawthorns to deliver its secret (S 193–95), he is luxuriating in the sight of water lilies which—just like the figurative flowers at Martinville, interestingly enough—seem, when the sun sets above them, to "blossom in the sky" (S 240). What the Martinville prose poem has to teach us, then, is that Marcel subliminally associates steeples with girls and with flowers as possessors of a feature which, within his idiosyncratic conceptual universe, comes to the fore in each, setting it apart from most of the other constituents of the visible world. And that feature, we may speculate, is its ability to call to him in a particular way, to set him dreaming, to invest him with belief, to promise him the object of his deepest desire.

The grail in question is not, as the novel's somewhat misleading title seems to suggest, "lost time." For it is not the past that its protagonist is pursuing across three thousand pages of peregrinations, but instead an enrichment of experience, an additional dimension, something more than he can readily perceive (under a limited definition, we might call this a desire for *transcendence*). To be sure, memory (of the involuntary kind) will ultimately prove one means to such enrichment. But it is only very late in the narrative that it does so, and even then Marcel considers it merely an intermediate goal, of strictly instrumental utility, and never an end in itself. Until the *matinée Guermantes*, he continually turns outside himself for inspiration, seeking release from the prison of his own consciousness and entry into a different domain. Everywhere he looks, be it at a geographical location, an interesting individual, or a collection of salon regulars, he thinks he sees *worlds*, which is to say systems that are both homogeneous and heteronomous, alien to everyday experience and at the same time perfectly coherent from within. Any manifestation that strikes him as unusual becomes a *sign*, a secret communication that stands in need of decoding, something that would yield a meaning if only one possessed the interpretive cipher, spoke the local language.[34]

The entire novel, in fact, presents itself as a relentless sequence of fascinations, one no sooner fading than it is replaced by another. Anything is worth attention that seems to hint at a world beyond Marcel's ken: magical names, like Brabant, Champi, Agrigente, La Raspelière, Saint-Euverte, and of course Guermantes; high-society salons; actors and actresses including Odette and La Berma; artworks including those of Bergotte, Elstir, and Vinteuil; hawthorns, trees at Hudimesnil, *poiriers* in Paris; places such as Balbec, Venice, and Doncières; milkmaids and other unknown women, like those of the Bois de Boulogne, around Méséglise, at Balbec, and in Rivebelle, or like the Putbus chambermaid and the ostensible Mlle d'Eporcheville; Gilberte and the agate marble she gives him, the Duchesse de Guermantes, Mlle Stermaria, Albertine, Andrée, Gisèle, the *petite bande* in general, and no doubt the thirteen others at Balbec.[35] If, therefore, Marcel's unconscious mind brings the Martinville steeples into connection with water lilies and legendary maidens, it is because all three represent classes of objects typically invested with what Marcel calls "prestige" or, more commonly, "faith" (*foi, croyance*).[36] Artworks, flowers, and young women have alike the power to summon a conviction on his part that they are home to a mystery he can share, residents of unknown worlds to which he may travel.[37]

Translated into propositional phrases, the steeples' revelation would run more or less as follows: "Your deepest desire, driving your perspective, is for transcendence; you seek that transcendence in natural objects, fellow human beings, and aesthetic artifacts; that is why we are linked, in your mind, to flowers and maidens, even though we might be linked to other things in other minds; what is behind us is this fact, and in general the fact that you have a unique and identifiable perspective." The images do not, in the end, teach us anything about the steeples themselves, but only (here again there is a Kantian flavor) about their place in Marcel's subjective conceptual framework.[38] What they bring to light is not so much a hitherto unremarked feature of, say, the color of the masonry as the information that buildings, girls, and flowers can all be invested with *croyance*—or rather, since even this last item is barely news to anyone, that *croyance* sits at the heart of Marcel's desire, ruling his perspective, almost exclusively responsible for the myriad serial infatuations related in the novel. (Just to emphasize the connection, he has the imaginary flowers being "*painted* upon the sky" and the girls emerging from a "legend.")

Were Marcel but listening, in other words, he would hear the images telling him a truth about his nature, one which brushes the surface of his consciousness at regular intervals throughout the novel (BG 194, GW 155, SG 560, C 120): that he perceives an aura around certain women, flowers, names, and locations only because he has projected it onto them in the first place; that when all the various haloes have faded it is the projection that remains, evidence of a unique and consistent point of view on the world. That is to say, "we end by noticing that, after all those vain endeavours which have led to nothing, something solid subsists, [i.e.,] what it is that we love" (GW 529). Or again,

> if the object of my headstrong and active desire no longer existed, on the other hand the same tendency to indulge in an obsessional day-dream, which varied from year to year but led me always to sudden impulses, regardless of danger, still persisted. The evening on which I rose from my bed of sickness and set out to see a picture by Elstir or a mediaeval tapestry in some country house or other was ... like the day on which I ought to have set out for Venice [S 559], or that on which I had gone to see Berma [BG 17–29] or left for Balbec [BG 303–4]. ... my musings gave a certain glamour [*prestige*] to anything that might be related to them. And even in my most carnal desires, orientated always in a particular direction, concentrated around a single dream, I might

have recognised as their primary motive an idea, an idea for which I would have laid down my life, at the innermost core of which, as in my day-dreams while I sat reading all afternoon in the garden at Combray [S 115–23], lay the notion of perfection.[39]

6. Two Objections: Image-Chains and Metonyphors

But can we really agree with Marcel that "something solid subsists," that there is a single, uniform perspective at work, consistently glamorizing particular aspects of experience? Some critics would dispute the idea. First of all, they would argue, Marcel produces too many metaphors. If, as I have claimed, the image in Proust brings together two disparate objects by means of a subjectively (unconsciously) necessary connection, then a given object A should only ever be linked to a given object B. Yet here in the Martinville passage we find four separate counterparts for the steeples, one indeed from each of the mineral, vegetable, animal, and human realms (pivots, flowers, birds, girls). Elsewhere in the novel we find similar cascades of correspondences, as for example when the narrator likens his future project to a military campaign, a spell of fatigue, a discipline, a cathedral, a diet, an obstacle, a friendship, a child, a new world, and, of all things, a dress (TR 507–9). Are we not simply dealing with an exceptionally fertile imagination, capable of converting anything into anything else? Should we not agree with Gaëtan Picon that in Proust things can be "not only themselves, but all the rest" (159; my translation; cf. Spitzer 457, Tadié 1971: 432)?[40]

If we consider the last-mentioned example closely, we find that the process of metaphorization is not after all as random as it might seem. Whether Marcel envisages the magnum opus as cathedral or dress depends, as it turns out, on which of its aspects is in view at the particular moment. For the fact that artworks appear to have two completely incommensurable sides, the "material" and the "ideal," has been a source of immense fascination and confusion to Marcel ever since his disappointing encounter with Bergotte: What connection, he wonders, holds between mere literary craft and the magic of personal expression (BG 167; cf. C 209, C 259, C 504–14)? How is it possible that composers can convey their inner world merely by rearranging musical notes that are available to all, notes that "the lay listener . . . may pick out on one finger upon the piano" (C 540)? It is no wonder, then, that he considers his own future production very differently depending on whether he thinks about the painstaking labor that will be involved or about the miracle of communication it will enable. "And—for at every moment the metaphor uppermost in my mind changed as I began to represent to myself more clearly *and in a more material shape* the task upon which I was about to embark—I thought that . . . I should construct my book, I dare not say ambitiously like a cathedral, but quite simply like a dress" (TR 508–9; my emphasis).

In the same way, the Martinville passage does indeed offer four separate images, but only one image per steeple-impression, the impression vary-ing—just as in a Monet series[41]—according to the time of day. The steeples remind Marcel of birds while the sun still gilds their peaks, but when the sun, having set, gives them a rosy glow, they are "*no more now than* three flowers painted upon the sky" (notice how the language registers a clear shift from one state to the next).[42] And when, finally, the steeples suggest legendary maidens, they are completely bathed in darkness. In the first two cases, we may imagine, Marcel focuses on the very tips of the steeples, the only portion still to be lit by the waning sun, and consequently selects relatively diminu-tive terms of comparison; in the third, the entirety of each steeple forming a homogenous whole, a single dark mass rising against the dusk, he selects something a little more substantial.

The prose poem is extremely careful, in fact, to emphasize that the images all belong to different intervals, attaching a temporal clause to each. The final sentence may well begin casually—"They made me think, *too*, of three maid-ens in a legend"—and thus appear to lend credence to the Picon-Spitzer view of Marcel as an expansive free-associator, but it almost immediately proceeds to inform us that "night had begun to fall," implicitly offering a perfectly sound reason for the change in analogy. What happens in this passage is almost exactly the same as what happens when Marcel elsewhere describes a set of rectangular pear orchards: "all these airy roofless chambers seemed to belong to a Palace of the Sun, such as one might find in Crete; and they reminded one *also* of the different ponds of a reservoir," he adds, "*when one saw . . . the light play upon the espaliers*" (GW 204–5; my emphasis).

The abundance of imagery does not, therefore, invalidate the principle that every connection is a (subjectively) necessary connection. It is still pos-sible to claim that the combination of a given perspective with a given object yields a regular and predictable term of comparison, just as mention of the Dreyfus affair, and only mention of the Dreyfus affair, brings out the phrase "well and truly" [*bel et bien*] in the Duc de Guermantes. "Five years might go by without your hearing him say 'well and truly' again," notes the narrator wryly, "but if, at the end of five years, the name Dreyfus cropped up, 'well and truly' would at once follow automatically" (C 43).

There is, however, a second and more serious objection. For a number of Marcel's metaphors depend not on a deep (perhaps unconscious) *analogy* between their elements but merely a *contiguity*, a strictly spatial adjacency. In such cases, the metaphor ("A is like B") is based on a metonymy ("A is next to B") and can be termed a metonymic metaphor or, to use a somewhat bar-barous shorthand, a *metonyphor*. When we are faced with metonyphors, so the argument runs, we stand to learn nothing about their user's perspective, since their selection depends only on extrinsic and haphazard circumstances. If, for example, Marcel spends some nine pages (GW 40–49) on a conceit in which high-society patrons of the theater metamorphose into tritons and nereids, their fans into foam, their hair into seaweed, and even their seats into cave walls, it is merely because the French word for the type of "box" in which they find themselves is *baignoire* ("bathtub"). The bulging eye of the Marquis de Palancy, behind its glass monocle, might not strike Marcel as the eye of a fish inside an aquarium were Marcel not sitting in the Opéra, his head filled with images of watery depths. In a laboratory, by contrast, it might remind him of a microscope slide; at the sea, of a lighthouse lamp. None of these metaphors can have anything to say about Marcel's mind, since each merely indicates the place in which he is physically located at the time of its production.

In the eyes of some readers—such as Gérard Genette, the first to detect the prevalence of "diegetic metaphors" in the *Recherche*—the metonyphor is not just prevalent but absolutely ubiquitous, with nary a trope remaining pure of metonymic contamination (1972: 45, 48). Certainly, some of the most widely used images in the novel do have propinquity as their basis. All of the maritime resonances surrounding Albertine, for example, owe their existence to the contingent fact that Marcel first saw her on the beach at Balbec (cf. Genette 1972: 46); had he met her in Paris, as would have been quite possible, he might have considered her more a pigeon than a gull, her eyes more like the Trianon lake than like the sea (BG 718–21). So, too, having once encountered Gilberte at Tansonville, he will unfailingly connect her with hawthorns (TR 443, S 261–62), rather than, say, the Champs-Elysées snow. In each case, two impressions that (quite by chance) come to strike the mind at the same time, such as the sound of waves crashing on the shore and the sight of a young girl pushing a bicycle, fuse into a stable synthesis. "An image of which we dream remains for ever stamped," Marcel explains, "by the association of colours not its own which may happen to surround it in our mental picture" (S 118). Sanctioned by repetition, the arbitrary link then ends up looking necessary (F 679–80), so that, for example, Albertine reminds Marcel of the sea, even when neither she nor it is present: "I had been quite well aware that this love was not inevitable . . ., sensing it to be vaster than Albertine, enveloping her, unconscious of her, *like a tide swirling around a tiny rock*" (F 679; my emphasis).

Nor are steeples exempt from the process. On the contrary, they seem to attract metonyphors like magnets (cf. Genette 1972: 42–44). If the Saint-Hilaire steeple resembles a pair of "hands joined in prayer" (S 87), convent steeples, quite appropriately, suggest nuns' coifs (S 91); if the pinkish steeple at maritime Saint-Mars has something of the salmon about it (SG 562), and if the steeples of Saint-André-des-Champs, rising above farmland, are "*themselves* as tapering, scaly, chequered, honeycombed, yellowing and friable as two ears of wheat" (S 205), the Balbec steeple, close to (and carved out of) the rocks, is "*itself* a rugged Norman cliff" (BG 322); and if, finally, Combray's spire is, at harvest time, as purple as the ripe grapes it overlooks (S 62), all of a sudden, when pastries are in the offing, it becomes "baked golden-brown *itself* like a still larger, consecrated loaf" (S 88). (As Genette points out, "itself" and "themselves" are sure-fire indicators of a metonymy lurking beneath the metaphor.)

A latter-day Genette might well be justified, therefore, in raising the question of whether any of the images in the Martinville prose poem falls under the same category. Its coda contains an undeniable example: "I never thought again of this page, but at the moment when, in the corner of the box-seat where the doctor's coachman was in the habit of stowing in a hamper the poultry he had bought at Martinville market, I had finished writing it, I was so filled with happiness . . . that, as though I *myself* were a hen and had just laid an egg, I began to sing at the top of my voice" (S 256–57). And surely the birds ("the three steeples were still a long way ahead of us, like three birds perched upon the plain") must also be somewhat suspect, since one could reasonably expect there to be rooks and ravens wheeling about the steeples, perhaps even nesting in their belfries.[43]

We must therefore meet head-on the challenge of Genette, for whom such heterogeneous tropes serve as evidence of a disconnect between intention and execution: as he sees it, Proust sets out to use images in order to shed light on the essence of the objects compared but fails, and fails necessarily, to do so.

How indeed could anyone imagine that a metaphor, that is to say a displacement or transfer of sensations from one object onto another, can lead us to the essence of that [second] object? How could anyone entertain the idea that the "deep truth" of a thing, that particular and "distinct" truth Proust is looking for, can be revealed in a figure of speech . . .? . . . wouldn't a description based on the "relationship" ["*rapport*"] between two objects be more likely to dissolve the essence of each? . . .

In between its conscious intentions and its actual achievement, a remarkable reversal besets Proust's writing: having set out to elicit essences, it ends up constructing, or reconstructing, mirages. (1966: 45, 46, 52; my translation and emphasis)

Being the charitable reader that he is, Genette goes on to label this apparent flaw an additional attraction of the novel, since what Proust actually does—namely, produce mirages—is more "modern," and therefore presumably more interesting, than what he *thinks* he is doing (53). Even more charitably, Paul de Man says that Proust himself may have allowed the metaphors to miscarry *on purpose*. According to de Man, it is Marcel and Marcel alone who believes in the possibility for metaphors to "pass the test of truth," to capture an adequate and necessary relationship between "the thing" (say, steeples) and "the idea of the thing" (say, flowers). As for Proust, he is fully aware[44] that "the relationship between the literal and the figural senses of a metaphor is always . . . metonymic" (71). The novel is, in a way, Proust's conscious attempt to expose the seductions of language, demonstrating that a link between any pair of objects can only ever be one of contiguity, a thoroughly contingent connection which has nothing to say about anything.

De Man's ultra-charitable reading has, when he adheres to it,[45] the advantage of accounting for Proust's palpable awareness of what is going on, plainly visible in the repeated instances on which he has Marcel draw attention to, and even theorize, the metonymic basis of some of his own metaphors.[46] If we return to our seat in the Paris Opéra, we find the long conceit quite explicitly introduced as a train of thought the Prince de Saxe triggers when he asks to be shown to his *baignoire*: "in uttering this sentence to the attendant, he grafted on to a commonplace evening in my everyday life a potential entry into a new world; the passage to which he was directed after having spoken the word 'box' and along which he now proceeded was moist and fissured and seemed to lead to subaqueous grottoes, to the mythological kingdom of the water-nymphs" (GW 41). And similarly, if we consider those links between a woman and a landscape which de Man finds so revealing, we find the adult Marcel fully cognizant of the mechanism subtending them:

> the passing figure whom my desire evoked seemed to be not just any specimen of the genus "woman," but a necessary and natural product of this particular soil. *For at that time everything that was not myself, the earth and the creatures upon it, seemed to me more precious, more important, endowed with a more real existence than they appear to full-grown men. And between the earth and its creatures I made no distinction.* I had the desire for a peasant-girl from Méséglise or Roussainville, for a fisher-girl from Balbec, just as I had a desire for Balbec and Méséglise. . . . That girl . . . was to me herself a plant of local growth, merely of a higher species than the rest, and one whose structure would enable me to get closer than through them to the intimate savour of the country. (S 220–21; my emphasis)

In the end, however, de Man's conclusion is just as unsatisfying as Genette's, for all the brilliance of the analysis in either case. For both critics appear to assume that an analogy succeeds *if and only if the term of comparison captures something essentially inherent in its target.* (Metonyphors miss the mark, on this view, by neglecting to elucidate the item they pick out, reflecting instead their own place of manufacture and nothing more.) It is a strictly binary choice: either A and B are linked by objective truth, or there is no real connection between them. Thus, in de Man's illuminating example, "an element of truth is involved in taking Achilles for a lion but none in taking Mr. Ford for a motor car" (14), there being apparently no third option; and "if the proximity between the thing and the idea of the thing fails to pass the test of truth," then it "remains reduced to 'the chance of a mere association of ideas'" (71).[47]

It should, however, be clear from the preceding discussion that the aim of a metaphor can be—and in Marcel's description *quite explicitly is*—to convey not an objective but a subjective connection between two impressions or ideas, and that this subjective connection can possess a type of local inescapability. Marcel, in other words, locates an intermediate position between the two de Manian extremes of thorough contingency and absolute necessity, and indeed considers his intermediate position the most interesting thing there is to say about metaphor. He would completely agree that no image captures a universally valid relationship between a pair of terms, but he would not conclude from there that all metaphors are entirely arbitrary, that all metaphors are (in the restricted sense de Man gives the term) metonymic.

And surely Marcel is right. In order to feel how poorly such a totalizing theory captures the nuances of writing in general and Proust's prose in particular, we need only open the *Recherche* to more or less any page. Granted, plenty of the images it contains depend on their local context, but just as many do not. When, for instance, Marcel compares his future masterwork to a cathedral, he is not standing in Notre-Dame but lying in his bedroom; the analogy with *dresses* may well be suggested by what he can see around him, but architecture comes up for no other reason than because it is part of his set of guiding preoccupations. So too,.when it comes to the Martinville passage, there seems to be a sliding scale, from the clear metonyphor "steeples = birds" at the one end to the bland, unobjectionable, almost factual comparison "steeples = pivots" at the other, with "steeples = girls" sitting firmly in the middle as a plain case of perspective at work ("steeples = flowers" may shade slightly toward the metonyphor, but even that is debatable). Here as elsewhere, the erasure of distinctions simply leaves readers fewer resources with which to tackle a text.[48]

7. Metonyphor and the Spatial Imagination

We can say, then, that Genette and de Man are a little overzealous when they tar all of Marcel's metaphors with the metonymic brush; that at least *some* of Marcel's metaphors indicate features of his perspective, and are to that extent necessary within his subjective world; and that we should not hold the images in the novel to standards of objective truth, since these are not the standards they set themselves. But this is not all that can be said in defense of the metonyphor. Quite surprisingly, it turns out that far from undermining Marcel's theory of the literary image, the metonyphor has if anything *more* to tell us about Marcel's perspective than do the various "pure" metaphors we see him produce.

Marcel says it himself: the reason that women find themselves linked, in his mind, to their geographical site, and that many gain their very "prestige" from the connection, is because he imagines that they can deliver the essence of a place. What he seeks in the peasant girls of Roussainville is, as we just saw, "the intimate savour of the country" (S 220–21); what he seeks in Mme de Stermaria is the *île de Bretagne* (GW 528–29); what he seeks in Gilberte is, among other things, the Tansonville hawthorns; and what he seeks in Albertine is, in good measure, the sea at Balbec. Thus, in general, the girls of the *petite bande* "were for me the mountainous blue undulations of the sea, the outline of a procession against the sea. It was the sea that I hoped to find, if I went to some town where they had gone. The most exclusive love for a person is always a love for something else" (BG 563). And thus, more specifically, when it comes to Albertine, "I cannot say whether it was the desire for Balbec or for her that took possession of me then; perhaps my desire for her was itself a lazy, cowardly, and incomplete form of possessing Balbec, as if to possess a thing materially . . . were tantamount to possessing it spiritually" (GW 480; cf. GW 496, C 81, F 744, TR 216).

Now if Marcel believes, at this point in his life, that a woman can initiate him into the mysteries of her birthplace, it is because, as he puts it, she seems to him "a necessary and natural product of this particular soil." His fantasy is that everything belonging to a given site shares a common essence, that there is so to speak a *Raumgeist* as well as a *Zeitgeist*, that there is some property held in common among all neighboring elements, that a town such as Balbec magically invests its buildings, streets, seas, and trees—even its name—with a single unique nature. For if it did not, then it would not have an essence, would not be a *world*, both consistent with itself and set apart from everything else,[49] and thus represent (as we saw earlier) the object of his deepest desire.

Metonyphors, therefore, are very far from being mute. If we bear in mind the fact that Marcel is not Proust but a character, designed to embody particular idiosyncrasies of vision, belief, and desire, we can see how such idiosyncrasies inform every aspect of his performance, right down to the way his imagery is constructed.[50] No, Proust does not set out to produce metaphors that illuminate the objects concerned, and unwittingly fail to do so; instead he sets out to produce metaphors that illuminate the subjectivity of the character he has created, metaphors that are in keeping with that character's fundamental disposition. So considered, the metonyphors succeed perfectly. To be sure, the steeples-birds analogy does not point to a law of Marcel's perspective in the way that the steeples-flowers analogy does, since in another context birds might easily be replaced by fish; but the very employment of a metonymic metaphor testifies, here as elsewhere, to a *higher-order law*, namely that every conspicuous component of a particular place finds itself subliminally connected to every other component of that place in Marcel's imagination.[51] The same rule applies to people as to cities: an aura-invested woman will function as a unified whole, so that her name, her face, her neck (C 94–95), the acacias under which she walks (S 602), and in general all surface manifestations become reliable guides to depth. Any book can be judged by its cover, any contiguous connection promoted to correspondence.

If, however, we already know this about Marcel, why do we need the metonyphors? If we already have all the evidence I have presented here for his fetishism of place, do not the metonyphors once again slide into redundancy, merely repeating over and over something of which we are fully aware? The answer to this question is what makes metonyphor more informative than any of the individual analogies. For the fact is that Marcel's explicit statements tend to concern his *past*, his "croyante jeunesse," the early and naive phases of his life. The narrator presents the *character* as subject to illusions of essence, but *himself* as free from them. What the metonyphors show us, since these images are produced by the narrator himself, is that *he has, at some level, never stopped believing in them*. Long after his intellect has given them up, his intuition remains firmly under their spell. Perspectival distortions, by definition, never fade; they just become more or less apparent.

Metonyphor, then, is a window onto Marcel's unconscious mind. We might call it his linguistic tic, the counterpart of Cottard's obsession with idioms or Legrandin's highfalutin diction, "these expressions alien to our thoughts which by virtue of that very fact reveal them" (TR 192).[52] Marcel's is fundamentally a *spatial imagination* (cf. Genette 1972: 46), clustering objects and individuals according to their geographical locality. It makes him arbitrarily separate the two *côtés*, the Guermantes and the Méséglise; conversely, it makes him consolidate memories from disparate epochs, both in his narration of walks there (S 190–262) and in his narration of the "stations du transatlantique" (SG 647–98); it even makes him consider time in spatial terms, labeling the periods of his life according to the room inhabited. And, of course, it makes him produce metaphors which are very, very frequently—but not always—of metonymic inspiration.

8. A Theory of Knowledge

"It was certainly not impressions of this kind that could restore the hope I had lost of succeeding one day in becoming an author and poet, for each of them was associated with some material object devoid of intellectual value and suggesting no abstract truth" (S 252). So says Marcel of the various stimuli that strike him on the Guermantes way, including those generated by the Martinville steeples. But as we saw above, the novel he ends up writing (or starting to write) has sensory impressions at its very heart, like precious stones set within a band of gold (TR 303). Marcel is, therefore, quite mistaken—or to be more precise, Marcel the *character* is mistaken; Marcel the narrator merely *pretends* to be, allowing his former self to usurp, as it were, his own voice. We are dealing here with a rather unusual form of free indirect speech, in which an assertion or thought of the early Marcel ("I said to myself, 'it is certainly not impressions of this kind that can restore the hope I have lost'") is taken up and rendered obliquely by the later Marcel.[53] This technique, which Richard Terdiman calls the *feint* (1976: 138–45), can be thought of as a long-range impressionism, an impressionism over time: once again, the narrator is registering an effect on the character before its cause, but here it is an effect on the character's *judgment* rather than on his senses (as in the optical illusion) or his mood (as in the pre-predication); and here we may wait a considerable period before the misconception is corrected, so that we may easily be deceived into taking the first statement at face value, into taking it, that is, as the narrator's own verdict on the situation.

Similarly, what the character considers a totally safe prediction of Albertine's behavior—"I knew quite well that she could not leave me without warning me" (C 537)—the narrator will, thirty pages later, acknowledge to have been a mere "hypothesis" (F 568); likewise, the statement "I learned . . . that Bergotte had died that day" (C 246–47) should really read "I was told by Albertine, who was lying, that Bergotte had died that day, whereas in reality he had died the day before." In both cases, as is typical for the feint, our confusion is compounded by the fact that the narrator employs verbs of firm conviction ("I knew," "I understood," "I learned") in order to introduce propositions he fully perceives to be false.

We should, therefore, be somewhat suspicious of Marcel's defeatist attitude toward impressions, and even if we are inclined to take it as definitive the first time we read *Swann's Way*, we know by the time we have finished the novel—some 4400 pages further on—that it belongs to a superseded stage of development, that he now recognizes the crucial role they have to play in the creative process. What, however, is behind his earlier failure to see the light? The answer is not (as one might expect) that a novel has no need of an "abstract truth," that it can do without a "philosophical significance of infinite value" (S 243), but instead that such truth and significance are available from unexpected sources. There are, after all, truths to be found in sensory impressions, and indeed truths of two different types. First, each impression incarnates a local, subjective "truth," a "law" of one's perspective, so that "truth" in this sense is interchangeable with "image": "certain obscure impressions, already even at Combray on the Guermantes way, . . . concealed within them . . . a new truth, a precious image" (TR 272). Second, the set of impressions considered as a whole, their very *existence*, communicates a universal, objective truth, namely that every human being has a unique perspective.

And so the Martinville passage, however disappointing at first glance, offers us nothing less than an unexpressed theory of knowledge. Three players are involved, the *data of sense*, my faculty of *intuition*, and my *intellect*. In themselves, the data of sense are thoroughly chaotic (again, a Kantian point), coming across as a blurry mass of shapes and colors. Thus Elstir's studio is "the laboratory of a sort of new creation of the world . . . from the chaos that is everything we see" (BG 565), and the impression Marcel sets out to translate at Martinville is not "three steeples seen from a carriage" but merely a group of "shifting, sunlit planes" (S 254). It is intuition that first seizes on inputs from the external world, and intuition, as we recall, is the seat of the perspective, with its universal aspect generating optical illusions and its individual aspect generating the "truths" we were just discussing (that is, the idiosyncratic connections that form impressions and, by consequence, literary images). Only later does the intellect, presumably by examining the data supplied it by intuition and by applying certain laws of logic and nature, work back to the facts, the real-life sources of the confused sensations—back, so to speak, from prose poem to narrative.[54] We might map out the system as follows:

FACULTY INVOLVED	ITS YIELD
intellect	"objective truth"
intuition (individual aspect)	"subjective truth"
intuition (universal aspect)	"optical illusion"

The way a given object looks to us will thus inevitably depend on three factors, the epistemological, the ontological, and the axiological. Our picture will vary, first of all, according to what we can see of the object, the specific "aspect" our emplacement allows us to capture. "No doubt it was the same thin and narrow face that we saw, Robert and I. But we had arrived at it by two opposite ways which would never converge, and we would never both see it from the same side" (GW 209–10). Indeed, a face will appear different to the same spectator, given a change of viewpoint (Poulet 1952: 435): each time it reenters our field of vision, it "appears to us . . . from another angle and shows us a new aspect" (BG 677). And even just moving closer will "evoke out of what we believed to be a thing with one definite aspect the hundred other things which it may equally well be" (GW 499). Then again, external objects "change also in themselves" (C 83), so that—a second factor—the vista before us may alter, no matter how steadily we hold our position.

Finally and most importantly, there is what one might call the *focal point* of the perspectival painting, namely, that feature within the object depicted which my disposition makes me find peculiarly valuable and hence places at the center of my canvas, forcing the other elements to redistribute themselves around it.[55] If, for instance, I consider artistic creation paramount, I am likely to consider Elstir's stint as the asinine "Biche" in the Verdurin clan an aberration, a distraction from his true calling; if, on the other hand, I imagine that social elevation trumps all other concerns, I may lament his "defection," his reclusive existence in the studio at Balbec. (Similarly, a Dostoevsky might consider Rachel a talented actress once forced by hardship to sell her body, whereas a Zola might consider her a prostitute who has deceived her way to a career on the stage.) The Martinville steeples passage reveals all three factors at work in contributing to Marcel's perception. The location of the carriage affects his view of the steeples; the fading sunlight, as we have seen, dramatically modifies the impression they make; and of course his own sensibility determines the associations that immediately spring to mind, the flowers and girls that suggest themselves as ready comparisons for the dancing medley of lines and planes before him.

For all that, it is important to emphasize that the philosophy subtending Proust's novel is not a sweeping relativism, let alone a subjective idealism (pace Descombes 25, 45).[56] Gilles Deleuze may feel that when it comes to Proust "we are wrong to believe in facts, there are only signs" (90), but "in spite of whatever may stem from various subjective points of view"—Marcel says it himself—"the fact remains that there is a certain objective reality" (GW 780); "the subjective element that I had observed to exist . . . in vision itself did not imply that an object could not possess real qualities or defects and in no way tended to make reality vanish into pure relativism" (TR 326). Perspective does not change the facts on the ground, or altogether preclude access to them. If it makes them elusive, it is primarily by endowing them with a spurious *value*,[57] rendering some deceptively salient and others nearly invisible; if it thereby impedes their accurate assessment, it does not always rule the latter entirely out of bounds.

We know, for a start, that a world of perspective-independent objects exists outside of our mind.[58] The clearest proof is that life constantly manages to *surprise* us, defying any actual or even potential expectation on our part. Thus, when Marcel first visits the Grand Hotel at Balbec, "the impossibility of forming any idea of the manager, the Grand Hotel or its staff" suddenly gives way to "a whole frieze of puppet-show characters"; "there is perhaps nothing that gives us so strong an impression [as this] of the reality of the external world" (BG 332). Surprises can be unpleasant—Albertine's revelation of her connection with Mlle Vinteuil is "something which my mind would never have been capable of inventing" (SG 703)—or they can be welcome, as with "women whom it was impossible to imagine *a priori*" (C 26), women who provide "that element [of female beauty] which we are powerless to invent . . ., the only one that we cannot bestow upon ourselves, before which all the logical creations of our intellect pale, and which we can seek from reality alone: an individual charm" (BG 205–6). Either way, surprises prove to us that we have not dreamed the world, that it exceeds our oneiric capacity.

Furthermore, we know not just that the world exists but also, to some extent, what it looks like. To be sure, Marcel frequently laments that "we see, we hear, we conceive the world in a lopsided fashion," that "we have of the universe only inchoate, fragmentary visions, which we complement by arbitrary associations of ideas" (F 774–75). The universe he is referring to is, however, usually that of human beings, and in particular human beings in whom we have an emotional investment; the context here is his mistaking a Mlle Forcheville (actually Gilberte) for a Mlle d'Eporcheville, a name he in turn misremembers as belonging to a young woman who reportedly frequents houses of ill fame (SG 126–27, SG 166, C 106). Where the intellect has a reason to hope that things are one way rather than another—that the unknown woman, for example, is a debauchee—it fails to do its normal job of reconstructing facts and instead spins *hypotheses*, typically hypotheses that are as favorable as possible. (We shall learn more about these in the next chapter.) Normally, however, the intellect is perfectly capable of isolating facts (local objective truths) and, once sufficient data have been collected, of inferring from them to general laws (universal objective truths). When, in the course of the novel, we read a statement of apparently global application, it may therefore be one of three things: an objective truth (law of life); a subjective truth (law of Marcel's perspective); or a hypothesis (revisable theory). I raised in the introduction the possibility of confusion between subjective truths and universal objective truths (projecting what is true for me onto the entire human race, as though it were true for everyone). This chapter is, however, all about a case of subjective truths being taken for *local* objective truths, and it is to that specific error—which I mentioned at the very outset—that I now return by way of conclusion.

9. Marcel's Blind Spot

In this chapter, I have argued that the Martinville composition reveals something important about perspective; on my account, it is the existence of perspectives in general, and the nature of Marcel's perspective in particular, that sit "behind" the steeples and that render Marcel's prose poetic, making it the one and only piece of creative writing he completes in the course of the narration, endowing it indeed with the kind of "philosophical significance" that makes it a worthy precursor to the coming masterwork.[59] What is strange, given all of that, is Marcel's own obliviousness to its true value. Clearly he must sense, fairly early on, that it is an aesthetic product, since he sends it to the *Figaro* for potential publication; but he never seems to realize what follows—namely that it is, according to his own theory, a royal road to self-knowledge.

For an artwork, on his view, conveys its creator's perspective not merely to other people but also to the artist herself. "It alone expresses for others *and renders visible to ourselves* that life of ours which cannot effectually observe itself . . . [our] true life" (TR 300; my emphasis). (Recall that Marcel's own metonyphors reveal an unconscious attitude which his conscious mind strenuously denies.) Everyone, concurs the narrator of *Contre Sainte-Beuve*, has perspectival impressions, but few are "gifted" enough to notice; and of these few, still fewer have the "talent" to translate them into writing. "The fine things we shall write," he explains,

> if we have talent enough, are within us, dimly, like the remembrance of a tune which charms us though we cannot recall its outline, nor hum it, nor even sketch its metrical form, say if there are pauses in it, or runs of rapid notes. Those who are haunted by this confused remembrance of truths they have never known are the men who are gifted; but if they never go beyond saying that they can hear a ravishing tune, they convey nothing to others, they are without talent. Talent is like a kind of memory, which in the end enables them to call back this confused music, to hear it distinctly, to write it down, to reproduce it, to sing it. There comes a time in life when talent, like memory, fails, and the muscle in the mind which brings inward memories before one like memories of the outer world, loses its power. Sometimes . . . this time of life extends over a whole life-time; and no one, *not you yourself even*, will ever know the tune that beset you with its intangible delightful rhythm. (BSB 201; my emphasis)

Why do Proust's two narrators, in *Contre Sainte-Beuve* and the *Recherche*, think it impossible even to access our inner essence for ourselves—let alone to communicate it to others—outside of aesthetic production? The answer is that our true life, as we just saw Marcel put it, "cannot effectually observe itself." A perspective is something we look *through*, not *at*; we can never turn our gaze around, as it were, to stare at its own mechanism. Instead we always require an external object, something from which to work back in order to calculate, a posteriori, the nature of our subjectivity, its index of refraction. Just so, if we wish to determine the effect of a new pair of contact lenses, we need to train our vision on a distant tree, say, and not on the blank wall in front of us.

Now external objects can take various forms and offer different quantities of information. An artwork produced by someone else is perhaps the least informative, since it is so overwhelmingly about its creator that it reduces its consumers "to being no more than the full consciousness of another" (TR

297). If it is, nonetheless, also "a kind of optical instrument" (TR 322, 508) allowing its reader, viewer, or listener to "descend into [her]self" (C 206; cf. S 497), the descent is only into realms of experience common to all, and not into the most personal area of her soul.[60] Similarly, although less dramatically, love affairs may well reveal something about the nature of our personality, since (as I explained in the introduction) we can reconstruct post hoc the process that has all along been guiding our selection, but our vision is also clouded by the fact that each love object is an individual in her own right, so that it is difficult to separate out those signs that point in the direction of her perspective from the ones that point in the direction of ours.

We are left with two main sources of insight, namely memories and impressions. Neither is likely to distract us with glimpses (whether clear or indistinct) of anyone else's subjectivity, and both are at least somewhat illuminating when it comes to our own. Involuntary memory manifests the existence of an enduring component within us, that part which experiences the taste of, say, a small cake dipped in *tisane*, in exactly the same way at any given moment in our life (I shall return to this point in chapter 3). That said, involuntary memory does not tell us very much more; and it is not entirely free, in the end, from all distractions. For since there is an objective side to it, in as much as today's *tilleul* and *madeleine* really are the same type of thing as those of yesteryear, it is tempting for us to imagine that the entire miraculous phenomenon can be explained by reference to a previous episode. We can easily be led to misinterpret the epiphany as "meaning" Combray,[61] even though it must, as is plain, mean something far more consequential.

An impression, on the other hand, has no objective ("material") aspect. It connects the immediate sensory experience not with an identical sensory experience stored in the memory but with an entirely *disparate* object, conjured up from the *imagination*. And since no material explanation is available, the entire event must be understood as an effect of perspective: "whereas in memory th[e] vagueness may be, if not fathomed, at any rate identified, thanks to a pinpointing of circumstances which explain why a certain taste has been able to recall to us luminous sensations, the vague sensations given by Vinteuil coming not from a memory but from an impression (like that of the steeples of Martinville), one would have had to find, for the geranium scent of his music, not a material explanation, but . . . the mode by which he 'heard' the universe" (C 505).[62]

This is why inanimate objects like steeples do a better job of revealing our perspective than do artworks, lovers, and memories. For objects, like events, "in themselves are nothing" (TR 92); stripped of our *croyance*, the Bois de Boulogne is just a wood, the Grand Lac nothing more than a lowercase lake (S 606).[63] If, therefore, we see something in them—if they appear to have a value, a depth, a message to convey to us—then it is only because we have put it there in the first place. "We try to discover in things, which become precious to us on that account, the reflection of what our soul has projected on to them," Marcel explains (S 119). And if we wish to gauge that projection, we merely have to juxtapose the *factum brutum* with the mirage, measuring how much one departs from the other.

The steeples at Martinville should, by rights, constitute the perfect opportunity for self-discovery. Marcel has both the objective truth, reconstructed by intellect, and the perspectival distortion imposed by intuition, and he need only subtract the one from the other, the narrative from the prose poem, in order to learn important information about the way his mind processes experience. Yet as we saw in the first section of this chapter, he fails to do so, instead consistently situating the "depth" within the steeples, not only before the epiphany ("something more lay behind that mobility, that luminosity, something which they seemed at once to contain and to conceal"), but also during it ("something of what was concealed from me in them became apparent"), and even after it ("this page . . . had . . . relieved my mind of . . . the mystery which lay behind them").[64] How can we explain this lapsus?

It is, of course, perfectly in keeping with Marcel's character that he would make the mistake described. We saw earlier how congenially and irremediably predisposed he is to see truth and desirability (authenticity, uniqueness, value, depth) located in the external world, whether within the character of a woman, beneath the bark of a tree, or behind the syllables of a name. And just as the dying Bergotte is feverishly persuaded that the little square of yellow paint in Vermeer's *View of Delft* is "precious in itself" (C 244), regardless of its context—which is to say regardless of the perspective vision behind its placement—so Marcel, whose own theory clearly states that "everything is equally precious" and that value "is all in the painter's eye" (GW 576),[65] nonetheless decides at one point that Elstir's talent consists in an ability to locate inherently beautiful landscapes; "the fact that such objects can exist, beautiful quite apart from the painter's interpretation of them, satisfies a sort of innate materialism in us," he adds (BG 583).[66]

Marcel, in short, regularly contents himself with what he condemns as the "clumsy and erroneous form of perception which places everything in the object, when really everything is in the mind" (TR 323). His intuition continues to commit him to views his intellect has long abandoned. To put it another way, Proust deliberately has his character fail—and deliberately makes it clear to us, the readers, that he is doing so.[67] Quite premeditatedly, Proust is placing a distance between himself and protagonist and narrator alike, and reminding us that not two but three agencies are jointly responsible for the Martinville steeples section. For if the prose poem, with its series of subjective "truths," conveys the response of the character, and if the narrative version reveals the narrator correcting such immediate perceptions into objective fact, then the construction of the episode as a whole betrays the presence of an *author*, someone for whom many of the events are not true in any sense.

Indeed, Proust has gone to some trouble to take the events out of the realm of plausibility. When he originally published the piece in 1907, he set the journey in Caen, in front of the Saint-Pierre, Saint-Sauveur, Saint-Etienne, and Trinité churches, and had the first-person narrator share a vehicle with Proust's own companion Agostinelli; here, the town is the nonexistent Martinville, and the narrator's fellow inhabitants include Dr. Percepied, whose ridiculous name seems to have no other function than to undermine verisimilitude. Just as the novel as a whole presents a striking mixture of real and imaginary places—Paris and Venice, as against Combray and Balbec—and also of real and imaginary characters, such as Sarah Bernhardt and "la Berma," Dr. Dieulafoy and Dr. du Boulbon, Céleste Albaret and Françoise, so here Vieuxvicq sits side by side with Martinville. And thus we end up with three conceptual domains, occupied by character, narrator, and author respectively:

AGENT	DOMAIN	VISION OF STEEPLES
character	prose poem	subjective truth
narrator	narrative	objective truth
author	novel	unfettered fantasy

The crucial distinction, that is to say, between Proust and Marcel is not merely one of cognitive superiority (Proust understanding better than Marcel the mechanism of perception) but also one of increased *creativity*. For while Marcel's stance vis-à-vis the fictional world depicted in the *Recherche* is a largely passive one—he receives data from it, registers it, processes it, analyzes it, and to some extent acts upon it—Proust *invents* it, at the cost (if we are to believe him) of great personal effort.[68] What is quite fascinating is that Marcel, so far from concocting stories of his own, in fact dismisses fabrication as entirely irrelevant to artistic production. "It may be that, for the creation of a work of literature, imagination and sensibility are interchangeable qualities and that the latter may with no great harm be substituted for the former," he insists. "The essential, the only true book . . . does not have to be 'invented' by a great writer—for it exists already in each one of us. . . . The function and the task of a writer are those of a translator" (TR 307, 290–91).

Marcel, we are meant to infer, has almost everything right about perspective—located in intuition, it is first to reach the data of sense, generating optical illusions on the objective (common) side and combinatory images, which are only visible in aesthetic artifacts, on the subjective (idiosyncratic) side—but not quite. Something is missing from his account, something that Proust knows and that Proust wants us, too, to know, even though he does not always want Marcel to have it in mind. And that something is the crucial role of imagination in the business of being a self. For while my perspective is a fundamental part of who I am (Marcel calls it the "true self"), it does not exhaust my identity. Since I am also a chronological series of states, I require not only prose poetry, capturing the timeless essence of my *vrai moi*, but also a history by means of which to corral all the other *moi* under some kind of structure.[69] This, in part, is why the Martinville episode strikes us as strangely anomalous, a moment of intense artistic energy that nevertheless fails somehow to break the writer's block, a flaring match that burns alone and dies in the darkness.[70] And since many such structures are possible, I must (as will become clear in chapter 3) employ a certain degree of imagination in order to set one up and to endorse it as the appropriate arrangement of the material. Marcel's memoir, Proust is telling us, is already a piece of creative writing, whether he knows it or not; Marcel's future work of literature, his *oeuvre*, will be even less able to do without fiction; and what Proust is doing, in fashioning the *Recherche* from whole cloth, is something of another, and higher, order altogether.

2

Self-Deception (Albertine's Kimono)

When my love swears that she is made of truth,

I do believe her, though I know she lies.

—William Shakespeare, Sonnet 138

The main trajectory of *A la recherche du temps perdu* consists, as we have just seen, in Marcel's learning to abandon the quest for objective truth—for the way in which objects, and particularly people, are in themselves, outside of any (specific) observer—and to focus instead on *subjective* truth, on his own inner nature, the very perspective that made accurate knowledge of the external world so elusive (and so seemingly desirable) in the first place. There is, however, a further component to Marcel's *Bildung*. He must learn not only that knowledge is sometimes *inaccessible* (and, where accessible, almost always dissatisfying), but also that it is sometimes *unendurable*, that "truth, which is not compatible with happiness or with physical health, is not always compatible even with life" (TR 314). Shifting spires are not enough to complete an education: Marcel requires love, and in particular jealous love, to teach him the necessity of illusion and imagination in a happy life; to teach him, also, the *fragility* of our beneficent fantasies, and the convoluted strategies that can sometimes be required for their preservation. Astonishingly, and yet in the end quite plausibly, it turns out that one of the best ways of remaining in the dark is to head straight for the light, that a quest for knowledge may be the single most effective way of keeping our ignorance intact. To explain how this apparent absurdity can be justified is the task of the present chapter.

1. The Unpurloined Letter

Early in the fifth volume, we find Marcel living in Paris with his lover and "prisoner," Albertine Simonet. Albertine has given him cause for concern— her reticence, her conflicting statements, her circle of acquaintances all suggest to Marcel that she may be "guilty" of infidelity, both hetero- and homo-

85

sexual—and he monitors her movements, accordingly, with the energy and enthusiasm of a trainee inquisitor. Yet so far no conclusive evidence, either for or against such "guilt," has come to light. How is he to reach a verdict? It is certainly not by an appeal to precedent. Granted, he has heard in detail how the famous courtesan Odette de Crécy repeatedly betrayed Charles Swann (without ever entirely eradicating his belief in her fidelity) and having seen his friend Robert de Saint-Loup take up with a person of equally dubious pedigree, an actress Marcel once knew as a twenty-franc prostitute (BG 206–7, GW 209). But the examples of Odette and Rachel fail to help him: if anything, they *add* to the confusion, raising the possibility that he is unfairly tarring Albertine with the same brush.[1]

Nor can Marcel rely on his own unaided faculties, any more than he can rely on second-hand information. While truths about the world of social groups and physical objects may be culled by the intellect (TR 303) and truths about the self by intuition (via impressions), there is no organ, as Nietzsche would say (GS 354), for truth concerning other human beings taken individually. Unless they are creative artists, we recall, there is no way of accessing their genuine nature, no way of learning that "which cannot be transmitted in talk, even from friend to friend, from master to disciple, from lover to mistress, that ineffable something which differentiates qualitatively what each of us has felt and what he is obliged to leave behind at the threshold of the phrases in which he can communicate with others only by limiting himself to externals, common to all and of no interest" (C 343).

What Albertine has to say about her own activities and tendencies is therefore, by Marcel's own theoretical lights, doubly suspect. For one thing, no amount of accurate information conveyed "from mistress to lover" can tell him what he really wants to know, namely what Albertine's bisexual episodes (assuming there to have been some) have *meant* to her, what the experience has been like from *within*: "I would have liked to know not only with what woman she had spent that evening, but what special pleasure it represented to her, what was happening inside her at that moment" (F 735; cf. 709). While we need not conclude, as Gilles Deleuze does (123), that Albertine's essence is strictly reducible to her bisexuality—she is very much more than a sexual orientation, and every other law of her perspective is equally incommunicable in direct language—it remains clear nonetheless that her encounters with women form a particularly dramatic instance of the remoteness of her world, forcing Marcel to countenance a radical inaccessibility which in other situations he is able to ignore.[2] He may for example imagine that he knows how she feels about *him*, but "this love between women was something too unfamiliar; there was nothing to enable me to form a precise and accurate idea of its pleasures, its quality" (C 519; cf. SG 709). Even the sight of two laundry maids having sex, in one of the most extraordinary scenes of the novel, only serves to reconfirm the existence of "the curtain that is for ever lowered for other people over what happens in the mysterious intimacy of every human creature" (F 742).

And for another thing, many of Albertine's reports are straightforwardly false. That in itself might not matter were Marcel were in a position to distinguish the genuine from the counterfeit, to winnow out the fictions from among the facts. But in lieu of a lie-detecting agency all he has is an intellect, a faculty that places two or more claims (that Albertine was on intimate terms with Vinteuil's daughter, for example, and that they barely knew each other)[3] side by side and attempts, by so doing, to adjudicate between them. Now the intellect does perfectly well at making sense of disparate conceptual contents under ordinary circumstances[4]—that, after all, is its job, a job which no other faculty can perform, so that to a certain extent the prosperity of an individual depends upon its proper functioning—but when the mental states of a fellow human being are its target, and when there is reason to wish that they are one way rather than another, then it is easily confused.[5] For it is always possible to produce more than one reasonably plausible account incorporating two conflicting stories. The second might, for example, be an opportunity for its teller to come clean and recant an earlier deception; but what if it is the *first* version that is authentic, and the subsequent story simply a cover-up?

To take one instance, Marcel might very well think that Albertine is being honest when she admits to having had sexual relations with Gilberte—she could hardly be suspected, prima facie, of making up such a thing—yet he countenances, even here, a more "innocent" interpretation: "perhaps Albertine had told me this because she wanted to appear more experienced than she was and to dazzle me in Paris with the prestige of her depravity, as on the earlier occasion at Balbec with that of her virtue" (TR 25). To take another, Marcel might very well think that Andrée is being honest when she admits to having had sexual relations with Albertine—now that Albertine is dead and that Andrée herself has become intimate with Marcel, Andrée's loyalties presumably lie with him—yet what if Andrée only *wanted* to be Albertine's lover, envies Marcel for having actually *been* Albertine's lover, and now *pretends* to have been Albertine's lover, merely in order to extract a measure of revenge?[6] Given the irremediable indeterminacy (irremediable at least in the absence of concrete evidence), and given the ease with which the intellect can be corrupted by desire (SG 705), there is every temptation for the former to opt for as favorable a reading as possible. At such moments its function is one part ratiocination to three parts rationalization; in Proust, as Georges Poulet (1952: 432) is one of the few critics to have remarked, the intellect often looks less like the seat of clear-headedness than the home of bewilderment.

To be sure, the mind also houses a competing impulse, a dissenting voice that accuses intellect of making things just a little too convenient. Each time the *intelligence* concocts a reassuring explanation for a suspicious set of circumstances, the *faculté intuitive* (III:848) objects vociferously, seeking to protect the overall self from excessive (and dangerous) gullibility. Yet precisely because intuition is a producer of random hunches rather than of considered beliefs, it is no more trustworthy than its rival. All it can do is to endorse the pessimistic construction of events initially offered by the intellect, one which is just as probable or improbable as the optimistic construction endorsed by the latter. Although it may now and then appear to be truth-tracking (C 480, S 388), in fact it often goes *beyond* what is actually the case, overcompensating for the shortcomings of reason; if it happens more often to latch onto reality, this is merely due to the contingent fact that matters in Proust's world tend to be as catastrophic as they can be, not to the superior efficaciousness of one agency over that of the other. After all, to make things even worse (from an epistemological standpoint), life is not even *reliably* hostile: what Marcel calls "miracles" (BG 99, SG 38)—such, most famously, as the permission his father grants for his mother to keep him company at night (S 48)—do occasionally suspend the Proustian laws of nature. Thus, while jealousy may *look* like a quest for knowledge, and may perhaps incidentally *involve* a quest for knowledge, the one is not reducible to the other.[7]

The upshot, for Marcel as for Swann (BG 131), is a pair of "hypotheses" about his companion—that she is deeply committed to life with him, that she is not committed in the slightest—espoused by the intellectual and intuitive faculties respectively.[8] Both are equally conceivable, and both equally extreme (cf. Bowie 1987: 54). "I continued to live by the hypothesis which accepted as true *everything* that Albertine told me. But it may be that during this time a *wholly contrary* hypothesis, of which I refused to think, never left me," Marcel speculates. "So that what probably existed in me was an idea of Albertine *entirely contrary* to that which my reason formed of her" (C 465–66; my emphasis).[9] Neither hypothesis can be trusted, since both are contaminated by interest, the positive by that of love, the negative by that of jealousy.[10] In order to have any hope of being right, therefore, Marcel is forced to split the difference, arbitrarily selecting a midpoint in between the contribution of his drive toward doubt and that stemming from his impulse toward belief. "I tried," as he explains in another context, "to be 'objective' and, to that end, to bear in mind the disproportion that existed between the importance which Gilberte had in my eyes and that . . . which she herself had in the eyes of other people. . . . But I was afraid also of falling into the opposite excess. . . . I tried to discover between these two perspectives, equally distorting [*ces deux optiques également déformantes*], a third which would enable me to see things as they really were" (BG 221).

The ostensibly "objective" result is, however, merely a third hypothesis furnished by the hardworking intellect, a hypothesis which can lay claim only to greater statistical likelihood and which thus leaves Marcel scarcely advanced when it comes to the one question that fundamentally concerns him.

Is his instinct simply making Albertine out to be unfaithful, when in fact she is a paragon of virtue? Or is this theory itself just a convenient concoction on the part of "an intelligence that is on the whole optimistic" (BG 278)? He never can decide: "whether the intuitions . . . grasped more exactly than my reason Albertine's true intentions," he concedes, "that I find difficult to say" (C 468). After all of his interrogations, investigations, and ruminations, indeed even after Albertine's disappearance and death, Marcel is still not sure whether to pronounce her "innocent" or "guilty," with the result that in his narration he is forced to report as fact what, in an intriguing formulation, he admits never having been able to confirm: "we shall see all this—the truth of which I never ascertained—later on" (C 65; cf. F 843). As long as he is attached to Albertine, he is too close to see her clearly; once his jealousy has abated, he no longer cares enough to try.[11]

Thus Marcel cannot hope to solve the Albertine enigma using nothing but the resources of his mind. Neither can he extract the information from Albertine herself, of course, since her many denials—and even her few admissions, as we saw above—may well be invented on the spur of the moment, anticipating his perceived desires. And third parties are of no greater use, since to consult them is always to place oneself in a typically Proustian double double bind. For if the chosen spy is too remote from the suspect (Albertine in the present instance), he will not be in a position to find out the facts; if, on the other hand, he is too close, he will be unlikely to communicate them to the investigator (Marcel).[12] Conversely, should the spy be too close to the investigator, he may spare the latter's feelings and tell him nothing (cf. F 823), while if he is too remote, he may simply not bother to talk. The whole world, concludes Marcel, conspires to keep the jealous lover in the dark, "the kind out of kindness, the cruel out of cruelty, the coarse-minded out of their love of coarse jokes, the well-bred out of politeness" (C 401; cf. C 383–84, TR 24).

The one avenue that remains open to Marcel, if he wishes to learn for certain about Albertine's activities—about their bare facts, at any rate—is that of doing some prying for himself. His detective work, as he is well aware (SG 28), has always been most successful when carried out directly, so that Mlle Vinteuil and her unnamed female friend become the two women of whose lesbianism Marcel has absolutely no doubt. "This time at least, I had no need to 'seem to know,'" he observes; "I *knew*, I had *seen* through the lighted window at Montjouvain" (C 451; cf. S 224–30). Similarly, the sight of Charlus pursuing Jupien clears up once and for all the mystery of the former's previously unaccountable mixed signals, allowing Marcel's intellect, which had previously been spinning its wheels, to reach a definitive conclusion: "in retrospect, the very ups and downs of his relations with myself, everything that hitherto had seemed to my mind incoherent, became intelligible, appeared self-evident" (SG 19).

And a perfect opening to reach equally sound conclusions concerning Albertine—or rather, to judge by the first word of the relevant passage, a *series* of perfect openings—presents itself to him while she takes her afternoon nap. Her kimono is lying across the armchair, its pockets full of letters. All Marcel has to do is reach in and take them out. . . .

> Sometimes, when she was too warm, she would take off her kimono while she was already almost asleep and fling it over an armchair. As she slept I would tell myself that all her letters were in the inner pocket of this kimono, into which she always thrust them. A signature, an assignation, would have sufficed to prove a lie or dispel a suspicion. When I could see that Albertine was sound asleep, leaving the foot of the bed where I had been standing motionless in contemplation of her, I would take a step forward, seized by a burning curiosity, feeling that the secret of this other life lay offering itself to me, flaccid and defenceless, in that armchair. Perhaps I took this step forward also because to stand perfectly still and watch someone sleeping becomes tiring after a while. And so, on tiptoe, constantly turning round to make sure that Albertine was not waking, I would advance towards the armchair. There I would stop short, and stand for a long time gazing at the kimono, as I had stood for a long time gazing at Albertine. But (and here perhaps I was wrong) never once did I touch the kimono, put my hand in the pocket, examine the letters. In the end, realising that I would never make up my mind, I would creep back to the bedside and begin again to watch the sleeping Albertine, who would tell me nothing, whereas I could see lying across an arm of the chair that kimono which would perhaps have told me much. (C 89–90)[13]

Why does he not simply read them?[14] For such a perennially prolix narrator, Marcel is remarkably reticent on this point, not even offering a set of "hypotheses" to explain his decision, as he does for the initial movement toward the kimono ("perhaps I took this step forward also because to stand perfectly still and watch someone sleeping becomes tiring after a while"). To be sure, he provides a hint, couched between clandestine parentheses, that an alternative mode of operation may have been possible and desirable—"and here perhaps I was wrong"—but he does not lay out the decision process which led him to opt for one over the other. One thing, at least, is certain: Marcel is not just being polite. While it may not be the act of a gentleman to peruse a lady's mail while she sleeps, the interception of intimate correspondence hardly represents an invasion of privacy more egregious, more counter to an old-world code of ethics than Marcel's repeated efforts at surveillance—let alone his exploitation of Albertine's unconscious form in the shocking scene immediately preceding the kimono episode.[15] Besides, Marcel has displayed

precious little compunction about Swann perusing Odette's note to Forcheville (S 401), and only a modicum more at his own scrutiny, indeed verbatim transcription, of a letter home from Françoise's *valet de pied* (GW 776);
so too he has deliberately eavesdropped on (SG 1–44) and will deliberately
observe (TR 181–82) the Baron de Charlus in increasingly compromising
sexual situations.[16] In our passage, there is (as Bersani agrees, at 1965: 79)
nothing to suggest that scruples play the slightest part in his deliberations.
Instead, Marcel seriously considers the possibility that he should *regret* his
course of conduct, as though it were driven by weakness rather than moral
fortitude (we will see later that such regret would be misplaced, for reasons
of which Marcel himself is not fully aware). If, therefore, Marcel cannot
bring himself to read Albertine's *billets doux*, it is not because he has been
raised with better manners.

We have, in fact, to wait until the following volume of the long novel
before the mystery of the unpurloined letter finally yields its decisive clue.
All along, Marcel here admits, he has desperately wanted to believe in
Albertine's innocence, and has thus allowed himself to be ruled by his intellect which, in turn, was always in thrall to desire: "the objections against my
certainty of her guilt . . . were inspired in my mind [*mon intelligence*] only by
my desire not to suffer too acutely"; "my desire, by utilising the powers of
my intelligence . . . [,] had put me on the wrong track" (F 723, F 824). When
presented with opportunities to find out unpleasant facts, we may surmise,
he permitted his intellect to talk him out of exploiting them. The reason he
did not search the pockets of Albertine's nightgown is that he was afraid of
what he would find there, afraid of finding conclusive proof of infidelities
which, as it stood, he only suspected—evidence so overwhelming that it
would definitively disqualify the alternative "hypothesis."[17] He chose instead
to remain, as he puts it, in "a state of expectancy which does not leave us in
absolute despair" (F 621).

2. Necessary Illusions

Perhaps, though, we should say that the kimono episode is a triply special
case, Albertine being peculiarly untrustworthy, Marcel testifying to an
unusual (and reprehensible) degree of weakness, and love in any case representing a relatively minor aspect of existence. To address the first matter
first, Albertine's case may be a little dramatic, but all those we deal with, even
our closest companions, have faults we do better to overlook— "each of our
friends has his defects, to such an extent that to continue to love him we are
obliged to . . . ignor[e] them" (BG 439)—and all, conversely, are in possession of "home truths" we would greatly prefer them to keep to themselves
(GW 463). Next, as to the issue of Marcel's reaction, it is far from clear that
he should proceed any differently. Should he step up his surveillance (by

reading the letters, for example)? The trouble is that only one hypothesis can ever be proven, namely that of Albertine's "guilt." If Albertine is faithful, no amount of positive evidence can ever set Marcel's wary mind at rest, and his most zealous espionage can only serve to bring innocent, but seemingly suspect, incidents to light. "It is better not to know, to think as little as possible, not to feed one's jealousy with the slightest concrete detail," he himself recognizes (C 22). If, on the other hand, Albertine is disloyal, to know it for a fact will prove fatal to the attachment; truth may well cure jealousy, but it does so by exterminating love, a remedy as radical as decapitation for a case of influenza.[18] And while Marcel is perfectly capable of detaching himself from a partner (vide Gilberte), he can hardly hope, within the world of Proust's fiction, to find a significantly more monogamous replacement (translating again into a less pessimistic framework, we might say that there is no point replacing one imperfect friend with another under the expectation that the newcomer will prove utterly flawless).

So should Marcel not just abandon love as a lost cause? There are, to be sure, a number of critics who consider it a mere stepping-stone to the glorious revelation of the final volume, a foolish, frivolous, trivial, futile, and painful phase to be put aside as quickly as possible, an illusion to be surrendered in exchange for the certitudes of involuntary memory (Deleuze 39–42). After all, Proust and his narrator are unconditional alethophiles, or so the story goes, unwilling to rest content until the very last stock of fancy, even the type of fancy that can stand in an instrumental relationship to truth, has been uprooted from their minds.[19] Some of these critics (such as Bales 63, Maurois 220, Terdiman 1976: 229, and even Bersani 1965: 124–25) go so far as to imagine that Marcel withdraws to monastic seclusion at the end of the story, giving up the carnal altogether. But in fact Marcel suggests that a life of celibacy is (a) not what has been his situation since he retired from the *monde*, (b) not something he would ever want for himself, and (c) not possible in the first place, under any circumstances:

> [a] I remember the hot weather that we had then, when from the foreheads of the farm labourers toiling in the sun drops of sweat would fall . . .; they have remained to this day [*aujourd'hui encore*], together with that mystery of a woman's secret, the most enduring element in every love that offers itself to me. For a woman who is mentioned to me and to whom ordinarily I would not give a moment's thought, I will upset all my week's engagements to make her acquaintance, if it is a week of similar weather, and if I am to meet her in some isolated farm-house. (SG 320)
>   . . . we do not sufficiently reflect that the life of the writer does not come to an end with this particular work, that the same nature which . . . entered into his work will continue to live after the work has been

concluded and will cause him to love other women. . . . Indeed—as I was to experience later on—even at a time when we are in love and suffer, if our vocation has at last been realised . . ., we come to suffer from our love merely as we might from some purely physical disease in which the loved one played no part. (TR 311–13; translation modified)[20]

[b] . . . intervals of rest and society would at times be necessary to me and then, I felt, rather than those intellectual conversations which fashionable people suppose must be useful to writers, a little amorous dalliance with young girls in bloom [*des jeunes filles en fleurs*] would be the choice nutriment with which, if with anything, I might indulge my imagination. (TR 437–38)

[c] Amorous curiosity is like the curiosity aroused in us by the names of places; perpetually disappointed, it revives and remains for ever insatiable. (C 183–84)

Marcel has good reason for continuing his *légères amours* even as he dedicates his life to literature. For while no amount of shared affection can ever reveal the essence of another person, in love any more than in friendship—such communication being the exclusive province of art—erotic attachments are, as we saw in the introduction, particularly propitious when it comes to uncovering our *own* essence. The reason is that the very "temperament" that turns all love objects into what we want them (or fear them) to be, and thus prevents us from seeing them as they really are, also constitutes that which *we* really are at a fundamental level.

I had guessed long ago . . . that when we are in love with a woman we simply project on to her a state of our own soul; that consequently the important thing is not the worth of the woman but the profundity of the state; and that the emotions which a perfectly ordinary girl arouses in us can enable us to bring to the surface of our consciousness some of the innermost parts of our being, more personal, more remote, more quintessential than any that might be evoked by the pleasure we derive from the conversation of a great man or even from the admiring contemplation of his work. (BG 563–64)

If . . . Albertine might be said to echo something of the old original Gilberte, that is because a certain similarity exists, although the type evolves, between all the women we successively love, a similarity that is due to the fixity of our own temperament, which chooses them. . . . They are, these women, a product of our temperament, an image, an inverted projection, a negative of our sensibility. (BG 647)

Our passions, that is, may never reveal the "objective truth" about someone else (i.e., correspondence between our imagination and her reality), but they do communicate a "subjective truth" about ourselves (i.e., coherence among our various projections).[21] And they tell us more about this "innermost part of our being" than do the artworks of others or even our own involuntary memories, since the latter merely indicate the *existence* of an abiding temperament within us and never its specific *nature*. Far from being a distraction from creative activity, they positively serve it: just like Marcel, Bergotte entertains mistresses in his old age, simply "because he knew that he could never produce such good work as in an atmosphere of amorous feelings" (C 239).

This being the case, it is in our interest to preserve our illusions, precisely because they are *our* illusions, indicative of who, at a deep level, we are.[22] And it is not, as it happens, merely the illusions of love that the narrator learns to treasure. If we consider the kimono passage less from the point of view of Marcel's actions (as character) than from that of the manner in which he explains them (as narrator), we notice that the habitual dynamic of the obsessively analytical novel finds itself suddenly suspended, with Marcel signally failing—or refusing—to account for and to evaluate his actions, as he almost always does, in terms of their motives and their results. He disdains to speculate on the possible merits of finding out the truth ("and here *perhaps* I was wrong"); what is more, he even attempts to take the emphasis off his very desire to do so ("*Perhaps* I took this step forward also because to stand perfectly still and watch someone sleeping becomes tiring after a while"), to redirect attention away from the central issue.[23]

With his double doubt, his repeated "peut-être," Marcel reintroduces into the present the rhythm of his past hesitation. Even now, when he is no longer living but telling his story, he is still in flight from the facts; in spite of the years that have elapsed since Albertine's departure and demise, and in defiance of the elaborate machinery he habitually brings to bear for the dissection of his own minutest actions and impulses, he remains determined to be oblivious when it comes to certain matters. Whether it concerns Albertine's infidelities or his own attitude toward the truth, there comes a point at which Marcel, following a benevolent instinct of self-preservation, does not dare to look too closely, *does not want to know*. He is dimly aware that he has perpetrated a deception on himself, one which has allowed his love for Albertine to stay alive and will—*if and only if he fails to see through it*—continue to protect all future loves. Exactly what the trick consists in will form the subject of the following section.

3. The Slipshod Detective

So far we have found Proust's protagonist lingering in the shadows, shielding himself from any danger of stumbling across disaster. Ignorance, in turn, enables him to preserve uncertainty: when he harbors particular suspicions concerning Albertine's conduct, these suspicions are kept within a self-contained world of fancy, so far removed from reality that their occasional confirmation comes as an excruciatingly painful surprise. "In order to picture to itself an unknown situation," explains Marcel, "the imagination borrows elements that are already familiar and, for that reason, cannot picture it. But the sensibility . . . receives . . . the original . . . imprint of the novel event" (F 570; cf. SG 701, and S 516 for Swann's comparable experience). Finally, even what he knows for sure he is able in a sense to *forget*, simply by allowing intellect to overcome sensibility: "once [a doubt] is introduced into the fabric of our lives it enters into competition there with so many longings [*désirs*] to believe, so many reasons [*raisons*] to forget, that we speedily become accustomed to it, and end by ceasing to pay attention to it" (C 295–96); "let us bear in mind the numberless men who believe in the love of a mistress who [they know] has done nothing but betray them" (BG 72). Selective memory can at times serve knowledge (F 751) but is far more likely to protect against it. For all that it concerns involuntary memory, Proust's novel is just as much about *voluntary amnesia*.

If, however, we are right to suppose that the explanation for Marcel's behavior in the kimono scene is his desire to avoid full awareness, we are faced with another, equally troublesome question: why, when Marcel is at such pains to conceal the facts from himself, does he go to such lengths to expose them? Why send all his spies (first Andrée and the chauffeur, later Aimé and Robert) after Albertine, when knowledge of her doings is the last thing he wants?

A partial answer might be that he has as it were no choice in the matter, since jealousy in Proust is a self-sustaining mechanism.[24] Once set in motion, it seeks sources of doubt wherever and whenever it can, indifferent to the activity of the other faculties and indeed to the needs of the Self as a whole. Like Nietzsche's will to truth (GS 344), it is divorced from all instincts of utility, not to say self-preservation, so that Swann feels "as though [his] jealousy had an independent existence, fiercely egotistical, gluttonous of everything that would feed its vitality, even at the expense of Swann himself" (S 402; cf. 518).[25] It also has no necessary relationship to love, in spite of what many critics have thought. Far from being its inseparable counterpart, jealousy is but a perversion of the original desire,[26] and follows its own autonomous schedule: it often comes in late (S 327) and fades out early (S 432) or, inversely, lingers on after the love and/or its object are dead (F 661). It does not depend on the *fact* of being in love, the *object* of one's love or even the object of one's *suspicion*: "jealousy," as Marcel defines it, "is the painful extension of an anxiety which is provoked now by one person, now by another" (C 298; cf. 481). One could perhaps simply suggest, then, that there is no communication between the two drives, no way of predicting or explaining when one will take over from the other: sometimes Marcel will seek knowledge, driven by an imperious yet largely unconscious directive; sometimes, under the sway of the opposite impulse, he will curb his appetite for it.

Yet there is more that can be said about the relationship between the love-sustaining will to ignorance and the will to knowledge that serves, or appears to serve, jealousy. For *Marcel's spies are in fact never intended to gather the truth in the first place.* He knows, after all, that he will not believe what they tell him, since it is easy to discredit what we have merely heard and not seen for ourselves ("[things] which we have learned only through other people are such . . . that we have missed the chance of conveying them to our inmost soul; [their] communications with the real are blocked" [F 936]) and since, for the various reasons outlined earlier, no third party can ever be relied on to provide a jealous lover with sound information. Furthermore, Marcel seems always to select the worst possible candidates for the job. He prefers the word of Andrée, whom he has known to be "in league with Albertine" (C 72) since the second Balbec visit (SG 326) and to be a liar in her own right since the first (BG 636), over that of his own devoted Françoise (F 812, C 64–65); even when he has clear evidence that Andrée has deceived him concerning a day on which she acted as Albertine's chaperone (C 298), he still persists in using her as his most trusted delegate. Similarly, he continues to place at least some stock in his driver's dependability even after the latter has confessed to leaving Albertine alone all day.[27] "At all events, while retaining full confidence in the chauffeur," Marcel claims with revealing disingenuousness, "I no longer allowed [Albertine] to go out after this without the reinforcement of Andrée" (C 174). And when he debriefs these hopeless agents, he instinctively senses which circumstances to inquire about and which to leave alone. "As a by-product of the instinct of self-preservation," he explains, "the same jealous man does not hesitate to form the most terrible suspicions *upon a basis of innocuous facts*, provided that, whenever any proof is brought to him, he refuses to accept the irrefutable evidence" (C 105; my emphasis; cf. F 585).

The worse they are at reconnaissance, the more highly he prizes them: at the very apex of this relation of inverse proportion, Albertine, the least reliable of all possible witnesses, stands as Marcel's favorite source.[28] And if he periodically confronts her, tempting her to testify against herself, he only does so in hopes of being reassured, out of "a need to calm the agitation" (C 471); he only asks questions, as he later realizes, to which he is confident the answer will be "no."[29] When Albertine responds indignantly, he is secretly delighted (SG 307–8), and when she confesses he is shocked, more shocked than he would have been if he had ever really believed his own accusations. "I felt a stab in my heart as I listened to this admission of *what I had but faintly imagined*," he tells us (SG 271; my emphasis).[30] For what Marcel seeks, at bottom, is not the truth but a convincing lie, a lie with the power—like that of the maternal kiss (S 15, S 261, C 93)—to send all his doubts to sleep.

Even when Albertine is taking her afternoon siesta, it is to her that Marcel turns; he may not always look at her face during his jealous interrogations, when it might have something to reveal,[31] but he is careful to scrutinize it when it can show nothing. And he stares, in exactly the same way, at the kimono instead of at its contents. Our passage draws attention to the fact by surrounding its central clause—"as I had stood for a long time gazing at Albertine"—with a perfectly symmetrical system of repeated elements: the kimono as potential site of knowledge, Albertine asleep, movement away from the foot of the bed, the kimono; the kimono, movement back to the foot of the bed, Albertine asleep, the kimono as potential site of knowledge. We are invited to focus on Marcel's gaze, one directed at the kimono's surface just as it has been directed, moments earlier, at the surface of the sleeping Albertine. In each case Marcel gains a spurious sense of control ("when she was asleep, . . . I had an impression of possessing her entirely which I never had when she was awake" [C 84–85]) without, for all that, coming any closer to the true depth of the form in view. Perhaps his intense contemplation of the kimono is designed to fill it, as his imagination regularly fills the silent Albertine, with what he would like to see: other mail, perhaps, or no mail at all. Perhaps the three perfect-tense verbs he uses ("never once did I *touch* the kimono, *put* my hand in the pocket, *examine* the letters") to describe, in counterfactual mode, the gradual process of coming closer and closer to Albertine's correspondence serves to provide him with the fantasy of actually having examined it—a mere dream of knowledge, protecting him from its real-life counterpart.

Such, then, are Marcel's chosen paths to discovery: unreliable witnesses, indifferent details, silent surfaces. He chooses to look in the wrong places— among "the specific pledges that she gave me *and that I wanted to believe*, the negative results of my *incomplete* inquiries, [and] the assurances of Andrée, *given perhaps with Albertine's connivance*" (C 193; my emphasis)—for information he does not wish to obtain; his peace of mind requires that he employ sufficient resources to generate the illusion of knowing the truth, but that he stop short of those which risk actually uncovering it.[32] The point of all his surveillance is not to confirm his suspicions but to allay them with false evidence to the contrary, to provide a semblance of accuracy rather than the facts themselves, *to redouble his ignorance by making him forget that there is even anything left to know*.[33] It is to channel a doubt that can never be fully uprooted, not repressing it but, in the manner of Freud's celebrated *fort-da* game,[34] permitting it to play within carefully controlled conditions. Thus

I realised that if I had not until then suffered too painfully from my doubts as to Albertine's virtue it was because in reality they were not doubts at all. My happiness, my life required that Albertine should be virtuous; they had laid it down once and for all that she was. Armed with this self-protective belief, I could with impunity allow my mind to play sadly with suppositions to which it gave a form but lent no credence. I said to myself, "She is perhaps a woman-lover," as we say "I may die tonight"; we say it, but we do not believe it, we make plans for the following day. (F 694)

4. A Second-Order Will to Ignorance

Having learned the value of "self-protective beliefs," and indeed learned it so well that he does not attempt to know any more about *them* than he has to, Marcel stands almost at the end of his *Bildung*, on the verge of understanding what it takes to bring sense and structure into a life. (The next chapter will investigate how this final challenge is to be met.) He is at least partially aware that the compulsion to seek enlightenment—all his relentless suppositions, inquisitions, and investigations—can in fact be dictated by a more primordial drive, namely the instinct of self-preservation that keeps people happily ensconced in their blindness;[35] he recognizes, that is, that a *second-order will to ignorance*, a will to remain ignorant of the fact that one knows nothing, comes as a standard part of human mental equipment.

Proust, here, would entirely agree with Marcel. What is more, he would agree—unwittingly, as ever—with Friedrich Nietzsche, just as we saw the two independently reach the same conclusions about perspective in chapter 1, and just as we will see them independently reach comparable conclusions about selfhood in chapter 3. For Nietzsche holds a view that is strikingly similar to what I have been presenting, in the current chapter, as the position of Proust. Consider the twenty-fourth section of *Beyond Good and Evil*, which runs as follows:

O sancta simplicitas! In what strange simplification and falsification man lives! One can never cease wondering once one has acquired eyes for this marvel! How we have made everything around us clear and free and easy and simple! how we have been able to give our senses a passport to everything superficial, our thoughts a divine desire for wanton leaps and wrong inferences! how from the beginning we have contrived to retain our ignorance in order to enjoy an almost inconceivable freedom, lack of scruple and caution, heartiness, and gaiety of life—in order to enjoy life! And only on this now solid, granite foundation of ignorance could knowledge rise so far—the will to knowledge on the foundation of a far more powerful will: the will to ignorance, to the uncertain, to the untrue! Not as its opposite, but—as its refinement!

Even if *language*, here as elsewhere, will not get over its awkwardness, and will continue to talk of opposites where there are only

degrees and many subtleties of gradation; even if the inveterate Tar-
tuffery of morals, which now belongs to our unconquerable "flesh and
blood," infects the words even of those of us who know better—here
and there we understand it and laugh at the way in which precisely
science [*Wissenschaft*][36] at its best seeks most to keep us in this *simplified*, thoroughly artificial, suitably constructed and suitably falsified
world—at the way in which, willy-nilly, it loves error, because, being
alive, it loves life.

Like Proust, Nietzsche clearly considers the will to "ignorance, to the
uncertain, to the untrue" every bit as essential as the will to knowledge, every
bit as indispensable to a happy life.[37] Like Proust, furthermore, Nietzsche
presents the former as primary, the latter as its belated derivate and inden-
tured servant. Contrary to what one might imagine, the will to knowledge is
not something radically distinct from the will to ignorance but merely a new
form of it,[38] a "refinement," a subtle sophistication: the most strenuous efforts to gather information—those of science "at its best"—do the very *most*
to keep us safely cocooned in our "suitably falsified world." For science, by
always raising questions of fact (the *what* and the *how*), and by falsely assuming that learning is an end in itself (cf. GM III:24), shields itself from ever
having to raise questions of value (the *why*). As Nietzsche puts it, in a paraphrase of Pascal's 139th *Pensée*, "men pursue their business and their sciences so eagerly only so as to elude the most important questions . . ., that is
to say precisely those questions as to Whither, Whence and Why. Amazingly,
the most obvious question fails to occur to our scholars [*Wissenschaftler*]:
what is their work, their hurry, their painful frenzy supposed to be *for*?" (DS
8; my emphasis).[39]
 Science, then, turns out to be no more than a mechanism spontaneously
developed by mankind as protection against the dangerous insight that in and
of itself life has no meaning, human striving no point or purpose. Our tireless
pursuit of trivial facts simply serves to conceal from us that far deeper ignorance, and thus to *preserve* it, there being no other way it can be preserved
once the first rays of doubt begin to dawn on our cognitive horizon. We must
persuade ourselves that we are doing everything possible to discover the
truth, while continually investigating areas from which we know it absent;
we must, as it turns out, double our delusion, not only remaining unaware of
the state of affairs but *forgetting that we are unaware*, becoming ignorant of
our very ignorance. Because we appear to be on the trail of truth, we are pre-
vented from actually finding it, and even from realizing that we have found
nothing worth looking for (lest we embark on a more successful, and thus
life-endangering, hunt). The will to knowledge thus acts, in such cases, as
an aid to the will to ignorance—as the latter's "refinement"—by spuriously
convincing us that we have left no stone unturned. And all of us who "have

looked deeply into the true nature of things" (BT 7), not scientists alone, stand in need of Nietzsche's remedy. Or, to phrase the issue in terms more congenial to Proust, not just lovers mad with jealousy but all human beings endowed with excessive curiosity require the second-order will to ignorance, the drive to cease believing there is any more to learn.

3

Self-Creation (Odette's Face)

"And how is the book entitled?" asked Don Quixote.

"The 'Life of Gines de Pasamonte,'" replied the subject of it.

"And is it finished?" asked Don Quixote.

"How can it be finished," said the other, "when my life is not yet finished?"

—Miguel de Cervantes, *Don Quixote*

If there is one question that most haunts Proust through the thousands of pages in his novel, it is whether the Self—that shadowy and fragmented, indeed doubly fragmented, entity—can ever achieve any real degree of harmony.[1] Bringing together two strands of philosophical-psychological inquiry, Proust suggests that each individual is riven both synchronically, into a set of faculties or drives, and diachronically, into a series of distinct organizations and orientations of those faculties or drives, varying according to the phase of life (or even the hour of the day). He thus places his narrator, and indeed his reader, in a dual predicament. Not only do we change over time, he implies, so that it is difficult to pinpoint a common factor which would grant us the "personal identity" we seek (a term made popular by Locke, Hume, and their followers),[2] but we cannot achieve unanimity within ourselves at any given moment. In fact, the simultaneous multiplicity is even greater than Proust's sources (from Plato and Augustine to the French *moralistes*) acknowledge, since on his model the diachronic becomes synchronic: our various incarnations do not simply replace one another but remain with us forever, in the background of our consciousness, forming a complex geological structure of several superposed strata.

It would be a prodigious feat of escapology if Proust's narrator were to emerge from the above constraints clutching intact a convincing version of selfhood. Like any such version, his has to satisfy two conditions, namely coherence (identity with oneself) and uniqueness (distinction from other individuals). Marcel, in other words, has to find an element which sets him apart from other human beings, but which, unlike for example his (full-blown) love for Gilberte, is permanent; or, conversely, an element which guarantees a continuity across time and which, unlike for example his need to breathe, is peculiar to him. For a very long time he despairs of ever satisfying the twofold requirement: "my life appeared to me," he laments, "as something utterly devoid of the support of *an individual, identical and permanent self*" (F 802–3; my emphasis). He is, however, ultimately successful, and the burden of this chapter will be to explain how exactly he accomplishes his great escape, first by means of a hidden faculty (the perspective, or "tempérament") that he discovers and then, elegantly enough, by using one multiplicity to cure the other: using the synchronic division to impose order on a diachronically fractured Self. Marcel's solution, it turns out, is an existence cast in literary terms, a life in literature (a genre I shall term the aesthetic biography). As for *Proust's* solution, there are indications that it does not stop here but concerns, instead, a life lived *as* literature (or bioaesthetic), one in which experience is continually spun into art even as it unwinds.

Much, of course, has been made in critical circles of the Proustian Self and its vicissitudes, whether from a Freudian, a Humean, or even a Sartrean angle.[3] Almost all the analyses, however, seem to simplify matters by selecting one or other of the problems Proust wishes to deal with simultaneously, focusing either on the diachronic division to the near-exclusion of the synchronic or on the synchronic to the detriment of the diachronic.[4] In addition, as is understandable given the well-nigh irreducible complexity of the novel, the analyses often stop short of Proust's full account, resorting at one extreme to an uncritical acceptance of involuntary memory as panacea[5] or, at the other extreme, dismissing it out of hand and reveling in what are taken to be insoluble conflicts.[6] As for the few analytical philosophers who have commented extensively on Proust, they tend, for the most part, to view Proust less as a philosopher in his own right and more as someone who provides a convenient and vivid illustration of ideas to be found elsewhere.[7] In what follows, by contrast, I shall suggest that there is rigorous consistency, deep philosophical sophistication, and conceptual novelty in Proust's portrait of selfhood; that if we only have patience enough to tease out each thread, many (if perhaps not all) of its knots may eventually be unraveled.

PART I: PROBLEMS

1. Synchronic Division: Faculties and Drives

The idea that human inwardness (whether it is thought of as "soul," "mind," or "psychic apparatus") is or may be broken down into a set of separate parts has an extremely long history indeed. It is already implicit in the *Iliad* where, to take one example, the "heart" within Achilles' "shaggy breast" is "divided two ways" (ἐν δέ οἱ ἦτορ / στήθεσσιν λασίοισι διάνδιχα μερμήριξεν [book 1, 188–89]); and it is made explicit in the earliest texts of Western philosophy properly so designated, Plato's Socratic dialogues. In Achilles' case, the continuation (book 1, 190–92) indicates that his ambivalence takes the form of a choice between aims, namely immediate revenge upon Agamemnon and control over the "anger" (θυμός) that he feels. We might label the areas responsible for such aims, for the pursuit of particular interests or values, our *drives*, each one distinguished by its objective. Plato, of course, does not use the word, but his three components of the soul—τὸ λογιστικόν, τὸ θυμοηιδής, τὸ ἐπιθυμετικόν—could surely be classified in that way, as the horse-and-charioteer metaphor of the *Phaedrus* (246a-b, 253c-56c) makes plain. And so, conceivably, could Freud's superego, ego, and id, those agencies that strive for narcissistic satisfaction, self-preservation, and instinctual gratification, respectively.[8] In Augustine, on the other hand, the three segments of the soul are powers of the mind rather than orientations of activity, the terms "intellect," "memory," and "will" designating that which each part is *able* to do, as opposed to that which each *wants* to achieve. Here, therefore, as in Descartes's schema and (mutatis mutandis) that of Kant, we tend to speak of *faculties*.

Whether we consider the multiplicity in terms of drives or faculties, two central discrepancies and disagreements among the various theories and theorists will prove germane to our discussion. First, there is the relative complexity of each model, from Homer's apparently binary system to Plato's tripartite soul and thence to Nietzsche's elaborate picture in which the various drives are themselves agglomerations of an undefined number of subdrives (BGE 19). Second, there is what one might call the dynamic question, concerning the ways in which the parts relate to one another. It is particularly important to know whether they naturally or at least ideally work in concert (as in Aristotle's perfectly constituted soul, according to Cooper) or whether they are in eternal competition and conflict, and if the latter, which may gain control and under what circumstances. In order to explain how a subordinate drive may overpower a dominant drive, for example, it may be necessary to assume that an external event affects them in different ways, strengthening the former and weakening the latter. Such,

I submit, is the case with the Self in Proust: it is divided into at least three strictly synchronic components, each of which may come to dominate at any one time and all of which may never, perhaps, be brought into full alignment.

Thus far we have mostly been dealing with the intricate pas de deux performed by intuitive faculty (*faculté intuitive, intuition, sensibilité*) and the intellect (*intelligence, raison*). A third agency, however, always accompanies the other two, but silently, surreptitiously; if it is so frequently overlooked in Marcel's analyses of internal dissension, its very discretion is to blame. While intuition doubts and intellect rationalizes, will (*volonté*) makes the decisions, constantly providing the Self as a whole with what it needs, even while that quantity changes from one moment to the next. When, for example, Marcel has the opportunity to be introduced to Albertine, his *intelligence* assumes romance a foregone (and thus uninteresting) conclusion, his *sensibilité* demurs for opposite reasons, and his *volonté* studiously ignores both:

> My brain [*intelligence*] assessed this pleasure at a very low value now that it was assured. But, inside, my will [*volonté*] did not for a moment share this illusion, that will which is the persevering and unalterable servant of our successive personalities; hidden away in the shadow, despised, downtrodden, untiringly faithful, toiling incessantly, and with no thought for the variability of the self, to ensure that the self may never lack what is needed. . . . It is as invariable as the intelligence and the sensibility [*sensibilité*] are fickle, but since it is silent, gives no account of its actions, it seems almost non-existent; it is by its dogged determination that the other constituent parts of our personality are led, but without seeing it, whereas they distinguish clearly all their own uncertainties. So my intelligence and my sensibility began a discussion as to the real value of the pleasure that there would be in knowing Albertine. . . . But my will would not let the hour pass at which I must start, and it was Elstir's address that it called out to the driver. (BG 614–15)

There are, in short, at least three faculties sharing the Self between them, a triad of will, sensibility, and intellect that may owe something to the Cartesian model. Not only do the faculties frequently come into conflict, as when intellect clashes with instinct for power over the Self's overall attitude toward a subject (the two "hypotheses"), or when will bypasses them both in situations of decision making; they may even remain periodically unaware of each other's operations, if not existence—all of which poses a severe threat to any project of self-unification.

2. Diachronic Division: Sedimentation of the Self

As though matters were not problematic enough, Marcel's presentation (above) of his inner dialogue on the uses and disadvantages of meeting Albertine points toward an additional, entirely separate level of complexity afflicting the Self. Not only does Marcel portray it as a synchronically multiple entity, in principle resistant to synthesis, but when he describes one of its components as "the persevering and unalterable servant *of our successive personalities*," he intimates that it is no more uniform in the diachronic dimension. Our personality, on his view, has a way of changing dramatically over time, to such an extent in fact that today's "moi" cannot predict tomorrow's, nor even always remember that of yesterday (F 805); so radical is the rupture that it gives the impression of multiple deaths and rebirths over the course of a single life (BG 340, F 653), producing a series of "new selves" each of which should, according to Marcel, "bear a different name from the preceding one" (F 804; cf. BG 720).[9] With no solution of continuity between its various incarnations, the Self begins to look like a gallery of photographs taken at different stages of development. Just as we envisage other people in a succession of still frames ("I possessed in my memory only a series of Albertines, separate from one another . . . a collection of profiles or snapshots" C 192), so our own life disintegrates into an accumulation of apparently unrelated molecules of memory, the transitions between them unclear, their number limited only by the divisibility of time into smaller and smaller units. Indeed, it is in large part *because* we ourselves are constantly changing, both in the level of our knowledge and in our attitudes, that we see other people— indeed the entire ambient world—in the fragmented way we do.[10]

If, however, we really are recreated entirely from one moment to the next, how is continuity possible over time? How do we manage, on waking up, to recover precisely that *moi* we surrendered when we fell asleep (GW 110)? How, in particular, can we have that direct access to our old, departed selves which is the hallmark of involuntary memory—not merely the imaginative reconstruction of an earlier life, as though it were someone else's, but a genuine reexperiencing from within of the way our attitudes used to organize sensation, when "some former self . . . momentarily [takes] the place of the present self" (SG 581; cf. TR 284, BG 300)? These are questions Proust's narrator repeatedly raises, from the first section of the novel (S 49) onward. And the answer he ends up giving involves an attenuation of the rhetoric of death and rebirth, one which proves to have been somewhat misleading. For the old Marcels do not, as it turns out, disappear without a trace. All of the avatars remain forever within the mental apparatus as a ghostly residue, as the faint and often unconscious mnemonic trace of previous modes of being. We carry around with us, imprinted indelibly on our mind, a precise if inconspicuous record of every single phase of our development to date. The Self thus comprises a multitude of overlaid strata, each one representing a deposed *moi* from a different era of the individual's existence.[11]

When, therefore, Marcel refers to the "death" of a self, he means nothing more than its removal from power, its relegation from a position of predominance over the Self as a whole to a deeper, more hidden level of the mind. It may be *largely* displaced by a successor, but it is never exorcised entirely. As Marcel puts it—in an unusually pithy four-word sentence—"Rien ne se perd" ("nothing is ever lost," SG 34). Thus, for example, a belief in the magic of the Guermantes name never quite deserts Marcel, in spite of all the disenchantment to which it is subjected over the course of the tale. In the third volume alone, its prestige suffers at least three separate blows (GW 29, 280, 719), only to bounce back each time (30, 514, 744–45) with renewed vigor, so that the volume more or less ends on a renewed commitment to the illusion, catalyzed by an invitation from the Princess (779–80; cf. BSB 155). Even in the later volumes, after etymology has ostensibly reduced names to the arbitrary signifiers they really are (Genette 1969: 248), Marcel suffers periodic relapses into his fascination with the orange-tinted bisyllable. For while the Guermantes-acolyte no longer sits at the forefront of his Self, it is liable to return at any moment (albeit briefly) to prominence, "to renew [itself] in me" (F 773), "to draw up from the depths of my memory a sort of section of the past of the Guermantes, attended by all the images of seignorial forest and tall flowers which at that earlier time of my life had accompanied it" (TR 240; cf. 282).

In the same way, Marcel's love for Gilberte (at least for the Gilberte he knew as a young man) lingers on indefinitely.[12] He may imagine, at the start of "Place-Names: The Place," that he has rid himself of it forever, the relevant part of him having committed "suicide" (BG 255), yet he suddenly finds himself overwhelmed, immediately on his arrival at Balbec, by a recrudescence of the very same feeling (BG 300). Of course, it is possible to stop loving someone. It is just that the loving self does not, for all that, simply vanish; rather it takes a back seat, no longer preeminent but still, under certain circumstances, ready to reemerge and reassert its control. Indeed, the process of ceasing to love someone also turns on the synchronic-diachronic division of the Self. For since it still contains any number of avatars that are utterly indifferent to the loved one, one merely has to wait for these voters to reach a majority within the "commonwealth,"[13] for the *indifférents* within one to displace all the *passionnés*:

> I was not one man only, but as it were the march-past of a composite army in which there were passionate men, indifferent men, jealous men [*des passionnés, des indifférents, des jaloux*]—jealous men not one of whom was jealous of the same woman. And no doubt it would be

from this that one day would come the cure for which I had no wish. In a composite mass, the elements may one by one, without our notic-ing it, be replaced by others. . . . until in the end a change has been brought about which it would be impossible to conceive if we were a single person. (F 660, on Albertine)

These states of consciousness to which the person whom we love remains a stranger. . . We must seek to encourage these thoughts, to make them grow, while the sentiment which is no more now than a memory dwindles, so that the new elements introduced into the mind contest with that sentiment, wrest from it an ever-increasing portion of our soul, until at last the victory is complete. (BG 285, on Gilberte)[14]

What exactly is, then, the nature of all these subsidiary selves? Primarily, they consist in a set of identifications with different objects of desire, belief, and adherence. Thus we can demarcate a Marcel who seeks all the satisfac-tions of love in his mother, followed by a Marcel who idolizes Gilberte, then a Marcel who stalks the Duchesse de Guermantes, and finally a Marcel who keeps Albertine as his "prisoner" in Paris. ("There was not one of the years of my life that did not have, as a frontispiece," notes Marcel at TR 440, "the image of a woman whom I had desired during that year.") There is the Marcel who believes in Balbec as a magic world, divorced from the everyday world in which he lives, bathing in the mystery of its name and its reputation; there is the Marcel who believes the same about Venice; there is the Marcel who (at least in theory) no longer believes it about any place. Since external sites serve as boundary markers for an internal chronology (Poulet 1963: 12–13), the memory of a room (S 5–9) is also the imprint of a former self. We might term such local, time-bound selves the *moi-Gilberte*, the *moi-Albertine*, the *moi-Venise*, and so on.

Now within these categories there is a further subdivision, according to the specific attitude the subject takes toward the object in question. Thus, to return to Marcel's comment cited above, he contains (among other entities) the *moi-Albertine-jaloux*, the *moi-Albertine-indifférent*, and the *moi-Alber-tine-passionné*: "I developed the habit of becoming myself a different person, according to the particular Albertine to whom my thoughts had turned: a jealous, an indifferent, a voluptuous, a melancholy, a frenzied person [*un jal-oux, un indifférent, un voluptueux, un mélancolique, un furieux*], created anew . . . in proportion to the strength of [my] belief [*croyance*]" (BG 719–20). Here the balance is firmly shifted away from the outside world, the distin-guishing feature of each sub-self consisting in the relative importance within it of the various faculties which, as we saw above, vie for control over the psyche. Since only our faith in the uniqueness and mystery of a person has the power to render him or her desirable,[15] it is when Albertine finds herself invested without admixture by "croyance" that Marcel considers himself a *voluptueux*, and it is the total dissipation of that same faith which renders him *indifférent*. The *jaloux* emerges, presumably, when suspicion for the most part predominates over trust, the *mélancolique* when a bedrock of belief suffers the vague rumblings of subterranean fears of which it is, under such circumstances, completely at the mercy.

Each sub-self is, I would suggest, a hierarchical arrangement in which, as in a physical compound, the various parts, blended together in their relative proportions, combine to form what looks and feels like a single substance—the jealous, the melancholic, the indifferent man—and is thus able to determine what we refer to as our "self" of the moment (cf. Nehamas 1985: 181). We are not usually able to isolate, at the time, the elements of which it is made; thus it is only in retrospect, and working back from external evidence, that Marcel can reconstruct the full complexity of his state of mind during his disconsolate period. "I continued to live by the hypothesis which accepted as true everything that Albertine told me. But it may be that during this time a wholly contrary hypothesis, of which I refused to think, never left me; *this is all the more probable since* otherwise . . . my lack of astonishment at her anger would not have been comprehensible" (C 465–66; my emphasis). At the time, we impose a much simpler label on our state of mind, generating a hypostasized disposition which, we may speculate, solidifies into a conditioned reflex (what Marcel calls a "secretary of habit" [SG 187]).

At the lowest level, finally, the sub-self is further divided into a number of discrete fragments, each corresponding as it were to its respective date of manufacture (*moi-Albertine-jaloux-t$_1$*, *moi-Albertine-jaloux-t$_2$*, etc.). There are, we recall, not one but several Marcels who are jealous of Albertine—jealous, that is, of different Albertines: "I was not one man only, but as it were the march-past of a composite army in which there were passionate men, indifferent men, jealous men—jealous men *not one of whom was jealous of the same woman*." As Marcel gradually glimpses more and more of Albertine's "aspects" (without, of course, ever reaching a definitive moment of absolute knowledge), his picture of her, his notion of who she is, keeps changing; and thus his passion or his jealousy turns out to be a passion or a jealousy for a different Albertine (C 713).

It might therefore be more appropriate to label the lowest-level selves *moi-Albertine$_1$-jaloux*, *moi-Albertine$_2$-jaloux*, and so on, providing of course that *Albertine$_1$* and *Albertine$_2$* are not taken in any strictly objective sense. Each second-order self (what I have termed a "sub-self") is made up of several of these third-order selves; each emotional attitude toward a person, which we mistakenly treat as one extended event, comprises a plurality of separate attitudes. "What we suppose to be our love or our jealousy is never a single, continuous and indivisible passion. It is composed of an infinity of successive loves, of different jealousies, each of which is ephemeral, although by their uninterrupted multiplicity they give us the impression of continuity, the illusion of unity" (S 529). Deprivation accordingly affects a horde of bereft lovers, attached to a horde of departed beloveds: "at every moment, there was one more of those innumerable and humble 'selves' that compose our personality which was still unaware of Albertine's departure and must be informed of it. . . . In order to be consoled I would have to forget, not one, but innumerable Albertines" (F 579, 645). If, as Richard Terdiman (1976: 208) has pointed out, there are some twenty-two repetitions of the phrase "Albertine was dead" in the early portion of *The Fugitive*—including no fewer than four on the page that carries Marcel's self-comparison to a "composite army"—we are doubtless to imagine a different Marcel being notified on each occasion.

The final distribution of selves is predicated, in other words, not just on our attitude toward a given object but on what, amid the pandemic epistemological crisis that characterizes Proust's world, we take that object to be. The elementary, indivisible particles of which the Self as a whole is composed may thus each be defined as (1) a disposition toward a specific object of attention (2) comprising a certain hierarchy of faculties and (3) taking the object in its current, momentary form. And it is precisely the proliferation of such lowest-level selves, I would argue, that accounts for the constitution of the intermediate selves we investigated earlier. The relative proportion within each second-order self of, for example, faith and doubt should be understood as referring to the respective population sizes of the *croyants* and the *sceptiques*: when the skeptics outnumber the believers, the sub-self will take itself to be a *jaloux*. As we move up from the atomic level to the level of highest complexity, the genuine nature of the individual undergoes a series of abstractions (comparable to Nietzsche's "metaphors" in TL), our disparate loves reduced to a single passion, our various dispositions bracketed into the all-encompassing category of concern for a specific individual, and at last our several concerns brought together, in imagination, into an overall Self which—as if it were one and the same over the entire course of its life—dares to call itself "I."

3. Proust's Predicament

The result is an extremely complicated picture of the soul, one in which its multiplicity—"for duplication would not be a strong enough term" (F 664)—increases prodigiously. Where primitive descriptions viewed each human being as a vertex, with a single and immutable distinguishing trait (Samson's strength, for example); where doctrines of conversion (such as that of Paul) extended the point into a line, adding the possibility for a (solitary) moment of change in the course of a life; where theorists of the faculties (Plato, Augustine, the *moralistes*) engaged in plane psychology, considering the Self an entity with *depth*, fragmented and hierarchized vertically, Marcel's is a genuinely three-dimensional account, accommodating both synchronic and diachronic variations. "As there is a geometry in space, so there is a psychology in time, in which the calculations of a plane psychology would no longer be accurate," he writes (F 751; cf. TR 505–6, EA 253, *Letters* 226). For him, as we have seen, the Self ("*le* moi") is defined as the accumulation of its consecutive states ("*les* moi"), sedimented over time;[16] at any given instant, we are the sum of an extremely large set of existences, many of which are entirely unknown to us, and all of which cohabit simultaneously in the mind.

Although a certain debt to Henri Bergson is both clear and indirectly acknowledged (SG 522), this remains an extremely bold, controversial, and ingenious move on Marcel's (and, I think, Proust's) part. The image of the Self conveyed by the *Recherche* may be rebarbatively elaborate, but it has the merit of explaining a wide variety of phenomena that alternative schemata simply cannot capture: recidivisms of the soul, simultaneities of faith and distrust, lucid dreams, a confusion as to our location on waking, and above all the strange power of ancient memories over our present-day organism. The fact, as Marcel sees it, is that involuntary memory is really not memory at all. When an odor, texture, or sound returns us to a former state, we are not dragging into the light a set of impressions that have long since departed but, instead, summoning up a part of us that is still very much present within our mind. Only in this way is it possible to reexperience *from within* a situation we approached with a radically different set of attitudes, beliefs, and desires.

Nonetheless, as I mentioned earlier, this does leave us in quite a predicament when it comes to discovering (a fortiori communicating) a unity amid the multiplicity, a Self beneath the selves. Three criteria need, in fact, to be met if we are to convey our distinctive essence to other people. To begin with, there is the two-pronged ontological requirement that has been the substance of our discussion thus far: the Self must be a Self, namely both coherent and unique, in order for there to *be* a distinctive essence at all. The second and third requirements, epistemological and representational respectively, dictate that we must be able to have sufficient access to our deepest, darkest corners to satisfy the Delphic demands of self-awareness, and that we must then be able to express our findings in language. Now Marcel is reluctant to consider any of these requirements satisfied in advance. Although no one else can know us as well as we do—"experience of oneself . . . is the only true experience" (SG 434)—we do not, when it comes to it, know ourselves particularly well. Our very proximity to the object of study prevents us from gaining a clear view; the Self's relations with itself are never entirely disinterested, will-free (in Schopenhauer's terms), unmixed with libido (in Freud's). Thus Gilberte, Marcel concedes wryly, "understood me even less than I understood myself" (TR 2). Faint praise indeed for his own perspicacity.

And if there is no direct self-knowledge, it follows logically that there is no straightforward transmission of knowledge about the self: to paraphrase a Platonic point (*Symposium* 196e–97a), one cannot share what one does not have. Worse still, the contradictory nature of the Self makes complete candor problematic in the extreme. "If we are not altogether sincere in telling ourselves that we never wish to see the one we love again," for example, "we would not be a whit more sincere in saying that we do" (BG 269). Fortunately for Marcel (and for us), there is a solution to all three issues, involving involuntary memory, metaphor, and art; the rest of the present chapter will be dedicated to an exposition, and in many cases a hypothetical reconstruction, of that ingenious escape route.

PART 2: SOLUTIONS

1. The "True Self": Temperament, Taste, and Style

Involuntary Memory It is a well-known fact that the discovery of involuntary memory, in the experience of the madeleine dipped in an *infusion de tilleul*, is what rescues Marcel from the doldrums and finally allows him, after similar experiences at the Guermantes *matinée*, to begin writing his masterpiece. It is perhaps less well known exactly *how* the one leads to the other. Granted, involuntary memory releases hitherto buried memories—of Combray, for instance—and thus provides the work, whose material is Marcel's past life (TR 304), with some of its substance. More importantly, however, it offers at least a partial solution to the predicament of the Self, one which needs to be addressed before any autobiographical or quasi-autobiographical project may be undertaken. What involuntary memory gives to the future book is less its content than its *form*, if not its very condition of existence: a narrating instance sufficiently unified as to be able to say "I" and to speak for a multiplicity of selves in past and present tenses.[17]

In the first place, it should be noted that if involuntary memory restores lost time, it does so by restoring a lost self. What emerges from the cup of tea (S 63) is not really Combray per se but the Marcel who used to inhabit it (what we have been calling the *moi-Combray*) and who used to consider its every field and side street a source of magic and wonder (S 260); it is only because this former "moi" is returned to consciousness—because, that is, Marcel comes to reinhabit its precise organization of identifications and faculties—that Marcel is able to rescue the specific details of his childhood holiday home from oblivion. He not only hears the church bells and smells the hawthorns but holds the beliefs and feels the desires that went along with them: "so complete are these resurrections of the past . . . that they . . . oblige our eyes to cease to see the room which is near them . . ., they even force our nostrils to breathe the air of places which are in fact a great distance away, and our will to choose between the various projects which those distant places suggest to us; they force our whole self to believe that it is surrounded by those places" (TR 268).[18] There is, of course, an immediate and important consequence for self-knowledge. When involuntary memory reinstates a "self" that has long been forgotten, as though it were "dead" (i.e., permanently erased from the mental record), it holds out the hope that all of the other selves that go to make up the overall persona—at least the second-order selves (like the *moi-Combray*), if not the innumerable third-order selves—may similarly be resurrected.[19] Even if, from one instant to the next, we are privy to but a fraction of our soul's activity (SG 211), a cumulative awareness of its several states looms at least as a hypothetical prospect.

The epiphanies have, however, something far more crucial to teach us. The very fact that we are able to summon up the ghostly residue of a past self indicates an essential point of continuity between the latter and our present-day incarnation. If today's madeleine tastes the same as it did thirty years ago, it is because there must be a part of us at least that has not changed in between times, *a permanent aspect underlying all of the mutable selves.*[20] Thus we should not be misled by Marcel's claim that involuntary memory, in addition to catalyzing the emergence of this "true self," also provides insight into the secret essence of things ("the . . . habitually concealed essence of things is liberated and our true self [*notre vrai moi*] . . . is awakened" [TR 264]): what we discover is not the essence of cake and tea, eaten and drunk at different periods of our life—how could such a thing deliver the kind of bliss of which Marcel speaks in *Swann's Way* (60) and elsewhere?—but a hidden region of the Self, one which must be invariable since it is capable of experiencing the same tastes in the same fashion at a distance of decades.[21] "The being within me which had enjoyed these impressions had enjoyed them because they had in them something that was common to a day long past and to the present, because in some way they were extratemporal, and this being . . . [was itself] outside time" (TR 262). Although the "being" thus revealed remains indistinct for now, the mere notion of its existence is cause enough for joy.[22]

Perspective   Though he is not normally known for his reticence, Marcel declines to elaborate on the nature of the "true self" revealed during involuntary memory. We may, however, reasonably assume that what is in question is an aspect of the mind that organizes the data of sense in a comprehensive and consistent manner. For Marcel, as we recall from chapter 1, seems to share with Kant and with Nietzsche the idea that the data of sense are entirely unstructured in themselves, and that it is the human mind which makes them intelligible by classifying them under a set of schemata.[23] And while some of the schemata are objective (intellect allowing us, each in the same way, to isolate individuals), others are subjective (instinct forging more idiosyncratic associations): the way in which we see the world is not determined, as in Kant, by a uniform array of transcendentally necessary "categories" but, following Nietzsche, by our specific constitution—our "perspective" or *tempérament*—so that there may be as many arrangements as there are pairs of eyes.[24]

The genuine impact of involuntary memory thus turns out to be related to its unveiling of a hidden faculty within the Self. The simple act of remembering, and remembering from within—not just the facts of an experience (dates, times, names, places), as if it belonged to another person, but the subjective component, the way in which our taste buds receive information, the way (more importantly) in which we put things together—offers the sudden tantalizing glimpse of a possible identity consistent over time, and thus a partial and preliminary satisfaction of the ontological and epistemological criteria: involuntary memory indicates the existence of, and affords access to, a unique and diachronically stable self.[25] It also provides a powerful response to David Hume's typically dogmatic-slumber-shattering question. For Hume, the individual has a type of effective identity, as a "chain of causes and effects" (262), but possesses no *inner* coherence, no common element shared among the various impressions that make up the mind. "The identity, which we ascribe to the mind of man, is only a fictitious one," Hume writes (259); it is "nothing but a bundle or collection of different perceptions, which succeed each other with an inconceivable rapidity, and are in a perpetual flux" (252); "there is properly not *simplicity* in it at one time, nor *identity* in different" (253). Hence "when I enter most intimately into what I call *myself*, I always stumble on some particular perception or other. . . . I can never catch *myself* . . . without a perception. . . . When my perceptions are remov'd for any time, as by sound sleep; so long am I insensible of myself, and may truly be said not to exist" (252).

Proust (and others) might well think Hume is taking *esse percipi* a little too far here. More to the point, Proust would doubtless agree with Ricoeur (128) that Hume, whether wittingly or unwittingly, is in the above passage presupposing the very entity whose existence he denies. For if there is no *me* to be found, who is the *I* that is "always" looking for it? There must surely be a secret site of constancy after all in the "mind of man," a part of ourself which can never be seen since it is always doing the seeing, something *through* which, and never *at* which, we stare. "Throughout the whole course of one's life," Marcel confirms, "one's egoism sees before it all the time the objects that are of concern to the self, but never takes in that 'I' itself which is perpetually observing them" (F 628).[26] Marcel has to wait many years before discovering his *je* (the madeleine episode, although one of the first to be narrated, is chronologically situated toward the end of the tale, in between the visit to Tansonville and the climactic Guermantes *matinée*);[27] and as for David Hume, it would seem that he never did so.

Style   Now that involuntary memory has sketched the outline of the true self, all that remains is to fill in its specific details, to give a content to the form. Since the temperament, as we have seen, cannot be perceived directly—involuntary memory may indicate its *existence*, but can give few hints as to its nature—in order to register the latter we need to work back from its effects, from the template we project onto the indifferent material of our life and loves, the "negative" of our personality, as Marcel puts it, just waiting to be "developed."[28] Thus our various choices of partner shed light on the temperament which has, unbeknownst to us, been making the decisions all the time (BG 647). It is artistic creation, however, that provides the most perspicuous method through which to elucidate a temperament, allowing us to move from the latter's effects (in the case at hand, from the finished product) to their postulated cause.[29]

Just as, in ordinary life, what we "discover" in objects is only what we have put there in the first place[30]—a result which may be disappointing for those in search of objective fact, but is a godsend for those who seek *la vérité subjective*—so in literature that which a writer appears to see in things turns out to be nothing more, or nothing less, than the gleam of his or her own projections bouncing back. Thus "every fresh beauty in [Bergotte's] work was the little drop of Bergotte buried at the heart of a thing and which he had distilled from it" (BG 170). Marcel's wording here is perhaps a little ambivalent, but there is also a genuine sense in which Bergotte is extracting truths from the entirely fictional world of his creation: we identify with one side of the mind what we have just concocted with the other (cf. S 61), so that what we see is simultaneously "true" and "false," real and imaginary. One is reminded of a beautiful scene in the second volume—included, it seems to me, purely for its symbolic value—in which Marcel's mother places shells on the seabed so that Marcel may find them as he dives (100). Creation and discovery come together.

If, then, we wish to disclose the detailed composition of our true self, we can do little better than to approach our own writing from an outsider's position,[31] which is precisely how Marcel considers his Martinville steeples piece when it is finally published in the *Figaro* (F 770) and which is even, according to Marcel, how the great nineteenth-century novelists—glorious failures one and all—responded to their own creations. They "somehow botched their books," he ventures, "but, watching themselves work as though they were at once workman and judge, derived from this self-contemplation a new form of beauty, exterior and superior to the work itself" (C 207). The prefaces of the *Comédie humaine* or the *Rougon-Macquart*, drafted *après coup*, are a testament to what their respective authors have learned (about themselves, presumably) by writing them, rather than a reliable guide to what the reader is about to encounter; far from describing the contents of the opus at hand, they gesture toward a putative future effort which the recently accomplished process has, perhaps, made possible.

The view of art implied here is, of course, highly formalist in nature. It suggests that value is determined by the index of refraction alone, "genius consisting in reflecting power and not in the intrinsic quality of the scene reflected" (BG 176; cf. PM 201). Even if she wishes to convey her personal temperament, therefore, an artist can do without painting a self-portrait. Nor, when producing her landscape or still life, need she take an overt position on its contents: "since in a writer content is always appearance and form reality" (PM 191), it follows readily that "an artist has no need to express [her] thought directly in [her] work for the latter to reflect its quality" (GW 568). Given only a sustained effort to keep her style pure of contamination from outside influences and from the "common" parts of her soul (EA 366), her fundamental outlook will imbue it willy-nilly, as Bergotte's comes through in "le Bergotte"; all the rest—all the factual information about lineage, education, loves, and losses—can freely be left aside. For anything that can be communicated directly, to others or indeed to oneself, is by definition sharable, and hence common, and hence not worth communicating.[32] The nervous habit of twisting the wrist does not tell us anything about Charlus, since his brother the duke has it too; it is a superficial attribute, no more significant than hair color (or, for that matter, than sexual preference).[33] What truly indicates something about the deep structure of his personality is, rather, the end to which he puts it, "the individual expressing his distinctive characteristics by means of impersonal and atavistic traits" (F 935).[34]

The true self, in other words, cannot be *expressed in* but only *revealed through* language. It is not just perspective but first and foremost *style*;[35] which is why, *contre Sainte-Beuve* and with Mallarmé, the writerly persona is more authentic than the empirical human being.[36] (Of Bergotte, for example, Marcel says that "in his books . . . he was really himself" [BG 180]). As a musician of words, one is able to discover the true locus of coherence and uniqueness within oneself in "that song, different from those of other singers, similar to [one's] own, . . . that distinctive strain the sameness of which—for whatever its subject it remains identical with itself—proves the permanence of the elements that compose [one's] soul" (C 342–43). And one is able at last to communicate (to oneself as well, potentially, as to others) one's idiosyncratic view of the world, thus resolving the final difficulty, that of representation.

It is here that Proust, who has so far more or less kept company with Friedrich Nietzsche, finally moves beyond him, and, at the same stroke, beyond Marcel. Nietzsche, while starting from the same premises as does

Proust—first, as we just saw, that a direct, straightforwardly expressive autobiography is impossible; second, that every philosophy is an "unconscious memoir" on the part of its writer (BGE 6; cf. GW 402)—surprisingly fails to draw the same conclusion, and ends up writing *Ecce Homo*, against his "habits" and better judgment (EH 1). Marcel, too, indulges in self-description; from his point of view, we should not forget, the *Recherche* is the story of his journey toward literary inspiration rather than an example of its results.[37] Proust, on the other hand, writes a novel.[38]

We shall return to the relationship between Proust and Marcel in due course. In the meantime, we should take stock of where we have arrived in order to determine the distance that still remains before we can truly resolve the identity question as posed by the former. The chief result so far is that the enduring quality within us is not a desire for something specific, a fact to which the sequence of objects of attention, redheads (Gilberte), blondes (Mme de Guermantes), and brunettes (Albertine), from *duchesse* to *blanchisseuse*, eloquently attests; nor yet a *belief* in something specific (such as a life after death, about which Marcel cannot make up his mind); nor, finally, an intention to *do* something specific (as we found earlier, involuntary memory restores "various projects," none of which is a live concern any more). Instead it is our fundamental orientation, our overall framework for the organization of experience, a framework that becomes manifest in the way we look at (or smell, or touch, or taste) things: just as what fascinates us in those we know is their set of *qualia*, "that essential quality of another person's sensations" (C 206), so "our true life," in Marcel's definition, is "reality as we have felt it [*telle que nous l'avons sentie*]" (TR 277).[39] We deduce its existence from the phenomenon of involuntary memory, and derive its nature by working back from the effects it produces (particularly in various forms of artistic expression).

There is, however, still something missing. Involuntary memory may give us something "individual, identical and permanent" but it is not, strictly speaking, an individual, identical, and permanent *self*. Going back to the key passage cited earlier, involuntary memory summons up a "being *within* me" (TR 262): not the Self in its entirety, but only a tiny part of it, and not even a part that could ever speak for the whole. We recall that what is taken to be the "moi" of any given moment in time is the dominant disposition, brought to the forefront of consciousness—"the governing class identifies itself with the successes of the commonwealth," as Nietzsche puts it at BGE 19—and never the perspective, which is consistent, invisible, and utterly silent.

2. The Total Self: Aesthetic Biography

We could state Marcel's present problem another way by saying that time has intruded, just as it does in the final section of the novel, on his communion with the atemporal. In the shape of his own perspective, involuntary memory has given him the *depth* he has been looking for all his life; it has also restored to his universe an infinite *breadth*, made up of other people's perspectives;[40] but it has yet to provide the *volume* Marcel seeks (C 501, C 83, GW 495), namely a vision of his diachronic selves which would expand his newfound vertical axis into a genuine three-dimensional geometry, rather than simply leaving him a mass of chaotic fragments. He knows—has known, as it were, since the first pages of the novel, when the memories of rooms "would gradually piece together the original components of my ego [*les traits originaux de mon moi*]" (S 5)—that his Self as a whole comprises a large number of temporally layered sub-selves. What he does not know is how these layers connect, or may be made to connect. This is the objection posed by time, one whose dialectical incorporation into Marcel's two-dimensional schema will finally yield the long-desired volume.

The solution requires no more than Marcel turning upon himself a type of attention he has been lavishing on those around him. Thus "although Albertine might exist in my memory . . . subdivided in accordance with a series of fractions of time, my mind, reestablishing unity in her, made her a single person" (F 693); similarly, "sometimes I reproached myself for thus taking pleasure in considering my friend as a work of art"—the friend here being Robert de Saint-Loup—"that is to say in regarding the play of all the parts of his being as harmoniously ordered by a general idea from which they depended but of which he was unaware" (BG 432–43).[41] Marcel's comparison here becomes clearer when we consider the way in which we respond to an artwork, whether verbal or visual. Our interpretation of its various features—say, the little patch of yellow wall in the bottom right-hand corner of Vermeer's *View of Delft*, or the mysterious apotheosis of lowly Mme Verdurin into the Princesse de Guermantes at the end of Proust's *Recherche*—consists in regarding them all as belonging to a single overall plan, assigning each an identical source to which, somewhat loosely, we give the name of "author" or of "artist." When, as a result of staring harder at the canvas or reading further in the novel, we encounter new features, we tend to understand them in reference to that same monadic explanatory principle; if they will not fit within the latter's scope, we revise it accordingly. What we end up with, after an extended *va-et-vient* between fact and interpretation, is a single cause—Marcel's "general idea"—responsible for as many of the local effects as possible (Nehamas 1981).

Two consequences should be noted right away. The first is that any interpretation necessarily privileges certain elements and deprivileges others, "forcing, adjusting, abbreviating, omitting, padding, inventing [and] falsifying," as Nietzsche puts it (GM III:24). Some aspects of a work become virtually invisible under a particular reading, since they neither confirm nor infirm it, and so do not even bear the appearance of artistic choices; others, embarrassing for our "author" (that is, for our theory), may simply have to be overlooked as nonessential properties, if not outright mistakes. Conversely, there are elements that receive disproportionate attention, and there are also those that have, so to speak, to be read "between the lines."

Second, the figure of the "author" is invariably to some extent a regulative fiction, not just because it is very likely to differ from the empirical writer but also, and more importantly, because we can never be quite sure of having accounted for all of its actions. It is always possible that we have neglected a detail that would modify, at least to some extent, our understanding of the composition as a whole. Even if we are largely right, then, it would be fool-hardy of us to consider our interpretation definitive. And yet we do not have any choice; in order to make sense out of the data before us, in order to see them at all as a *set* of data, grouped together and cut off from their fellows in other texts or canvases, we need to conjure up a rational principle of inclusion and exclusion.

When, therefore, Marcel views Robert as if the latter were a Holbein, he implicitly attributes to him an extrinsic source of intentional design[42] and thus substantially falsifies not only Robert's actual nature but even the way he appears in Marcel's own mind. The only manner in which Marcel can picture the motley acts, aspects, and attitudes of Robert as part of a unified system is by imagining—erroneously—that they all serve a single purpose, as they would, ideally, if he were the protagonist of a story or the subject of a portrait. Marcel is aware that in itself Robert's life holds no such consistency, being made up of discrete instants of innumerable profusion and governed by no external force, but he is still charmed by the possibility of forcing it into fictional shape. And it may well be that he also realizes the implication for his own case. That is, it may well be the desire to introduce an artificial structure into his own life, as he has into that of Robert and of Albertine, which determines the form of his third major piece of writing (counting the Martinville steeples prose poem as the first and the memoir we are reading as the second), the project he begins at the very end of the *Recherche* and which he describes, with eager anticipation, as "life . . . realised within the confines of a book [*la vie . . . réalisée dans un livre*]" (TR 507). If Marcel chooses the fictional autobiography as his third and final genre, it is perhaps because he recognizes in it a golden opportunity (although, as we shall soon see, not the *only* opportunity) to turn his own existence into a work of art, to bring all of his selves and sub-selves finally into alignment, to produce what one might call the total Self.

"How happy would he be," Marcel continues enthusiastically, "the man who had the power to write such a book! . . . he would have . . . to accept it like a discipline, build it up like a church, follow it like a medical regime . . . , cre-ate it like a new world." Once again, we notice a strict alternation between the language of discovery ("accept," "follow") and that of invention ("build," "create"). For Marcel's ideal work has to be a mixture of sincerity and fancy, whim and necessity. It may well be an accurate account of (nearly) all known aspects of the Self, a faithful reproduction of Marcel's own traits in those of his protagonist; but Marcel will also, for reasons spelled out above, be forced to attenuate, simplify, exaggerate some, perhaps exclude others,[43] and in any case add in that purely imaginary element which is their mutual interdependence. The myriad synchronic-diachronic slices of a Self, we recall, bear little or no intrinsic relation to one another, either of continuity (since the world is, as Marcel would say, recreated anew every instant) or of causality (since new lowest-order selves are often generated by unpredictable incursions from the outside world, rather than from internal sources); they only begin to gain patterning and legitimation by reference to an entity outside of their number, an agent who might with singularity of purpose have *willed* all of the separate events and states. That is, while it may not be possible to detect a causal relationship between any given pair of selves, we may perhaps envisage such a relationship leading from both to their common product.

The relationship in question will in all instances conform to one of three separate schemata. In the first, the present-day agent affirms, or at least is taken to affirm, each past avatar as an indispensable step on the path to becoming the unified entity he or she is today; we could not be who we now are, according to Nietzsche's "eternal recurrence" doctrine (Nehamas 1985: 150–69), unless we had lived exactly the life we have, right down to the last detail. Thus in a typical fictional autobiography, the character's apparently haphazard thoughts, feelings, and actions start to make sense, or must be seen to make sense—such is the challenge, for example, of Joyce's *Portrait of the Artist as a Young Man*—as necessary staging-posts on the way to fame, fortune, and/or happiness.[44] A second model, making less stringent assumptions about the distinction (or lack thereof) between essential and accidental features, presents the years of wandering as ultimately incidental in relation to today's persona, but necessary as a measure of the distance traveled; necessary, that is, in relation to a narrative whose purpose is to stage the transformation from Saul to Paul. "The picture of what we were at an earlier stage . . . we must not repudiate," Elstir explains to Marcel (BG 606), "for it is a proof . . . that we have, from the common elements of life, . . . extracted something that transcends them."

Finally, and most interestingly for the case at hand, the narrator may acknowledge the importance of his or her former selves simply because they are also his or her *present* selves, synchronic-diachronic sediments remaining within the mind as deposed leaders waiting, perhaps, to return to power. The various *moi*, in other words, function neither as earlier stages of *giovanile errore*, subsequently overcome, nor as ingredients that are all required for the production of a successful life, but instead as integral and persisting aspects of who the narrator is today. *The Magic Lantern* will employ this third type of structure: for although Marcel, rather like the Nietzsche of *Ecce Homo*, ends up embracing sickness (TR 525) and suffering (GW 641) as having proven beneficial to his vocation, his narrative will not be able to make sense of the past altogether in such a straightforwardly causal manner. Instead it will have to incorporate ostensibly abandoned positions, just as Vinteuil incorporates fragments of his earlier efforts, which "had been no more than timid essays, exquisite but very slight, beside the triumphal and consummate masterpiece now being revealed to me" (C 335), into the glorious *septuor*. The total Self, like one of Vinteuil's symphonic compositions, will have to suggest a strictly aesthetic, not logical, principle of organization holding among its diverse features; as in "those finished works of art . . . in which every part in turn receives from the rest a justification which it confers on them in turn" (GW 737),[45] the separate components will gain legitimacy not by conforming to a preexisting value system against which all are measured alike but for their contribution to a whole which, taken together, they form.

It might be objected that although the *process* involves illusion, there is nothing to stop the *product*, like another Galatea, from achieving the status of authentic existence—nothing to stop the second nature, in Nietzsche's expression (HI 3), from becoming a first. Just as a literary or artistic masterpiece acquires a certain physical presence, an unchanging inner unity that is there to be discovered (rather than created) by the reader or viewer; just as, to return to our earlier scientific metaphor, a chemical reaction forges disparate substances into a new and stable compound; so, one might argue, the total Self is something that needs to be created from motley fragments of raw material, but that subsequently transcends them, leaving their dispersion far behind it and swelling the ranks of current facts about the world. Why should we not be able to take the result of the fiction and apply it to our actual life? Why should the total Self it conveys not be who we really are at that point, a genuine and abiding synthesis of our every aspect?

The answer is that no definitive assessment can be made, *even of who we are today*, without the absolute certainty that we have done all the changing we are going to do. Any nontrivial shift will immediately invalidate, by retroaction, a narrative that is either Pauline or Nietzschean in structure: since such narratives are teleological, giving sense and necessity to the events they contain only in relation to a single culminating state, to continue the story beyond its present conclusion would not merely be to extend it by a few lines but to alter it profoundly, reassigning values *all the way back to the start of the book*.[46] If, for example, Saint Augustine were seriously to question the completeness of his conversion from "darkness" to "light," his tale would start to look less like that of Saint Paul and more like that of Saint Teresa, more a matter of repeated lapses and revivals than of a solitary, decisive *metanoia*; no longer the balance-point of his entire career on earth, the "tolle, lege" epiphany would instead constitute just one of many realignments in the direction of God.[47] Or what if Vinteuil, having been spared death, had gone on to write an *octuor*, a still more glorious symphonic composition, incorporating the *septuor* as well as the sonata? In that (similar, but nonmoral) case, the *septuor* would slip down the hierarchy of incidents in Vinteuil's life, finding itself relegated from crowning glory to midsized stepping-stone.

Again, in the scheme of Mme Verdurin's will-to-social-power, where her decision to come out in favor of Dreyfus should be placed depends on *when* we ask the question. At the time, it looks like an "enormous setback" (C 312), attracting to her salon only those who are outlawed by the Faubourg Saint-Germain, and thus placing her "on the lowest rung of the social ladder" (SG 195). But later, when the dust has settled, Mme Verdurin's *dreyfusisme* turns out to have been the very motor that has driven her upward progress, since she now has a monopoly on the erstwhile outlaws (Anatole France, for instance), and since no one now cares about where anyone stood on the Affair. The very same fact receives two entirely opposite, and yet equally legitimate, interpretations, thanks to the passage of time and taste.

Perhaps it might be said that religious conversions, artistic achievements, and promotions to princess are exceptional circumstances, ones with which we are unlikely to meet in our everyday routine. What is surely quite common, however, is the experience of meeting again, after a gap of several years, a person to whom we have paid little or no attention, and proceeding to fall in love. The person in question would almost certainly be entirely absent from any autobiography predating the *coup de foudre*. Yet one postdating it would include not just the story of the courtship but also, in earlier volumes, memories of a love overlooked (no doubt with some proleptic gestures of the form "little did I know that one day . . ."). And *My Life* is, as it happens, just such an autobiography. To Marcel, Albertine Simonet is, at first, only a name; when presented with the opportunity to meet her, he passes it up, being in love with Gilberte (BG 277). Why, then, is the adolescent Albertine in his narrative at all? Why bother so much as to mention the relinquished encounter, "this insignificant seed" (TR 312)? The reason is, of course, that the seed has grown into a plant that casts a modified balance of light and shade over the course of his early years. The non-event has *become* something worth talking about.

In short, whenever a life is considered from a teleological standpoint, any new departure, any new encounter, any new climate will transform not only what *is*, but also what *was*; reaching back into the past, it causes minor episodes to *have been* momentous, momentous episodes to *have been* minor, "enormous setbacks" to *have been* the greatest possible contribution to an eventual triumph. Nor do we need, really, to do anything, or undergo anything, in order for such geological upheavals of our various strata to take place. For "in the absence of an outer life, incidents are created by the inner life too. . . . Even if one lives under the equivalent of a bell jar, associations of ideas, memories, continue to act upon us" (C 22). Thus sometimes, "without my having seen Albertine, without anyone having spoken to me about her, I would suddenly call to mind some memory of her with Gisèle in a posture which had seemed to me innocent at the time but was enough now to destroy the peace of mind that I had managed to recover" (SG 275).[48] Given continued rumination, fresh layers of chiaroscuro can always overlay our picture of the past.

As a result, not even the third (nonteleological) model can yield a Self resilient enough to withstand the onslaught of time; here too, tomorrow's version of today's total Self and today's version of today's total Self part company. For previously unseen sub-selves may at any moment float to the surface of consciousness, complicating the picture of who we are (who we are, on the third model, being in good measure the sum of who we have been), and what we already know—our picture of Albertine at a particular time, which is also a $moi\text{-}Albertine\text{-}t_n$—may itself, under the pressure of reevaluation, begin to signify differently. Hence "no matter at what moment we consider it, our total soul has only a more or less fictitious value, in spite of the rich inventory of its assets, for now some, now others are unrealisable" (SG 211; cf. BG 141).

Should we, then, have been so rash as to publish our autobiography before the thunderbolt (or revelation, or reevaluation) strikes us, a simple postscript is not going to suffice: we will, instead, have to come up with an *entirely new edition*, thoroughly revised. And that means that no version can ever be considered definitive. For if we are able to give a single series of incidents a pair of distinct interpretations, then it cannot be the case that either interpretation is the correct one. We cannot be confident that we understand our life, *even up to now*, unless we are sure that we have reached the personal equivalent of the End of History—something Marcel, for one, considers an impossibility.[49] In the meantime, to say of a given arrangement that it is *the* total Self, to be able to claim, without reservation, that one is and can only be that person and no other, involves a considerable suspension of disbelief.[50] Marcel seems to become aware of the fact when, on meeting Mlle de Saint-Loup, he begins to picture his life as a complex geometrical figure with her as its central node: "Was she not—are not, indeed, the majority of human beings?—like one of those star-shaped crossroads in a forest where roads converge that have come, in the forest as in our lives, from the most diverse quarters?" (TR 502). "*Are not, indeed, the majority of human beings?*": Marcel knows he could easily pick another character around whom to base his configuration, a configuration which would doubtless look somewhat different as a result. Thus, however we label the act that squeezes together the multifarious selves and sub-selves (falsification? rearrangement?), and whatever we think about the status of its product (fabrication? reality?), we must surely allow that *unqualified* faith in the *unique* fitness of the latter is only possible in literature—only possible, that is, if we turn ourselves into a *character*. The total Self, as constructed/conveyed in the fictional autobiography, may be honest in all its details (at least all of those it knows about), but must at the same time be profoundly dishonest in its most basic presupposition.

3. An Evolving Self: The Bio-Aesthetic

Proust may, however, be hinting at an even bolder solution. He may be suggesting, that is, that life in literature—necessitating, as it would, a fictional autobiography issued in an endless series of revised editions—is not a serious option, and that a second, more attractive possibility remains open. Yes, "life realised within the confines of a book" *would* be a wonderful thing (note the conditional mood Marcel uses throughout the relevant passage), but we do not have to go quite that far, since life itself *is already* literature (indicative mood), if one only knows how to see it. "Real life, life at last laid bare and illuminated—the only life in consequence which can be said to be really lived—is literature, and life thus defined is in a sense all the time immanent in ordinary men no less than in the artist. But most men do not see it because they do not seek to shed light upon it. And therefore their past is like a photographic darkroom encumbered with innumerable negatives which remain useless because the intellect has not developed them" (TR 298–99).

Real life, that is, is *inherently* literary, even for the inartistic, who are merely unaware of its existence at a subterranean level of themselves.[51] In order to bring it into the light, we do not have to channel our life into writing: on the contrary, we need only introduce literature into our life, "developing" the various images that lie dormant in the mind and thus, in compliance with the Pindaric injunction invoked by Nietzsche and Marcel alike (GS 270/SG 368), becoming who we are. For we *are* already a set of disparate elements; whether or not we then *become* a whole of which they are parts depends on the success of our attempts at self-unification, on the measure of artistry we import into our existence. Instead of life in literature, the ultimate answer turns out to be life *as* literature.[52] Instead of the aesthetic biography, what one might term the *bio-aesthetic*.

And the key model here is not Marcel or even Charlus, as one might expect, but Odette—or rather Mme Swann, for it is in the later stages of her life (subsequent to her *dame en rose*, "Miss Sacripant," and Odette de Crécy phases) that she discovers, and invents, her personal style. "Odette had at length discovered, or invented, a physiognomy of her own, an unalterable 'character,' a 'style of beauty,' and on her uncoordinated features . . . had now set this fixed type, as it were an immortal youthfulness," judges Marcel. "Odette's body seemed now to be cut out in a single silhouette wholly confined within a 'line' which . . . was able to rectify, by a bold stroke, the errors of nature" (BG 264–65). So successful is she, in fact, that she is still immediately recognizable years later, unlike any other guest at the Guermantes *matinée*: "Only perhaps Mme de Forcheville . . . had not changed" (TR 366–67).

The reason that Odette's achievement counts both as discovery and as invention hinges, as we saw earlier, on the two senses of the word "style." As a perspective, it is a genuinely existing quantity that Odette must first locate; as a specific, externally visible organization of her various "uncoordinated features," predicated on that perspective, it is a work of art and indeed artfulness, correcting the imperfections of nature. Using her own body as the material for an organic, extratextual "artwork," and rigorously obeying a law that she herself has set,[53] Odette is the very figure of the dandy in the *Recherche*. And in all of this she obeys Nietzsche's dictum, doing the one thing that (in a sardonic allusion to Luke 10:42) he claims is "needful," and in almost exactly the way he suggests:[54]

> One thing is needful.—To "give style" to one's character. . . . Here a large mass of second nature has been added; there a piece of original nature has been removed—both times through long practice and daily work at it. Here the ugly that could not be removed is concealed; there it has been reinterpreted and made sublime. . . . In the end, when the work is finished, it becomes evident how the constraint of a single taste governed and formed everything large and small. Whether this taste was good or bad is less important than one might suppose, if only it was a single taste![55]
>
> It will be the strong and domineering natures that enjoy their finest gaiety in such constraint and perfection under a law of their own. . . . For one thing is needful: that a human being should *attain* satisfaction with himself, whether it be by means of this or that poetry and art. (GS 290)

Proust does not have Marcel say it—perhaps he cannot—but the end-goal of the quest, the solution to the twofold problem of the Self, is not involuntary memory, not metaphor, and not even *la vie réalisée dans un livre* (Proust's novel is, after all, not the autobiographical fiction Marcel has in mind; the *Recherche* is not *The Magic Lantern*). There is a further stage to be reached beyond it, namely the process of giving style to one's character in everyday life, reinterpreting, concealing, foregrounding, even inventing elements *de toutes pièces* if necessary, but optimally preserving as much of the given arrangement as possible and aiming for a maximal multiplicity beneath the single controlling principle.[56] ("I was delighted by the multiplicity which I saw in my life," echoes Marcel at SG 590). As for the principle of organization, we have seen that it depends in part on a condition that is impossible to satisfy, namely a clean break with the past, a telos guaranteeing the retrospective position and value of the separate events in one's narrative. For Nietzsche and, I would argue, for Proust, it is preferable to *imagine* such a telos and live accordingly than to face the fact of its nonexistence. The way to give style to one's character is to posit a point of future completion and work back from there; it is to take up residence in the *future perfect*.

> Try for once to justify your existence as it were *a posteriori* by setting before yourself an aim, a goal, a "to this end," an exalted and noble "to this end." Perish in pursuit of this and only this—I know of no better aim of life than that of perishing, *animae magnae prodigus*, in pursuit of the great and the impossible. (HI 9)
>
> Only artists . . . have taught us the art of viewing ourselves as heroes—from a distance and, as it were, simplified and transfigured—the art of staging and watching ourselves. Only in this way can we deal with some base details in ourselves. Without this art we would be nothing but foreground. . . . it taught man to see himself from a distance and as something *past and whole*. (GS 78; my emphasis)[57]

Proust's narrator relocates to this particular temporal zone on a number of occasions (again something of a rarity in the French novel, though one might compare the climax of Flaubert's *Sentimental Education*), particularly during his *remedia Gilbertae amoris*.[58] In general, however, one might argue that the adoption of a fictionally futuric perspective is the inevitable destination of a novel whose sentences often delay completion inordinately, whose hero begins a novel without finishing it, and whose entire world is governed by a law of serial misconception. At any given moment in our life, runs the corollary, we should not be asking what we are—for we will always only be a tangle of unfulfilled possibilities—but wondering, instead, what we *will have been*. To think autobiographically is, in fact, to conjure up an idealized future self and to account for one's current constitution in terms of it. Thus an autobiographical text, or even a life lived in the autobiographical mode, is part of a narrative continuum that extends beyond the present moment, tracing the various lines of one's development toward their point of convergence at infinity, an ideal telos from which one projects, "as it were *a posteriori*," consistency and indeed purpose into a life of chaos and contingency. One manages to speak as it were from beyond the grave, to write one's own epitaph; but always in the awareness that this is a fantasy, and a transitional one at that.

For perhaps amid the generalized fabrication a different kind (or higher level) of honesty can remain in play—an honesty, precisely, with regard to the deception. Perhaps, that is, Proust considers authentic selfhood to involve not just illusion but *lucid* illusion. Cases of conscious fantasy abound in his novel,[59] and there are even the beginnings of a suggestion as to how the

strange feat may be achieved: as long as the mind is synchronically split—
into a part that sits at the forefront of consciousness and speaks, as "I," for
the entire individual (the "self"), a part that does the deceiving (the "delusion"), and finally a part that registers the event (the "lucidity")—invention and awareness may be simultaneous.[60] Just as Marcel's synchronically
divided Self is capable of holding two separate images ("stills") of Albertine,
taken by separate segments of the diachronically divided Self, at once in
view, *perceiving* their discrepancy and *imagining* a connection, so Proust in-
sinuates that we are able to bring the power of lucid self-delusion to bear on
our own fractured subjectivity, to forge an acknowledgedly fictional unity out
of the endlessly proliferating *moi*. What enables us to heal the diachronic rift
is, in fact, the very schism of the Self with which this chapter began; like the
côté de Méséglise and the *côté de Guermantes*, the two types of division have,
somewhat improbably, come together in the end.

Again it must be conceded that Proust is rather reticent, far more so even
than Nietzsche, in outlining the image of a life lived as though it were a work
of art. We have reached the area of greatest speculation, one to which only
the internal ironies of the *Recherche*, and the external discrepancies between
it and what we may postulate about Proust's actual project, can drive us. All
we can know is that the hesitant Bildungsroman Proust delivers is hardly the
novel saturated with metaphor and self-confidence that Marcel promises us;
and that there is simply too much else in it besides autobiography, whether
actual or fictional. I would therefore propose that we see the novel not as
Proust's own life "realised in a book," all of its individual acts and aspects
forged into a unity, but precisely as *one more act* in that life. If it ends up
imprinting a type of aesthetic order and justification on Proust's existence,
it does so not by transforming it directly into literature but by giving it a
retrospective meaning as the preparation for this great work.[61] It is not an
autobiography but, instead, "an aim, a goal, a 'to this end,'" an example of
the type of perfection we have to posit if we are to consider ourselves the possessors of a unified Self. To the artist, each successive artwork is, like a carefully chosen outfit for the dandy, merely the *outward sign* of a *single* coherent
organization of the inner Self, an organization which, like Elstir's manner,
may well change over time[62] and which, like the great nineteenth-century
novel, is always something of a failure.

Proust, it seems to me, understands more clearly than Marcel the instrumental and transitional role of fiction writing, its function as a stepping-stone
on the path to becoming who one is, rather than as that activity itself; his *Recherche* represents, in fact, not so much a way of siphoning life off into the
literary realm as a single part of an inverse process, namely the importation
of aesthetic modes into the day-to-day. With Oscar Wilde, Proust might well
have claimed to have put only talent into his written works, reserving all his
genius for the mode of being he practiced. But he cannot, of course, say so

directly. All he can do is to offer us a series of hints and a pair of models, one of which (a partial success) is Mme Swann, the other (a full success) being himself. And his own life is not to be taken as a model in every detail—not, that is, as a model of content, but merely as one of form. He is not suggesting that we all become novelists, still less that we all write write *A la recherche du temps perdu*. On the contrary, as his narrator reminds us, the only way to emulate a paradigm is to defy that paradigm: "you can make a new version of what you love only by first renouncing it" (TR 525). Not everyone has to be an artist; but anyone who wishes to possess a unified Self has to be an artist of life.

CODA

Style (Proust's Sentences)

Inconceivable boredom associated with the most extreme

ecstasy which it is possible to imagine.

—Henry James on Proust

Complaints about Proust's style started pouring in even before his first volume came off the presses. Jacques Normand, summoned to provide a report for the Fasquelle publishing house in 1912, famously lamented that "reading cannot be sustained for more than five or six pages. . . . one can set down as a positive fact that there will never be a reader hardy enough to follow along for as much as a quarter of an hour, the nature of the author's sentences doing nothing to improve matters" (15). "After the seven hundred and twelve manuscript pages," he went on, "after infinite amounts of misery at being drowned in a sea of inscrutable developments and infinite amounts of maddening impatience at never returning to the surface—one has no notion, none, of what it's all about. What is the point of all this? What does all this mean? Where is all this going?—Impossible to know anything about it! Impossible to say anything about it!"[1]

Contemporary victims of the *Recherche* might very well sympathize with these feelings. Still, as the long-suffering Normand already surmised, the novel's apparent weaknesses are amply compensated for by its strengths; from a certain point of view, indeed, they *are* its strengths. The various idiosyncrasies of Proust's style—labyrinthine complexity at every level, chronological confusion, an overwhelming atmosphere of uncertainty—find their justification as the reflection of, or in some cases the impetus to, a particular vision of existence. Specifically, they map or model the structure of the Self as Proust sees it, namely as an entity divided not only from the outside world (other minds included) but also from within, into different faculties or drives at a synchronic level and into discrete temporal segments on the diachronic. They thus echo the three-dimensional Proustian psychology we explored in chapter 3; but as we saw in chapter 1, they also intimate the outline of an *individual* subjectivity, namely that of the narrator; and they may, finally, be designed to train readers into producing a coherent and unique identity of their own. Reinforcement, revelation, cultivation: this coda will trace all three ambitions across the range of initially "maddening," ultimately inspiring, stylistic quirks of *In Search of Lost Time*.

1. Narrative Sequence

A first set of perplexities concerns temporal structure. Even leaving aside the issue of external chronology (that is, the relative order of historical developments alluded to, such as a Russian Revolution that seems, here, to take place in 1916 [TR 158]), internal chronology poses serious problems of its own. It is not always easy, where indeed possible, to reconstruct the sequence of events: thus, for instance, Marcel meets the *dame en rose* when, by his own account, she should already have metamorphosed into the more decorous Mme Swann. What is more significant and more difficult to explain[2] is the fact that "today," the narrator's present, designates not one period but a minimum of three. The visit to the Bois de Boulogne, after which he concludes that lost time cannot be regained, takes place "this November" (S 598, 606), meaning at most a month ago; yet the Guermantes *matinée*, which convinces him otherwise, is "aujourd'hui même" (IV:622); and there are also brief but telling references to a now that postdates the epiphanic climax, overshoots the beginnings of the literary "vocation" and even, as it turns out, outstrips the lifespan of Proust himself. For though Proust would die in 1922, he granted his more fortunate character at least enough longevity to receive a letter from the Baron de Charlus in 1926 (TR 167–68; cf. Steel 57, 180).

Part of the problem, of course, is that Marcel does not recount his life story in linear fashion. From the description of a given period he omits details as important as his first sexual experience, with a cousin who is mysteriously absent from the family portrait in *Combray*,[3] so that when he later refers back to them, in a "paralipsis," it is often impossible to date their original occurrence.[4] Others, inversely, he reveals ahead of time, only to withhold them from us when the appropriate moment arrives: thus, most shockingly, his account of the long years between Albertine's disappearance and the *matinée Guermantes* fails so much as to mention the madeleine episode (Genette 1980: 45, 66), in spite of the fact that it should, by rights, have improved his rather disconsolate mood. And then, some memories (such as the first evidence of Albertine's potential bisexuality)[5] jump the queue, impatient to be disposed of, while others, by contrast, are detained temporarily "for the convenience of the tale," ending up as belated flashbacks. By delaying the revelation of Charlus's homosexuality from the end of *Le côté de Guermantes* until the beginning of *Sodome et Gomorrhe* (GW 786, SG 1), Marcel neatly separates two phases of life—that of an interest in the Faubourg Saint-Germain, that of a fascination with homosexuality—which, in reality, overlap.

To be sure, the majority of the narrative, from *Nom de pays: Le nom* onward, conforms in a broad sense to calendar time. But thanks to the extreme waywardness of the earlier sections, this very conformity is made to look like a conscious stylistic decision. And even when the events we see are presented in order, huge gaps regularly remain between them. Tens, sometimes hundreds of pages are spent on a period of hours (such as the *matinée Guermantes*), while the intervening weeks, months, and sometimes years (such as those immediately preceding the *matinée*) are simply overlooked, held off until later, or (as at the end of each visit to Balbec) dealt with in a few lines. Like the *Iliad*, Proust's *Recherche* suggests a span of several years by narrating a limited number of individual days (three of which account, between them, for the majority of *La prisonnière*). Or are they even that? To compound our bewilderment, what seemed like a single episode, such as the first day of winter on the Champs-Elysées (S 563–65), turns out to be the description of a repeated state of affairs (the average winter day [Genette 1980: 116]) or at least of one event which stands for many (a typical winter day [Terdiman 1976: 185]). Conversely, a quotidian habit mutates without warning—that is, without surrendering its imperfect tense—into a particular occurrence: "Every evening I would beguile myself [*je me plaisais*] by imagining this letter. . . . Suddenly I stopped [*je m'arrêtais*] in alarm" (S 581; translation modified).

We find ourselves, in short, faced with an exorbitant abundance of material, clustered in scenes that hover uncertainly between events and habits and among which it is frequently difficult to discern clear logical or chronological links (Poulet 1968: 327, 1963: 52–56). And we cannot even determine, a priori, which incidents are going to prove consequential in the long run: by the time the protagonist receives an impossible telegram from a long-dead Albertine (F 889), we may well have forgotten the idiosyncratic way Gilberte scrawls her signature, a detail casually mentioned some three thousand pages earlier (BG 101) and responsible, as it turns out, for the confusion. Similarly, Albertine—who will be the almost exclusive focus from the end of *Sodome et Gomorrhe* to the middle of *Albertine disparue*—starts out as merely the niece of a certain Bontemps couple whose home Marcel, still obsessed with Gilberte, refuses to visit (BG 277; cf. TR 312). A motif which begins *pianissimo*, as Spitzer puts it (416), may end up taking over the entire composition.

To understand the various vicissitudes to which linear time is subject in the novel, we need to return to the portrait of human interiority it espouses, one in which the overall Self ("le moi") is made up of myriad smaller selves ("les moi"). Each minor self, we recall, is a snapshot of the psyche at a given interval, capturing in particular the primary object of adherence (Combray,

Balbec; Gilberte, Albertine) and the subject's momentary attitude toward it: thus Marcel is made up (among other things) of several selves which love Gilberte and even more which love, or (increasingly) distrust, Albertine. As the years go by, so our Self expands—grows "taller," in the narrator's image (TR 531)—to encompass all the diachronic selves accumulating within it, diachronic selves which are not just passive memory-traces but also active participants in the psychic apparatus, citizens of the "commonwealth," each with full voting rights. While they may occasionally join forces to vote en bloc, the diachronic selves have no contact with one another (S 529); time breaks down into a series of discrete instants, and the Self fractures into a plurality of segregated *moi*, united only by a fantasy of cohesion.

If the narration of the *Recherche* is characterized by a pandemic discontinuity, the structure of the Self is responsible. Marcel's past life—which is also the very substance of his present life, as the opening pages make clear—consists in a collection of mutually isolated phases:[6] at the highest level of the hierarchy, the Combray era, the Doncières era, the Paris era, the Tansonville era; lower down, the period of love for Gilberte, the period of love for Albertine; then within each love the stage of passion, the stage of jealousy, the stage of forgetting; deeper still, the separate "steps" made, say, by the passion;[7] and finally the individual days, which keep resurfacing even amid the "iterative" scenes. And if the narrator tends to move with improbable freedom in the fourth dimension, it is because all of these moments are available to the mind simultaneously, arrayed, like the notes of a familiar piece of music, in space rather than in time.[8] It is not that the mind is indifferent to or incapable of chronological sequencing, as may be the case in Robbe-Grillet or Beckett; instead, the linear thrust of most of Proust's narrative suggests that each minor self knows its precise place, while the deviations from this norm—which stand out all the more vividly against such a conventional background—imply that the various selves, for all their monadic insularity, may yet be subsumed under an overall pattern.

Now this pattern is, of course, profoundly subjective. What Marcel gives us is not his whole life story, but only what he remembers at the time of writing; and of what he remembers, only those aspects which, at that juncture, seem important to him, because they currently correspond to a sizeable subpopulation of selves; and the important aspects, finally, in the order his mind imposes on them, with artificial partitions—as between high society and homosexuality—often inserted. Hence the prolepses (Marcel writes, for example, that Albertine "had certainly no conception of what she was one day to mean to me") and the syllepses, as when we hear several of Albertine's alibis, or see her in various incarnations, all at once.[9] Hence, too, the ellipses and paralipses: events which, when they happened, doubtless seemed of immense moment to the protagonist (his first sexual experience, for example) find themselves relegated to a lower echelon.

The obvious corollary—that the arrangement, having changed once, may change again—is by no means lost on Proust's narrator. He knows full well that the only reason he now bothers to mention the intrinsically insignificant and declined invitation which would have brought him into earlier contact with Albertine, the only reason it has a place in the story he tells about himself, is that Albertine subsequently went on to become his second great love. And at any instant another equally decisive transformation may occur, sending fresh seismic shocks through the geological strata of his mind, forcing a reevaluation of much that has gone before. The most serious breach of chronological propriety, namely the multiplication of present moments, finds its explanation herein: Marcel must, as we saw in the introduction, already have made a number of returns to his account. The apparently homogeneous narrative of the *Recherche* in fact comprises several superimposed layers, each one deposited by a separate narrating instance, a separate diachronic *moi*.

And just as the Self, on the theoretical model delineated above, breaks down into subunits, so we may discern, even within the reign of a single narrating persona, more local variations. Subtle shifts in tone are detectable across the main body of the novel, from the bright, extroverted shades of the first third to the dark insularity of the last;[10] in addition, its narrator gradually countenances a greater degree of complexity in the world, acknowledging for example that societies and individuals change in and of themselves, as well as in relation to the observer.[11] Finally, it may even be possible, as we saw in chapter 3, to make out elementary diachronic selves in the twenty-two repetitions or variants of the phrase "she was dead" in the early portion of *Albertine disparue*: it is as though, on each occasion, Marcel were breaking the news, as he would put it, to "one . . . of those innumerable and humble 'selves' that compose our personality" (F 578–79). Proust, in other words, is using the temporal aspect of his narrative to convey an inner tridimensionality, to make powerfully palpable an existence that not only incorporates a multiplicity of minor selves but also—even when one is merely narrating one's life, and thus barely living it—changes across time.

2. Point of View

About the visit to the Bois de Boulogne, Proust was unrepentant. "I am obliged to depict errors," we recall him telling Rivière, "without feeling compelled to say that I consider them to be errors." And his narrator must feel the same way, for he readily puts forward a view of the protagonist, long since superseded, as though it were his own. Such legerdemain is on display from the very opening scene: with the sleeper now fully awake, we are assured, all the furniture has returned to its proper configuration (S 9); but no, nearly two hundred pages later the desk moves to where the fireplace was, the window displaces the desk, a door supplants the window, and what we took to be reality turns out to have been illusion all along (S 263–64).[12] At a more local level, we are often asked to visualize the way something strikes an observer (usually the protagonist) rather than, or at least prior to, the way it actually is. "A stout lady came up to me and greeted me," writes Marcel at TR 428, only mentioning on the following page that this "stout lady" is in fact Gilberte, his own childhood sweetheart and widow of his best friend;[13] and inanimate objects, whether the erratic bedroom furniture mentioned above, friendly houses that scurry to see one off (SG 538, 548) or—as we saw in chapter 1—the huddled Martinville steeples, appear to move under their own power. To borrow Spitzer's biblical image (465), the *Recherche* is a novel in which the hills really do skip like lambs.

And if it is relatively straightforward to read such personifications as mere figures of speech—to interpret what looks like a statement of fact by the narrator as a ventriloquism of the protagonist's first impressions—things become trickier in relation to assessments of other characters (is Albertine really bisexual, or is it just a case of the jealous imagination run riot?) and positively bewildering when it comes to appraisals of life in general. We are repeatedly forced to recognize, as we saw in the introduction, that opinions expressed in the *Recherche* are not necessarily those of its writer, indeed not even necessarily those of its most mature narrator. Just as the "facts" with which we are presented may really be subjective perceptions, so the "truths" may belong to (a) the protagonist, (b) the narrator at one or another stage of his development, and/or (c) Proust, there being no obvious discriminating marks between those that are spoken by each.

In fact, if we include the protagonist (whose voice is, strictly speaking, only heard through that of the narrator), we may detect at least five narrative instances all sharing, whether overtly or covertly, the first-person pronoun. We can tell, to start with, that the narrator is not strictly equivalent to the protagonist, since the former knows more about their joint existence, simply by virtue of having lived longer. This narrator announces his separate presence by ironizing or critiquing his former self, by proleptically gesturing toward the latter's future (his own past), or by focusing on the act of recollection rather than on the memories themselves.[14] But he, in turn, must bifurcate into an entity that merely knows more about the *protagonist* and one that also knows more about *everyone else*, namely the omniscient narrator who, instead of being forced into making hypotheses and deductions, can directly declare, in each case, the facts concerning a given character's state of mind (that of Bergotte, say, in his final moments [C 244–45]).

Now while the omniscient narrator may differ from the focalized narrator, the two share a belief that what they are describing is real; they are therefore distinct from the "author," that voice which dialogues with the "reader" (SG 69–70, C 57) and which tells us that nothing we have read, saving one tiny detail, is true. Finally, there is someone who views the novel neither as the narrator's reality nor as pure fabulation but as the reality of Marcel Proust: this is the persona which describes Tissot's portrait of Charles "Swann" in such detail that it is impossible not to understand the referent as Charles Haas (C 262–63), which claims to have written *Les plaisirs et les jours* and translated *Sésame et les lys* from Ruskin's original (TR 521, 206), and which, sadly enough, is outlived by all the others.

Nor will the various speakers cooperate, any more than will the different faculties within Marcel's mind. Instead, they collide and contend in subtle combinations, beyond even those envisaged by Bakhtin (324). Protagonist and narrator coexist uneasily in cases where narrative time is deliberately confused with narrated time ("I have no time left, *before my departure for Balbec . . .*, to start upon a series of pictures of society")[15] and in the free indirect speech that Proust, while borrowing it from Flaubert (EA 286), no longer restricts to outside characters. When, for example, the narrator states "I kissed the agate marble, which *was* the better part of my love's heart" (S 583, emphasis added), the main verb may belong to him alone but the subordinate clause clearly consists in a transposition of the *protagonist's* thoughts, long since repudiated.[16] The two narrators clash when, for instance, we are told first what the elegant men in their carriages are saying about Odette and then that there is no way for any of it to be heard;[17] when, on the other hand, it is a question of everything in the novel, with the sole exception of the Larivière family, being "fictif" (IV:424), the omniscient narrator (who can know about, but must believe in the reality of, the Larivières) comes into conflict with the author. And when, finally, we hear Albertine saying "'My—' or 'My darling—' followed by my Christian name, which, if we give the narrator the same name as the author of this book, would be 'My Marcel' or 'My darling Marcel'" (C 91), we are scandalously placed in the simultaneous presence of a narrator—who treats characters like Albertine as if they were real human beings and himself as someone capable of being addressed by or otherwise interacting with them—and, there is no other way around it, the writer Marcel Proust.

Viewpoint thus dramatizes a consciousness that is thoroughly fractured within itself—at a synchronic as well as a diachronic level—and equally divided, what is more, from the world outside. At every turn, the mind runs up against a "barrier of perception" (TR 420) interposed between it and its objects (all the more so, of course, when the target is another human being, who may well be seeking not to be known, and whose deepest essence can, in any case, never be accessed directly). If we wish to discover the truth about people, we need to split the difference between "equally distorting" hypotheses (BG 221); if we wish to find out the facts about inanimate entities, such as the actual location of a fireplace, we have to bring a secondary, rational mechanism to bear on the sense data to which we have already given a subjective and indeed thoroughly individual arrangement. And this is partly why Proust's literary impressionism, which gives us both the object (Gilberte) and the way it appears ("a stout lady"), does so in reverse order.

Proust's point is, however, as much an axiological as an epistemological one: what ultimately counts for us, what constitutes our world (the world *die uns wirklich etwas angeht*, in Nietzsche's phrase),[18] is not matter itself but the way in which our perspective filters it, bringing disparate objects into contact with one another, forging new combinations, and ultimately determining what we consider of value. The crucial aspect of Marcel's *Bildung*, one might almost say, resides in his realization that instead of forcing his way through to the facts, at great intellectual and emotional cost and with little informational gain, he should instead be looking—a Copernican turn—at the agency responsible for their persistent and consistent distortion.

Focalization, in the *Recherche*, thus conveys the structure of subjectivity. But it also conveys the structure of *a* subjectivity, a particular one, that of Marcel. The metaphors he consistently uses—young girls, for example, being incessantly seen as flowers, and flowers as young girls[19]—hint at an idiosyncratic conceptual framework; so too, as we saw in chapter 1, do the higher-order laws governing image-formation, such as Marcel's tendency to associate in thought two objects that he finds contiguous in space; and so, finally, do the treacherous maxims. For while some of the them carry absolute truths (subscribed to, we have to assume, by Proust), and others are hypotheses provisionally concocted by Marcel, there still remain those which, while they do not vary, are also not presented as absolute, and these, I would argue, mark the boundaries of the character's moral universe.

3. Sentence Structure

Chronology may be complicated and viewpoint variable, but if there is one single factor preventing us from reading more than six pages in a sitting then it is, as Jacques Normand was well aware, the notorious structure of the Proustian sentence. Although Proust is perfectly capable of being more concise when he so chooses (as in the brilliantly laconic "Peut-être" of II:72, producing a characteristic effect of bathos), the longer periods are so numerous, and their combined effect so powerful, that one has the overwhelming impression of a novel written entirely in distended, convoluted, barely legible blocks. It is not just that they stretch to improbable lengths (a little under three Pléiade pages, on one occasion: III:17–19) but also, and especially, that they tend to grow from the middle, so that in a sense their true dimension is rather one of *depth*. Just as at the macroscopic level, so at the microscopic the external boundaries in Proust are always predetermined—if some of the sentences and indeed the novel as a whole remain "unfinished," it is not because they lack satisfactory resolutions but because discrepancies and lacunae linger amid the minor clauses and smaller scenes—yet in the interstices, dividing a subject from its verb, a cause from its effect or a subplot from its dénouement, new material may at any moment muscle its way in, clad in a convenient pair of commas.[20]

When the narrator, to take a relatively brief example, wishes to describe his physical attraction to Albertine as unabating, he only reaches the second word before having to interrupt the thought to explain why it is of interest, namely that it marks a point of divergence from the Gilberte scenario [1]. But he now has to explain what exactly has changed, which means prefacing the disanalogy with [2] a general statement and [3] a detail or two about the specific mode of association with Albertine. The sentence may now continue, but it cannot yet end. Five words before the full stop, Marcel as it were draws himself up short, remembering two very important restrictions: first, that his way of loving may not be universal (he interjects the quasi-ubiquitous "pour moi" [4], and appends a parenthetical disclaimer for good measure [5]); second, that the revelation is occurring to him, like almost all knowledge, after the event [6]. The result translates as follows: "In Albertine's case, [2] thanks to a wholly different life shared with me [3] where no fissure of distraction or obliviousness had been able to penetrate a block of thoughts in which a painful preoccupation maintained a permanent cohesion, her living body had not, [1] like Gilberte's, ceased one day to be that in which I found what I [6] subsequently recognized as being [4] to me ([5] what they would not have been to other men) the attributes of feminine charm" (F 677–78).[21] A sentence like this one is not a marathon but a Zenonian hundred-yard dash, in which writer and reader alike could easily reach the finish line were it not for the necessity to reach the halfway mark, and before that all the halfway marks in between.[22]

One reason for the unusual intricacy is, of course, that the reality Proust is talking about is unusually intricate, given his remarkable sensitivity for subtle nuances. Not all the sentences, however, are content simply to mirror that reality; instead, some actively attempt to *reduce* its complexity (Spitzer 400–402, Milly 164–87), and do so by the time-honored method of collection and division, bringing a pair of items together ("just as . . . so") or marking a line of fissure within what looks like a single item ("sometimes . . . sometimes," "on the one hand . . . on the other"). The active stance reaches a higher degree of intensity when simplification becomes falsification, when the divided items in question turn out to be more or less continuous (as most famously in the case of the two *côtés*), the collected items radically heterogeneous (as when, to cite a minor example, the servants zeugmatically set themselves to "watch the dust . . . and the excitement . . . subside" [S 123]). Even the proliferating paradoxes which, on the one hand, are an apt reflection of life's enigmas function, on the other, to scale those enigmas down from a multidimensional conundrum to a set of straightforward binary oppositions.[23]

At its limit, style forces an obdurately chaotic material into the merest semblance of order, whether sound pattern as rich as "petit, trapu, étêté et têtu" (I:414)—a double-binary *combinatoire* of vowels (u/-) and consonants (pt/tt)—or a chiastic construction of the form "opposées et complémentaires, c'est-à-dire propres à satisfaire nos sens et à faire souffrir notre coeur" ("our opposite and our complement, apt, that is to say, to gratify our senses and to wring our hearts" [II:248/BG 647]). Occasionally, and most often at moments of the greatest tension for the character, Marcel's prose even ends up in an alexandrine or a perfect octosyllabic couplet (complete, in the following instance, with internal rhyme):

J'ouvris la fenêtre sans bruit
et m'assis au pied de mon lit . . . (I:32)[24]

Inevitably perhaps, one central reality the sentences both reflect and shape is that of the Self. In addition to the perennial "pour moi," several of the layered qualifiers (*peut-être, sans doute*) and associated locutions (*comme si, semblait, paraissait*) evoke the monadic isolation of a psyche which, when confronted with a potential object of knowledge, is continually thrown back on conjecture. Even when the object concerned is his own interiority, the narrator finds the epistemological predicament equally intractable, so that he is reduced at one stage to reporting, rather hesitantly, that he acted "perhaps [*soit*] out of duplicity, perhaps [*soit*] in a genuine access of affection" (GW 130). Such optimistic and pessimistic hypotheses may, as we recall from chapter 2, spring from rival sources of speculation about human agents, each designed not so much to track the truth as to exaggerate in its own way, and together providing impulses to action that are both simultaneous and contradictory. (Thus Marcel, in the case at hand, could very well be sincerely tender *and* guileful at one and the same time, especially given his theory of multiple motivations.)[25] The various disjunctions ("perhaps . . . perhaps," "whether . . . . or," "either . . . or," "neither . . . nor") remind us of their existence; for their part, the various oppositions, exclusions, and concessives that control so many clauses and even developments spanning several pages ("granted *a* . . . but *b*," "if not *a* . . . then at least *b*," "not only *a* . . . but also *b*") may represent efforts to steer a path between Scylla and Charybdis.

Analogously, we often feel the presence of multiple *diachronic* selves coursing through the finely textured prose. Occasionally a group of narrators will gather in a single paragraph, all using different tenses to discuss the protagonist and each other: "These . . . young playmates did not seem to me to be very many [*first narrator giving protagonist's impression*]. But recently I thought of them again, and their names came back to me [*first narrator referring to himself*]. . . . Another name came back to me later [*second narrator correcting first narrator*]" (SG 255–56). Or a sentence describing an act of recollection will contain a present-tense narrator describing the scene today, a past-tense character—such as the "intermediary subject" who stays up late remembering rooms—and as it were a pluperfect character, object of the latter's memory. "Then the memory of a new position would spring up [*unfocalised narration*], and the wall would slide away in another direction [*focalisation through the intermediary subject*]; I was in my room in Mme de Saint-Loup's house in the country; good heavens, it must be [*focalisation through the Tansonville self*] ten o'clock, they will have finished dinner!" (S 6; cf. Muller 79).

It is such diachronic selves, in their dense and labyrinthine configurations, that the skein of prose is primarily designed to follow. For the total Self, as we recall from chapter 3, consists in a hierarchy of hierarchies: just as Vinteuil's oeuvre as a whole comprises several works, each of which contains fragments of earlier pieces, each of which in turn involves a complex configuration of individual notes and timbres, so Marcel's life—the thought strikes him, precisely, while he is listening to Vinteuil's *septuor*—can be seen in terms of a series of love affairs, with every affair going through its own diverse stages, and any given stage incorporating multiple two-dimensional time-bound selves. Like Vinteuil's early compositions in relation to the masterwork, so the Gilberte episode proves to have been mere preparation for the magnum opus that is "l'amour pour Albertine":

> And I could not help recalling
>   by comparison
> that,
>   in the same way too,
> I had thought of the other worlds
>   that Vinteuil had created
> as being self-enclosed
>   as each of my loves had been;
>
> whereas
>   in reality
> I was obliged to admit that
>
> just as,
>   within the context of the last of these
>   —my love for Albertine—
>   my first faint stirrings of love for her
>   (at Balbec at the very beginning [BG 510],
>   then after the game of ferret [BG 680],
>   then on the night when she slept at the hotel [BG 699],

then in Paris on the foggy Sunday [CG 529],
then on the night of the Guermantes party [SG 181],
then at Balbec again [SG 246],
and finally in Paris [C 1]
    where my life was now closely linked to hers)
had been,

so,
    if I now considered
    not my love for Albertine
    but my whole life,
my other loves too had been no more
than slight and timid essays
    that were paving the way,
appeals
    that were unconsciously clamouring,
    for this vaster love:
    my love for Albertine. (C 335–36)

The total Self, in short, is an "orchestration"[26] of selves both diachronic (melody) and synchronic (timbre); and nothing could more perfectly render such an orchestration than the multilayered hypotaxis of Proust's writing. Indeed, the very sentence that makes the analogy between life and music (and which I have indented, above, so as to bring out its breakneck syntactical swerves), contains at least four nested layers, with the seven separate phases of the love affair—like the seven notes in the *septuor*, perhaps?—all occupying the two ground floors, huddled together between a pair of parentheses. For Proust's long sentences are not merely a repository for vast quantities of unruly and heterogeneous material; instead, through subordination, they already begin to suggest the relative positions of the items listed, intimating (rather as the prolepses, ellipses, and paralipses do) that *a* is more important than *b*, that all *c*'s are governed by *d*.

The example just given is quite a striking one: while he listens to the music, Marcel suddenly surveys his life from a radically new vantage point, considering incidents that were, at the time, of great significance to him—a first touch, a first attempted kiss, a first kiss—from the point of view not of their own inherent affective power but of their contribution, as mere "raw material" (TR 504), to his overall being. Even the Montjouvain episode, which has so tortured his imagination, likewise finds itself reduced to a mere brushstroke on a crowded canvas, an intrinsically valueless token in a rule-based game. (See sentence 2 in the appendix.) It is as if, to change the metaphor once more, Marcel were taking all the love letters he had ever received, ordering them by size and color, and turning them into a frieze.

4. Spiritual Exercises

In order to live up, as a novelist, to his own aesthetic and philosophical principles, Proust has a challenge to face that is even greater, perhaps, than the challenges posed by knowledge, illusion, and selfhood. For he needs to convey, in a more or less seamless narrative flow, (1) the way things appear to him,[27] (2) the way things appear to his protagonist, and (3) the way things must appear under all perspectives. To date, those critics who have taken Proust's perspectivism seriously have tended to equate Proust and Marcel, leaving themselves but one "vision" to account for; those, conversely, who have distinguished between author and narrator have also been liable to dismiss the idea that an artwork can somehow body forth the world of its designer.[28] In the few pages that remain to me, I intend to fill the gap, testing out the hypothesis that Proust's literary practice is entirely consistent with his literary theory.

We have already seen that Marcel's individual perspective emerges through various pores in the surface of the text, whether in a subset of the maxims he trots out, in a branch of the image-network he forges, in the mechanism of image-production he employs, or in his (inadvertent) strategies, large- and small-scale, for selecting and ordering his material.[29] We have seen, further, that certain aspects of sentence structure, along with a separate subset of the maxims—the accurate ones directly, the antithetical pairs obliquely—reflect the way Proust and Marcel would agree that things quite simply are in themselves. So far, we are dealing with domains under Marcel's purview, areas in which Marcel makes the (conscious or unconscious) decisions and which therefore cannot offer any evidence, assuming (*ex hypothesi*) that stylistic habits can count as evidence, as to Proust's attitude. What, then, of the domains belonging exclusively to Proust? What of storyline and characterization, in neither of which Marcel has any say, Proust's malleable invention being, from Marcel's standpoint, unalterable biographical *datum*? What, indeed, of the choice of mode and genre? And what, finally, of the narratorial horde, uncomfortably packed into a single, overcrowded first-person pronoun?

As it happens, a number of the devices listed above implicitly reendorse the same, "objective" portrayal of human existence. For one thing, the very fact that Marcel possesses, and unwittingly betrays, an idiosyncratic point of view—the fact that Proust has opted to present him as a decidedly un-Musilesque "man with qualities," endowing him with a series of propositions and dispositions that map his "world"—tells us something about Proust, confirming that perspective is, so to speak, part of his perspective.[30] For another, the laws of emplotment unique to Proust's fictional universe, laws which hold always and only within it, bear out Proust's (partial) alignment with his narrator.[31] Thus the law of double irony[32] accords with the general air of pessimism pervading the *Recherche*; the law of minor circumstances later proving significant corresponds to the note of caution vis-à-vis the total Self; and the law of characters returning under unfamiliar guises conforms to a widespread skepticism concerning knowledge of other minds. That there are, in the novel, enough cases of *anagnorisis* to satisfy a battalion of Aristotles (Robert's actress girlfriend turning out to be Rachel the prostitute, the *dame en rose* and "Miss Sacripant" both turning out to be Odette, the man having himself beaten at Jupien's seedy hotel turning out to be Charlus . . .) coincides with Proust's position that each individual is changeable and multifaceted, and that no single (visible) facet can capture his or her essence. If Rachel the actress is also "Rachel quand du Seigneur," this means that her proficiency on stage cannot fully define her—but neither would it be closer to the mark to say she is "really" a prostitute, any more than that Charlus is "deep down" a homosexual and "superficially" an aesthete, a socialite, a snob.

Matters are a little more complicated when it comes to the juxtaposition of omniscient and nescient narrators, yet I would hazard a guess—in company with Bersani (1965: 240) and Jones (177)—that it offers Proust a way to dramatize, in an overtly artificial manner, his (and Marcel's) attitude toward perception.[33] Though we know, in the abstract, that our perspectival prism bends the light it receives, we can only measure its degree of refraction against an original straight line: "it is by looking at the clock that one establishe[s] as being merely a quarter of an hour what one had supposed a day" (SG 519). Vistas of the world outside Marcel's head serve, perhaps, as just such a clock, allowing us to assess the quantity and quality of distortion (and how much more interesting a subjective vision is than the unvarnished reality). What is more, they hint at a particular brand of pleasure Proust derives from writing fiction, a thoroughly *personal* pleasure, that of "trying on all forms of life, one after the other," until everyday anxieties "cease for a moment to tyrannize" over him.[34] The combination of indulgence (in the form of the impossibly omniscient narrator) and restraint (in the form of the focalized "I") may indicate that *Proust loves to have it both ways*, facing up to the remoteness of other minds while, at the same time, reveling in the (lucid) dream that we can, for a spell, inhabit them.

For it has to be remembered that Proust's literary output, unlike Marcel's, is highly creative. Whereas Marcel's *oeuvre* is a lightly stylized autobiography that could equally well be composed by "a man born . . . without imagination" (TR 307), Proust's novel—"this book in which there is not a single incident which is not fictitious" (TR 225)—is not only invented but knowingly, ostentatiously so. Just as Proust departs from his character in having a distinct mechanism of perspectival valuation, indirectly disclosing a desire (say) to live different lives, rather than a desire (say) to seize the essence of a place, so too he implicitly chides Marcel for recognizing the necessity of illusions (as we saw in chapter 2) but not appreciating their fundamental role in self-fashioning (as we saw in chapter 3). The "universe that Proust sees" (to paraphrase TR 299), and to which Marcel is blind, is one in which every memoir is immediately out of date, and in which, as a result, it is preferable to bring the power of conscious self-deception to bear on our *present* existence, as past of a putative future, on that unified agent in other words which, according to an acknowledged fantasy, *will have been* who we are.

The gap that opens up, at such crucial junctures, between Proust and his sometime spokesman intimates something even more important. It suggests, namely, that Proust's novel incorporates a third level of communication, over and above the direct transmission of purportedly objective laws and the indirect transmission of perspectival laws (whether belonging to Marcel or to Proust). Far from being simply informative, the *Recherche* is, in addition, potentially *formative*; while we may look to it for teaching, we should also, and all the more so, use it for *training*.[35] For in order to absorb the multifarious effects of Proust's carefully layered prose, we need to deploy, simultaneously, our various types of readerly "attention."[36] And perhaps by so doing we may train our faculties—the intellect that produces pleasing pictures, the *volonté* that acts as if they were true, the instinct that senses they are not—to work together, so that we are ultimately able to pull off the act of deliberate and lucid self-delusion required to see our inner volume as a coherent whole.

As for the other mission of the Proustian spiritual exercise, it is to impart, as it were, the virtue of patience. By continually forcing us to go back and reread (Milly 202), the narrative repeatedly reminds us—in the foreshadowings and prolepses of the complex chronology, the twists and turns of the syntax—that we cannot know anything (even our own lives) all at once, that enlightenment is always retrospective and often long in coming, if indeed it ever does come. At times we receive more overt encouragement to retrace our steps, as when Marcel himself structures an episode (say, the description of Swann's visits, S 16–29) in such a way that he, and we, keep returning to earlier motifs; or when a sentence follows a hybrid logic, neither paratactic nor hypotactic but *recursive*. When, for example, Marcel suspects Albertine of having been with another woman on his second arrival in Balbec but decides not to confront her just yet, he tries quite hard to explain:

> *Perhaps the habit*
>   that I had acquired
> of nursing
>   within me
> certain desires,
>
> *the desire* for a young girl of good family
>   such as those I used to see pass beneath my window

escorted by their governesses,
 and especially for the girl
 whom Saint-Loup had mentioned to me,
 the one who frequented houses of ill fame,
the desire for handsome lady's-maids,
 and especially for Mme Putbus's,
the desire to go to the country
 in early spring
 to see once again
   hawthorns,
   apple-trees in blossom,
   storms,
the desire for Venice,
the desire to settle down to work,
the desire to live like other people—

perhaps the habit of storing up,
 without assuaging,
all these desires,
 contenting myself with a promise
   made to myself
 not to forget to satisfy them one day—

perhaps this habit,
 so many years old already,
of perpetual postponement,
of what M. de Charlus used to castigate
 under the name of procrastination,

had become so prevalent
 in me
that it took hold of my jealous suspicions also
and,
 while encouraging me to make a mental note
 that I would not fail,
   some day,
 to have things out with Albertine
   as regards the girl,
     or possibly girls
             (this part of the story was confused and blurred
             and to all intents and purposes indecipherable
             in my memory)
   with whom

—one or many—
Aimé had met her,
made me also postpone this inquest. (C 106–7; translation modified)

This one sentence encapsulates the variety of effects produced by the ex-asperatingly engaging Proustian style. Insistence on point of view emerges in the triply repeated "in me," as well as in the cautious "perhaps" for specula-tion about Albertine's activities; and speculation extends, here as elsewhere, to Marcel's own behavior. The anaphoric *desire . . . desire . . . desire* perfectly captures the multiplicity of simultaneous drives, some of which, it should be noted, are sediments of old diachronic selves (the fascination with haw-thorns dates from Combray, the lure of the Putbus's chambermaid only since Doncières [SG 127–29]); at the same time we sense a beginning of order, as a partial hypotaxis divides the groups (women, places, activities) into subgroups (chambermaids, daughters of aristocrats) and these in turn into specific cases (Mlle de l'Orgeville). Above all, however, the narrator perfectly matches the protagonist for tactics of deferral, twice interrupting and re-turning to the main line, qualifying his qualifiers. . . . One has the impression that sentences, in Proust, hardly dare to reach their conclusion, as if they were all too aware that new facts and reinterpretations of existing data can, at any moment, upset their delicate balance. The total Self is always incom-plete, contingent, subject to infinite revision, and, to that extent, fictional; though we need to believe, at least with one part of ourselves, in the fiction. And lessons like these, which we learn from the style far more than from the direct statements, are to be applied to our own lives, if we are to turn them, too, into works of art.

APPENDIX

In what follows, I offer a gallery of specimens that seem to me to exemplify, particularly powerfully, certain sentence-types to be found throughout the novel (albeit not always in so dramatic a fashion). Translations have been modified so that, in each case, the English sentence structure falls into line with the French.

As in the coda, I present the sentences in indented form, with a view to bringing out both the general density of their hypotactic layering and the specific elements of their arrangement (binaries, recursive patterns, and so forth). Besides, I also have a suspicion that they may just be easier to absorb this way.

SENTENCE I: ALBERTINE AND MOREL

Comment aurais-je pu deviner
  alors
ce qu'on me dit ensuite
  (et dont je n'ai jamais été certain,
    les affirmations d'Andrée
      sur tout ce qui touchait Albertine,
        surtout plus tard,
      m'ayant **toujours** semblé fort sujettes à caution
      car,
          comme nous l'avons vu autrefois,
          elle n'aimait pas sincèrement mon amie
          et était jalouse d'elle),
ce qui
  en tout cas,
    si c'était vrai,
me fut remarquablement caché
  par tous les deux:
qu'Albertine connaissait beaucoup Morel? (III:420)

Another "Zenonian hundred-yard dash," this sentence is an object lesson in how the mind can, under pressure, turn a simple question into an impossibly abstruse enigma. The nucleus, represented in the original by the first and last five words, is straightforward: "comment aurais-je pu deviner . . . qu'Albertine connaissait beaucoup Morel?" ("how could I have guessed . . . that Albertine was on the best of terms with Morel?"). It is repeatedly interrupted, however, by qualifications, justifications, and justifications of justifications.

To start with, an opposite (optimistic) hypothesis makes its appearance almost immediately: perhaps Albertine was *not* on the best of terms with Morel, in which case there is no point asking the question. This being the hypothesis of the intellect, it is appropriately backed up by argument (Andrée may be lying), and that argument in turn backed up by a causal explanation (Andrée is jealous of Albertine). It is not entirely convincing: Marcel says he has "always" distrusted Andrée, "especially later on"; the two temporal adverbs stand in a certain amount of tension.

How could I have guessed
  then
what I was told afterwards
  (and of whose truth I have never been certain,
    Andrée's assertions
      about anything that concerned Albertine,
        especially later on,
     having **always** seemed to me to be highly dubious,
      for,
        as we have already seen,
      she did not genuinely like my friend
      and was jealous of her),
something which
  in any event,
    if it was true,
was remarkably well concealed from me
  by both of them:
that Albertine was on the best of terms with Morel? (SG 586)

Next, Marcel feels compelled to defend his obliviousness, saying that he had no way of knowing what was going on; and he interrupts his excuses, for good measure, to give voice once again to the optimistic hypothesis ("if it was true").

What we are left with is a muddle, and the impression of a mind spinning its wheels in irremediable uncertainty, moving from ignorance to blind guesswork and thence to total confusion. At first Marcel knew nothing; later he learned that Albertine and Morel were in cahoots; later still he put that idea into question, ending up worse off than he started (still as ignorant, but even more racked with doubt).

The sentence is as contorted as the mind that produced it. It not only speaks of but also *instantiates* the intellect's failure to reach reliable conclusions concerning other minds. And it intimates, sotto voce, the one success to which intellect can still aspire: that of rationalizing away what we do not wish to believe.

SENTENCE 2: THE "IMPURE ELEMENTS" OF THE VERDURIN SALON

Pour cette fête-ci,
les éléments impurs
   qui s'y conjugaient
me frappaient
   à un autre point de vue;
certes,
j'étais aussi à même que personne
   de les dissocier,
   ayant appris à les connaître séparément;
mais surtout les uns,
   ceux qui se rattachaient à Mlle Vinteuil et son amie,
   me parlant de **Combray**,
me parlaient aussi d'Albertine,
   c'est-à-dire de **Balbec**,
   puisque c'est parce que j'avais vu
      jadis
   Mlle Vinteuil à Montjouvain [S 157–63]
   et que j'avais appris l'intimité de son amie avec Albertine [SG 499],
   que j'allais
      tout à l'heure
      en rentrant chez moi,
   trouver
      au lieu de la solitude,
   Albertine qui m'attendait;
et ceux qui concernaient Morel et M. de Charlus,
   en me parlant de **Balbec**,
      où j'avais vu
         sur le quai de Doncières
      se nouer leurs relations [SG 254–55],
   me parlaient de **Combray** et de ses deux côtés,
      car M. de Charlus était un de ces **Guermantes**,
         comtes de Combray,
         habitant Combray
            sans y avoir de logis,
         entre ciel et terre,
            comme Gilbert le Mauvais dans son vitrail [S 103]

(continued)

In the case of this gathering,
the impure elements
   that came together therein
struck me
   from another aspect;
true,
I was as well able as anyone
   to dissociate them,
   having learned to know them separately;
but the first set,
   those which concerned Mlle Vinteuil and her friend,
   in speaking to me of **Combray**,
spoke to me also of Albertine,
   that is to say of **Balbec**,
   since it was because I had
     long ago
   seen Mlle Vinteuil at Montjouvain [S 224–33]
   and had learned of her friend's intimacy with Albertine [SG 702]
   that I was
     presently,
     when I returned home,
   to find,
     instead of solitude,
   Albertine awaiting me;
and those which concerned Morel and M. de Charlus,
   in speaking to me of **Balbec**,
     where I had seen,
       on the platform at Doncières,
     their intimacy begin [SG 352–53],
   spoke to me of **Combray** and of its two ways,
     for M. de Charlus was one of those **Guermantes**,
     Counts of Combray,
     inhabiting Combray
       without having any dwelling there,
       suspended in mid-air,
         like Gilbert the Bad in his stained-glass window [S 145],

(continued)

et Morel était le fils de ce vieux valet de chambre
   qui m'avait fait connaître la dame en rose [S 74]
  et permis,
    tant d'années après,
de reconnaître en elle Mme **Swann** [CG 257]. (III:769)

    This is an archetypical synthetic sentence, one which brings together disparate aspects of a single life. It does so in terms both of time and of space, yoking two distant epochs—first, a childhood of stained-glass windows, a *dame en rose*, and a revelation at Montjouvain; second, a return visit to Balbec, where Charlus meets Morel and where Albertine drops her bombshell—and also, in a chiasmus, two different sites (Combray to Balbec, Balbec to Combray). In fact, the spatial fusion is double: not only does the imaginary conceptual barrier between Balbec and Combray start to fall, since Charlus and Albertine seem to straddle both domains, but even within Combray, it turns out that "Swann's way" and the "Guermantes way" can hardly be the hermetically sealed entities they once appeared to be, if Morel can shuttle between them, now identifying Odette, now consorting with the Duc de Guermantes' brother. Marcel is beginning to glimpse here a lesson he will fully learn on meeting Mlle de Saint-Loup (TR 502), daughter of Gilberte (a Swann) and Robert (a Guermantes).

while Morel was the son of that old valet
    who had introduced me to the lady in pink [S 103–8]
    and enabled me,
        years after,
    to identify her as Mme **Swann** [GW 361]. (C 353)

What is particularly delightful about this sentence is that it reveals an unconscious commitment to the very notion it denies. What the sentence *says* is that Balbec is much the same as Combray, and that the two "sides" of Combray are much the same as one another. The world does not fall neatly into sites of virtue and sites of vice, sites of nobility and sites of rustic authenticity; it has no "joints" along which it could be carved. What the sentence *does*, however, is to use precisely those joints as a way for Marcel to organize experience in his mind. While implicitly recognizing that his way of imposing order is nonobjective ("the impure elements . . . struck *me* . . . spoke to *me*"), and even that he himself could impose order in other ways, Marcel continues to use his own mental geography as a convenient device, one of his numerous useful (perhaps indispensable) fictions.

SENTENCE 3: THE JAPANESE FLOWER

ET COMME
dans ce jeu
   où les Japonais s'amusent
     à tremper
       dans un bol de porcelaine rempli d'eau
   de petits morceaux de papier
     jusque-là indistincts
     qui
       à peine y sont-ils plongés
     s'étirent,
     se contournent,
     se colorent,
     se différencient,
     deviennent des fleurs,
     des maisons,
     des personnages
     consistants et reconnaissables,

DE MÊME
   maintenant
toutes les fleurs de notre jardin
et celles du parc de M. Swann,
et les nymphéas de la Vivonne,
et les bonnes gens du village
et leurs petits logis
et l'église
et tout Combray
et ses environs,
tout cela
   qui prend forme et solidité,
est sorti,
   ville et jardins,
de ma tasse de thé. (I:47)

If involuntary memory consists in a moment of contraction by analogy (this madeleine *is like* that madeleine), followed by a period of dilation by contiguity (that madeleine *stood next to* the rest of Combray), then it is only appropriate that the madeleine episode should conclude with a sentence that begins by setting up a parallelism as its overarching structuring principle ("just as . . . so") and goes on to generate two long paratactic sequences, their thoroughgoing lack of subordination reinforced in the second case by the relentlessly repeated "and." With hypotactic structures bookending the sentence, it forms a perfect chiasmus, enfolding parataxis within hypotaxis just as the madeleine "contains" Combray.

There is something touchingly traditional about the degree to which presentation, here, mirrors proposition. As the second paratactic sequence progressively

AND AS
in the game
    wherein the Japanese amuse themselves
        by steeping
            in a porcelain bowl full of water
        little pieces of paper
            without character or form
            which,
                the moment they become wet,
            stretch
            and twist
            and take on colour
            and distinctive shape,
            become flowers
            or houses
            or people,
            solid and recognisable,

SO
    in that moment
all the flowers in our garden
and in M. Swann's park,
and the water-lilies on the Vivonne
and the good folk of the village
and their little dwellings
and the parish church
and the whole of Combray
and its surroundings,
all of that,
    taking shape and solidity,
sprang into being,
    town and gardens alike,
from my cup of tea. (S 64)

gathers pace (by losing punctuation) and takes us farther and farther afield—from Léonie's room to the garden, and then to Swann's park, followed by the "whole of Combray" and even "its surroundings"—it is almost possible to feel Marcel's childhood home emerging from the cup of tea. So too, in the first paratactic sequence, the pieces of paper communicate their twisting to the sounds, "s'étirent" stretching to "se contournent," "se contournent" metamorphosing into "se colorent." The sentence, with its time-honored, almost poetic perfection, rounds off *Combray I* in the way that a rhyming couplet rounds off a blank-verse scene in Shakespeare.

SENTENCE 4: THE WATER-PIPE MEMORY

Et au moment où je raisonnais ainsi,
le bruit strident d'une conduite d'eau
   tout à fait pareil à ces longs **cris**
      que
         parfois
         l'été
         les navires de plaisance faisaient entendre
         le soir
         au large de Balbec,
me fit éprouver
   (comme me l'avait déjà fait
      une fois
      à Paris,
      dans un grand restaurant,
    la vue d'une luxueuse salle à manger à demi vide, estivale et chaude)
bien plus qu'une sensation simplement analogue à celle que j'avais
   à la fin de l'après-midi
   à Balbec
   quand
      toutes les tables étant déjà couvertes de leur nappe et de leur argenterie,
      les vastes baies vitrées restant ouvertes
         tout en grand
      sur la digue,
         sans
            un seul intervalle,
            un seul "plein" de verre ou de pierre,
         tandis que le soleil descendait lentement sur la mer
         où commençaient à crier les navires,
   je n'avais,
      pour rejoindre Albertine et ses amies
         qui se promenaient sur la digue,
    qu'à enjamber le cadre de bois à peine plus haut que ma cheville,
      dans la charnière duquel on avait fait
         pour l'aération de l'hôtel
      glisser
         toutes ensemble
      les vitres qui se continuaient. (IV:452–53)

Marcel is here experiencing his fourth involuntary memory at the Guermantes *matinée*, one which restores to consciousness the self that inhabited Balbec. The total disposition of that self is resurrected simultaneously—the sight of tables, bay-windows, setting sun and sea, the sound of foghorns, even the future-directed contemplation of a possible walk outside—and the length and density of the sentence seeks in part to render that complexity of mental image.

What stands out, however, is the fact that the sound of the foghorns ends up buried in the very deepest level of the hypotaxis, so deep that it might go entirely unremarked on a cursory perusal. Although the first part of the sentence makes it

And now again, at the very moment when I was making these reflexions,
the shrill noise of water running through a pipe,
   a noise exactly like those long-drawn-out **cries**
     which
        sometimes
        in summer
     one heard **the pleasure-steamers** emit
       in the evening
       as they approached Balbec from the sea,
made me feel
   —what I had been made to feel
     once before
     in Paris,
     in a big restaurant,
   by the sight of a luxurious dining-room, half-empty, summery and hot—
something that was not merely a sensation similar to the one I used to have
   at the end of the afternoon
   in Balbec
   when,
     the tables already laid and glittering with linen and silver,
     the vast window-bays still open
       from one end to the other
     on to the esplanade
       without
         a single interruption,
         a single solid surface of glass or stone,
       while the sun slowly descended upon the sea
       from which the steamers began to emit their cries,
I had,
   if I had wished to join Albertine and her friends
     who were walking on the front,
merely to step over the low wooden frame not much higher than my ankle,
   into whose groove
     so that the air could come into the hotel
   they had wound down
     all at one go
   the continuous range of windows. (TR 266)

clear that this sound is what provides the link to today's sensory experience (a similar noise, made by the plumbing in the Guermantes' residence), it recedes, in the
second half, into the background. And in fact it is only appropriate that it do so. For
involuntary memory is only possible on condition that the sensation be eminently
forgettable, so that the intellect overlooks it and fails to record a (voluntarily accessible) memory. The "cry" of the ships *has* to have escaped Marcel's notice—just
as, in the second half of our sentence, it may very well escape the notice of a casual
reader.

SENTENCE 5: THE BLOW TO THE HEART

Certes, ce coup physique au coeur
   que donne une telle séparation
   et qui,
      par cette terrible puissance d'enregistrement
         qu'a le corps,
   fait
      de la douleur
   quelque chose de contemporain
      à toutes les époques de notre vie
         où nous avons souffert,
—**certes, ce coup au coeur**
   sur lequel spécule
      peut-être
      un peu
      —tant on se soucie peu de la douleur des autres—
   celle qui désire donner
      au regret
   son maximum d'intensité,
      soit que la femme
         n'esquissant qu'un faux départ
      veuille seulement demander des conditions meilleures,
      soit que,
         partant pour toujours
            —pour toujours!—
   elle désire frapper,
      ou pour se venger,
      ou pour continuer d'être aimée,
      ou
         dans l'intérêt de la qualité du souvenir
            qu'elle laissera,
         briser violemment ce réseau
            de lassitudes, d'indifférences,
            qu'elle avait senti se tisser,
—**certes, ce coup au coeur,**
on s'était promis de l'éviter,
on s'était dit qu'on se quitterait bien. (IV:8–9)

This sentence is a tour de force, a veritable compendium of Proustian devices. It falls into three sections, three ways of considering that "blow to the heart": first in terms of its post-hoc effect on the sufferer, next in terms of its putative benefit to the inflictor, and finally in terms of the sufferer's earlier fantasies about it. Before the event, Marcel believed he could avoid it, believed that he was in full control, the subject of every sentence (just as "on" is subject of the main verbs at the end); afterward, however, he realizes the extent to which events and emotions always have us at their mercy ("nous," in the first section, is only the subject of a doubly

To be sure, the physical blow to the heart
  which such a parting administers,
  and which,
    because of that terrible capacity for registering things
      with which the body is endowed,
  makes
    of the pain
  something contemporaneous
    with all the epochs in our life
      in which we have suffered
—to be sure, this blow to the heart
  counted on
    perhaps
    a little
    —so little compunction do we feel for the sufferings of others—
  by her who wishes to give
    to the regret she causes
  its maximum of intensity,
    whether because,
      her departure being only a sham,
    she merely wants to demand better terms,
    or because,
      leaving us for ever
        —for ever!—
    she desires to wound us,
      either in order to avenge herself,
      or to continue to be loved,
      or
        (with an eye to the quality of the memory
          that she will leave behind her)
      to destroy the web
        of lassitude and indifference
        which she has felt being woven about her
—to be sure, this blow to the heart,
we had vowed that we would avoid it;
we had assured ourselves that we would part on good terms. (F 571)

subordinate verb). The third section accordingly registers a tone of tragic resignation, poignantly simple in its parataxis and almost lyrical in its rhythmic, assonant
anaphora: "**on s'était** promis de l'éviter, **on s'était** dit qu'on se quitterait bien."

Each section is, in other words, very different. We are dealing here not just with
a recursive sentence but with one whose refrain ("ce coup au coeur") undergoes
variations, as if to suggest that our returns to the past reveal not only new information but also new aspects of old information, new perspectives upon what we
already knew.

Inevitably perhaps, the middle section is the most complex, since it involves speculation as to the contents of another mind. It nests its subordinate clauses obsessively, hedges itself about with qualifiers ("peut-être," "un peu"), and incorporates the usual two hypotheses about Albertine: (1) she's really leaving (conjecture of the intuition); (2) she's only pretending to leave (conjecture of the intellect). Underneath the first hypothesis, further, a pair of *sub*hypotheses remind us of Marcel's theory of multiple motivations. For if Albertine is really leaving, then it is in order to wreak her revenge, or in order to leave while Marcel is still in love with her, *or both at once*.

As well as hinting, via the hypotheses, at the synchronic division of personality, the sentence also points to the persistence of diachronic selves. In the midst of a lucid, detached, even pedantic dissection of Albertine's motives, suddenly a different voice makes itself heard, one for whom the issues being discussed are live, painful topics, not just fodder for reflection: when the adverb "for ever" is repeated, suddenly acquiring an exclamation mark, we understand it to be carried by a *moi-Albertine*, ostensibly "dead," resurfacing amid a sea of indifference. Love, in Proust, never fully dies.

Could it be this point of pain, tucked away in the heart of the sentence and deep within the hypotaxis, that Marcel is trying to avoid by speaking of his own specific predicament in such general terms? Is that why there is no "je" in the sentence, but only "nous" and "on"? Certainly there is a hint of irony here between Proust and his narrator, not least when the latter deploys an inset maxim—"so little compunction do we feel for the sufferings of others"—in the middle of his tirade. Marcel may very well complain about Albertine's disregard for his feelings; but what of *his* disregard for *hers*? Isn't it this disregard that really explains her flight? And isn't it a mark of his *continued* apathy that he does not even list this among the reasons he offers, "so little compunction do we feel for the sufferings of others"? How typical of Proust's world that Marcel is, here, right for the wrong reasons, and that we are obliged to take the maxim seriously while at the same time casting the gravest of doubts on its speaker.

NOTES

Introduction

1. An exhaustive list of philosophers to whom Proust has been compared—including Plato, Leibniz, Bergson, Schelling, Schopenhauer, and Nietzsche, all of whom I discuss below, but also the pre-Socratics, the neo-Platonics, Descartes, Spinoza, Locke, Kant, Hegel, Kierkegaard, Emerson, Husserl, Heidegger, Sartre, and Merleau-Ponty—may be found in Large (18–20nn58–60). Like Large, I believe that Proust is (without his knowledge) closer to Nietzsche than to any other philosopher, although Proust also goes *beyond* Nietzsche in certain respects.

I discuss Proust's response to Locke (and Hume), and his para-Nietzschean departure from Kant, in chapter 3. In as much as Sartre takes his inspiration from Nietzsche, the overlap between the former and Proust, elegantly explored by Bersani in *The Fictions of Life and Art*, is also a genuine one; further than that, however, I do not think we should go. We should certainly not hold, with Pauline Newman, that Marcel's "being" is identical to "the sum of his phases" (123; my translation): she herself acknowledges elsewhere (43, 129, 137) that the idea of a *vrai moi* is thoroughly antithetical to Existentialist principles. As for the remaining philosophers on Large's list, there is some overlap between their views and those of Proust (particularly in the case of the phenomenologists), but differences tend to outweigh similarities in each case.

2. It is true that Deleuze concedes (correctly) that "Proust's singular essences [are] closer to the Leibnitzian monads than to Platonic essences" (156n102). But this is in a footnote; in the main text, Deleuze states quite clearly that "Proust treats the essences as Platonic Ideas and confers upon them an independent reality" (42).

For a categorical rejection of the idea that Proust is a Platonist, see Benjamin 1968: 210.

3. In general, the (rare) metaphysical speculations in the novel tend to be couched in cautious modal verbs. Thus for example the excursus on ethics: "everything is arranged in this life *as though* we entered it carrying a burden of

obligations contracted in a former life. . . . All these obligations, which have no sanction in our present life, *seem* to belong to a different world, a world based on kindness, scrupulousness, self-sacrifice, a world entirely different from this one and which we leave in order to be born on this earth, before perhaps returning there to live once again beneath the sway of those unknown laws which we obeyed because we bore their precepts in our hearts, not knowing whose hand had traced them there—those laws to which every profound work of the intellect brings us nearer. . . . So that the idea that Bergotte was not dead for ever is by no means improbable" (C 245–46; my emphasis). Note the concluding triple negative; Marcel does toy for a while with the idea of the soul's immortality, but his last word on it—"eternal duration is promised no more to men's works than to men" (TR 524)—is extremely pessimistic, and lends no comfort to those who wish to view Marcel (a fortiori Proust) as a believer in reincarnation, anamnesis, and so on. (For involuntary memory as anamnesis, see Shattuck 144.)

4. In his own name, while discussing the work of Gustave Moreau, Proust writes that "a painting is a kind of revelation of a corner of a mysterious world some of whose other fragments are known to us, in the form of canvases by the same artist. . . . The country of which artworks thus provide fragmentary manifestations is the poet's soul" (EA 365–66).

Elsewhere in the *Recherche*, Marcel describes Elstir's canvases as "fragments of that world of new and strange colours which was no more than the projection of that great painter's peculiar vision" (GW 573–74); and "just as there was a certain world, perceptible to us in those fragments here and there . . . , which was Elstir's world, the world he saw, the world in which he lived, so too the music of Vinteuil extended, note by note, stroke by stroke, the unknown, incalculable colourings of an unsuspected world" (C 339–40). For his part, the narrator of *Contre Sainte-Beuve* finds in Baudelaire's poetry "phrases from a planet which he alone has lived in and which is like nothing we know of," a planet which turns out to be "[the] world of Baudelaire's mind, [the] country of his genius, of which each poem is only a part and which, as soon as we read it, rejoins other parts we know already" (BSB 99, 101).

5. As Duncan Large points out (30–31), Henry attempts to solve this problem by attributing a theory of perspectivism to Schopenhauer. See 1981: 87 and 2000: 64–65. Translations of Henry's work are my own.

Henry is not alone: Luc Fraisse and Sybil de Souza write that art, on Proust's account, uncovers "the thing in itself" (Fraisse 33), an eternal and universal "transcendent reality" (de Souza 111). My translation of both quotations.

6. That is, Proust agrees on the need for self-deception. He is, however, not quite as pessimistic (Schopenhauerian) as his narrator. See below, on the "Laws of Love."

7. That Henry has had some success in displacing prior modes of interpretation is evident from Luc Fraisse's recent study, *L'esthétique de Marcel Proust*, in which the specificity and "irreplaceable role" of art (56) is reduced to its capacity to make philosophical ideas more vivid.

8. Such readings were already current in 1914, causing Proust some consternation. "I have enough to do," he wrote to Henri Ghéon, "without trying to turn the philosophy of M. Bergson into a novel!" (Corr. 13:39).

9. See *Carnet* 113 and nn. 483–85; Corr. 12:295–96; EA 254; Painter 2:52–53; Shattuck 148; Tadié 1996: 163, 450–51; and I:cxxx.

10. *Matière et mémoire*, qtd. in Shattuck 144. Compare also Bergson's remark that "we forget nothing. . . . everything we have perceived, thought or wanted, since the first stirrings of our consciousness, persists indefinitely" (*Oeuvres* 886; qtd. in III:1557n2; my translation) and Chessick 22. There is a moment at which Proust's narrator explicitly critiques Bergson's presentation—"We possess all our memories, but not the faculty of recalling them, said, echoing M. Bergson, the eminent Norwegian philosopher. . . . What, then, is a memory we do not recall?" (SG 522)—but this is probably not a serious divergence.

11. *Matière et mémoire*, qtd. in Shattuck 140. Chessick (27) agrees that Bergson has a theory of involuntary memory, and Terdiman (1993: 188) adds that the idea originally comes from Théodule Ribot's 1881 study *Les maladies de la mémoire*. Proust's stated view is that "the distinction between involuntary memory and voluntary memory . . . not only does not appear in the philosophy of M. Bergson, but is even contradicted by it" (EA 254; cf. *Letters* 227); it is quite possible, however—especially given the discussion of Bergson at SG 521—that Proust simply failed to read the relevant passages.

12. In Bergson, the Self is *apparently* riven into myriad temporal slices, while the *true* Self is a unity that simply unfolds over time (*Creative Evolution* 220). In Proust, by contrast, the temporal selves are not just figments of my imagination but have a genuine (albeit inferior) existence; and the "vrai moi," for its part, is entirely static. Proust's true self cannot, therefore, be a replica of Bergson's, as Chessick claims (28). "No Bergsonism, then," concludes Picon correctly; "there is a permanency here . . . something atemporal" (179; my translation). For similar rejections of "Bergsonism," see Shattuck (145), Poulet (1963: 9–10), Genette (1966: 55), Jauss (132), Champigny (131), and Raimond (437).

13. It is not quite clear what Ellison means by *"stricto sensu,"* since as far as I know people are still reading the novel. What is clear is that Ellison's argument tends to work as follows: (a) the novel claims that object *A* has quality *f*; (b) the novel claims that object *B* also has quality *f*; (c) the reader becomes utterly confused; (d) the novel is therefore unreadable. To take one example, since Marcel states that both music and lies are routes to the unknown, "Proust has rendered reading 'impossible' by making judgmental choices undecidable" (176). Ellison's argument is (deliberately?) hard to follow. If I tell you that there are two different ways to reach my house from yours, will you be constitutionally incapable of picking one? Will I have rendered driving impossible?

14. Vincent Descombes explicitly rejects the *moraliste* reading. In theory, he writes, "the scenes of the hero's apprenticeship make sense in the language of an infra-personal psychology: The agents mentioned are the mental faculties (memory, sensation, intelligence, etc.)"; in reality, however, "the novel is a genre based

on extroversion. In a *novelistic* narrative, agents must be characters and not mental faculties" (133). Descombes's argument does not strike me as decisive, since the faculties are clearly not the *only* agents in the *Recherche*, and reference to them does not conflict with reference to other types of agent. Furthermore, it is puzzling to find such forthright definitions of the novel from a critic who castigates the kind of "essentialist reasoning" that "commits itself shamelessly to ignoring outright what most deserves our attention: the diversity of narrative forms" (86).

15. The knowledge yielded by involuntary memory (including the understanding of involuntary memory itself!) comes not through reasoning but through epiphanic *insight*. It is thus "more precious" than "truths which the intellect educes directly from reality" (TR 303).

16. Compare Nietzsche's early view that truth "kills itself": "Everything which is good and beautiful depends upon illusions: truth kills—it even kills itself (insofar as it realizes that error is its foundation)" (TL 176: 10).

17. Cf. "the maxims of [Norpois's] political wisdom . . . were as powerless to solve questions of fact as, in philosophy, pure logic is powerless to tackle the problems of existence" (GW 325).

18. "Our *intuitive* radiography pierces them, and the images which it brings back, far from being those of a particular face, present rather the joyless universality of a skeleton" (BG 648; my emphasis); "I had been quite well aware [*j'avais bien senti*] that this love was not inevitable . . . , sensing it to be vaster than Albertine, enveloping her, unconscious of her, like a tide swirling around a tiny rock" (F 679). The first statement is, of course, something of an exaggeration: while it is true that Albertine is not uniquely destined for Marcel, neither is it the case that any other woman will do equally well. Instead there are, on the Proustian view, numerous replaceable *tokens* of a nonetheless neatly demarcated *type*. Intuition may *imagine*, in its typically cynical way, that specific partners are "nothing" in themselves (TR 313), "interchangeable instruments of a pleasure that is always the same" (S 222); in reality, however, it has selected them on the basis of identifiable features of personality. It simply lacks awareness—as is, after all, only to be expected—of what it has been doing.

19. I am aware that *instinct*, *sensibility*, and *intuition* are not entirely synonymous in themselves; they are, however, used more or less interchangeably in Proust. At most, they represent separate aspects of a single component of the mind, namely, the individual perspective that filters incoming data, produces unreasoned judgments about them (intuition), imposes valuations upon them (sensibility), and generates impulses based on those valuations (instinct).

That *the unconscious* is, in Proust, another term for *instinct* is confirmed by the pairing of "my intelligence and my unconscious" at F 709, since elsewhere (e.g., C 468, C 495, TR 275) the habitual opposition is between intellect and instinct. Similarly, art is characterized both as the intellectual "translation" of sensibility (TR 307) and as the movement of unconscious contents into consciousness (TR 274, EA 288). The correspondence bears out the same point: "just as, while reading Stendhal, Thomas Hardy or Balzac, I have pinpointed deep features of their *instinct,*" Proust writes, "so, while reading myself, I have elicited post hoc some constitutive features of my *unconscious*" (Corr. 12:180; my emphasis). We should be somewhat circumspect, however: although Proust does refer to the *Recherche* as "an attempt at a sequence of novels of the unconscious" (*Letters* 226, EA 253–54), he is taking the term in its pre-Freudian, more inclusive sense. Proust did not read Freud.

20. This idea—that "a book is the product of a different *self* from the self we manifest in our habits, in our social life, in our vices" (BSB 76)—is, of course, the very core and motor of *Contre Sainte-Beuve*. That the narrator of *Contre Sainte-Beuve* is here speaking for Proust can be deduced from the preface to Jacques-Emile Blanche's *Propos de peintre*, where Proust makes a similar statement in his own name: "Jacques Blanche's mistake as critic, like Sainte-Beuve's, is . . . that of explaining the true Fantin or Manet, the one that is only found in their work, on the basis of the mortal man" (EA 273–74). Furthermore, the events depicted in the *Recherche* repeatedly bear out the theory. Of the three main artists, Marcel quite plausibly writes that "the prudish respectability of the one [Vinteuil], the intolerable defects of the other [Bergotte], even the pretentious vulgarity of an Elstir in his early days—for I had discovered from the Goncourt Journal that he was none other than the 'Monsieur Tiche' whose twaddle had once exasperated Swann in the Verdurins' drawing-room—prove nothing against them: their genius is manifested in their works" (TR 42). Even minor characters, and real-life artists to whom passing reference is made, conform to the rule: Charlus, the sensualist, would have written great novels (C 292); Morel is cowardly and grasping (e.g., C 212); Octave is fatuous (TR 58); and Laclos—conversely—has a higher standard of morality than his novels would suggest (TR 280).

21. "The thing fashioned itself in my head in two different ways . . . The first is the traditional essay. . . . The second begins with the story of a morning" (Corr. 8:320–21). See Schmid 63 for a brief history of publication. On generic hybridity, compare Barthes 1986a: 278, Genette 1980: 259, Picon 200, and Spitzer 460–61.

22. See the epigraphs to this chapter, which hail from S 598, TR 530, and Corr. 13:98–100, respectively. (The "moment from long ago" referred to at TR 530 is Swann's fateful visit on the night of the *drame du coucher*.)

23. One example of an infelicitous use of pronouns: "Proust's entire novel rests on certain privileged moments in which spontaneous memory opened up for *him* the door to authentic memory. *He* could so easily never have eaten that madeleine dipped in a cup of tea from which all the memories of Combray and of *his* childhood emerged" (Newman 30; my translation and emphasis; the same formulation is repeated almost verbatim at 105, and again at 111–12).

For Brian Rogers, similarly, it goes without saying that the madeleine scene is "Proust's own experience"; the only question is whether it is rendered directly or whether it is mediated by intellect. "Are the narrator's impressions of a forgotten past, for example, as he slowly savours the madeleine's taste, Proust's own experiences, or the bathing of an indefinable experience in the light of his cool and lucid intelligence . . .?" (1965: 200).

As for Sybil de Souza, she claims not only that the madeleine episode is a genuine memory for the author—Proust attempts, on her account, "to plumb the depths of that pleasure *he* felt while drinking a certain cup of tea" (110; cf. 34, 40, 44, 46, 95)—but also that its authenticity *matters*. "Facts and things interest Proust only if they contain an element of objective reality," she writes. "Thus the little incident of the madeleine dipped in a cup of tea derives its significance from belonging to a real past" (143). My translation and emphasis.

24. Compare also the start of Derwent May's *Proust*: "Marcel is not the same as Proust. . . . Proust drew deeply on his own experience for the portrait of Marcel; nevertheless, Marcel is always seen as a character, the object of scrutiny and sometimes of irony. We are dealing with a created world . . . , not just a remembered one. Proust did indeed have an experience like Marcel's over the tea; but . . . . it was a piece of moistened toast that he tasted early in 1909, and it was his childhood visits to his grandfather that he then recalled" (1). Similarly, Shattuck writes of Proust that "in January 1909, he apparently had an unexpected and compelling surge of memory over a cup of tea into which he dipped some dry toast" (15–16). By contrast, William Carter, author of a more recent biography of Proust, is careful to treat the toast-and-tea scene of *Contre Sainte-Beuve* as a "draft" for what will become the madeleine episode (466–67), and Roger Duchêne calls it an "expérience personnelle—ou prétendument personnelle" (602).

25. The Gallimard Folio edition of *Contre Sainte-Beuve* compounds (or at least abets) the felony by adding the initials "M. P." after what it calls the "Preface." There is no evidence that Proust intended the relevant pages to be taken as his own words, rather than those of his narrator. For some reason, Bernard de Fallois must just have decided to "improve" on Proust's manuscript. Why? Like so much else in this domain, de Fallois's decision is simply baffling.

26. JS 488. *Jean Santeuil* also narrates other instances of involuntary memory, notably the images of Brittany which come to mind while the hero is in the mountains and at Lake Geneva: "It was not the timid fingers of the sun feeling their way through clouds and touching the leaves though not yet fully lighting them, nor the chaste caress of the familiar wind, that had not changed. It was that in himself he felt the presence of a something else which had stayed the same, even though he was aware of it only at special times" (399–400); "Could it be that beauty and joy for the poet resides in an invisible substance which may perhaps be called imagination, which cannot work directly on immediate reality, nor yet on past reality deliberately remembered, but hovers only over past reality caught up and enshrined in the reality now present? It is as though before the eye which sees it now and saw it long ago, there floats divine imagination, which is perhaps the source of all our joy, something that we find in books, but only with the utmost difficulty in things around us" (407; cf. S 114, TR 263); "And this deep-dwelling pleasure . . . shows, because of the happiness we feel when we are freed from the present, that our true nature lies outside of time, and is forced to feed on the eternal" (410; cf. TR 264).

George Painter admits that "similar events . . . had happened throughout his [Proust's] life, and had been recorded again and again in *Jean Santeuil*" (2:147). It is not clear why he nonetheless considers the purported toast episode to have been "momentous."

27. Ellison is so keen to find oedipal dramas everywhere in the novel that he diagnoses Marcel's failure to kiss Albertine, in the second volume of the novel, as deriving from Albertine's taboo status (160): "Albertine's body is," he explains, "*possessed* by the phantom of the mother, who is a tabooed object" (154). But as is quite plain from the passage, Marcel does not hesitate in the slightest; if his effort to kiss Albertine goes awry, it is quite simply because "Albertine had pulled the bell with all her might" (BG 701).

Perhaps the most astonishing claim Ellison makes in the whole essay is that "Proust recognizes . . . that he is unable to love a woman as a woman—that is, as a physical presence to be desired for itself" (162). It is as though Ellison is so convinced the *Recherche* is a true autobiography that he has not bothered to look anywhere else for details about Proust's life, to the point of remaining unaware of Proust's homosexuality. (Compare also Sybil de Souza, who declares, equally bewilderingly, that "love remains purely subjective for Proust: thus the mistresses he loved the most never matched up to his love for them" [99; my translation].)

28. That Marcel and Proust are identical is clearly something for which Chessick does not feel he has to argue, so patently obvious is it to him. "Proust's novel actually opens with an attempt to force his will upon his mother," he writes, as though it went without saying that Marcel is Proust and Maman Proust's mother (28); the fact that Marcel "remains fragmented to the very end" thus constitutes, for Chessick, ample evidence that "Proust's effort to restore his neurotic and fragmented self . . . failed for him personally" (34–35). Compare Terdiman who, like Chessick, reduces Proust's skepticism to a derivate of his private obsessions (1976: 201) and, like Ellison, uses events in Marcel's life to undermine the involuntary memory theory (1993: 239).

29. Conversely, the real-life Céleste Albaret ends up *divided* into two separate characters in the *Recherche*, one of whom bears her name, the other ("Françoise") taking her job, so to speak, as the narrator's long-time domestic servant. On more than one occasion (e.g., SG 336), both are named on the very same page. So, too, are Robert de Montesquiou and the Baron de Charlus (SG 134), Charles Haas and Charles Swann (GW 794), Sarah Bernhardt and "la Berma" (S 102), Thibaud and Morel (C 63 and 383), Maspéro and Brichot (C 441), Potain and Cottard (S 265), Mme de Sévigné and Mme de Beausergent (BG 313), and the Empress Elisabeth and Mme de Villeparisis (GW 252). Elstir and Whistler both appear in the Goncourt diary fragment read by Marcel (TR 27, TR 33); for her part, the ailing grandmother is treated both by the well-known Dr. Dieulafoy and by the imaginary Dr. du Boulbon (GW 407–18, 459–60, 466–68). For some of these points, see Muller 112 and 166–67.

30. C 244–5. As Gérard Genette points out, autobiographers are really not supposed to be omniscient (1980: 208; cf. Martin-Chauffier 66, Cohn 60).

31. See O'Brien 1949. Gaëtan Picon, whom we saw above attributing a memory of Doncières to Proust, even though Doncières is a fictional location, also

believes more generally that the *Recherche* is "Proust's confession" (168; my translation). "The narrator," he writes, "does not say, 'Here I am, a timorous old baby, a sadomasochistic homosexual'"—but he *is* one, Picon believes, since he is identical to the author (101; my translation).

32. Both Maar (1997: 176) and O'Brien (1949: 943) cite, as further evidence for the "transposition" theory, Marcel's remark to the effect that "The writer must not be indignant if the invert who reads his book gives to his heroines a masculine countenance" (TR 321). But while this statement may perhaps be taken as *license* granted by Proust for readers to imagine Gilberte (say) as a man, it does not quite count as *encouragement*. The example Marcel goes on to give, namely of Charlus seeing the face of Morel in Musset's faithless woman from *La nuit d'octobre*, suggests that such readers sometimes do violence to the text—forgivable violence, but violence nonetheless.

33. Cf. Levin 650. And cf. Edmund White, who concedes that "it would be a mistake to see all of Proust's women as disguised men . . . some of the female characters are unquestionably, quintessentially womanly, such as Odette . . . or the duchesse de Guermantes or the actress Berma" (24, 25).

O'Brien, by contrast, clearly feels it helps his case that *Albertine*, *Gilberte*, and *Andrée* are all names with male equivalents (1949: 937)—hinting, presumably, at the true face beneath each mask. In his view, Gilberte is just as "unfeminine" as Albertine: "Proust had the right, and possibly even the power, to create an unquestionably feminine Gilberte or Albertine as the object of Marcel's passion, but the fact remains that he did not do so" (1950: 653).

34. Even Justin O'Brien admits (1949: 940n10) that Marie Nordlinger and Louisa de Mornand are involved.

35. In the preface to *Dates*, Jacques-Emile Blanche famously claimed that some of Proust's female characters are based on male models and vice versa, "so much so that one could say *he* instead of *she* [il *au lieu d*'elle]" (1921: xv–xvi). Yet even Blanche did not consider Proust to have operated a straightforward transposition; instead he told Proust that "the art with which you create, or rather recreate, your characters is one of the rarest and most complicated mental operations" (xiv). Responding to Blanche, Proust took him to task for his preface, with its "thousand elements that will be distorted (like the *he* which could be read as *she*, etc.)" (Corr. 20:67; letter dated January 16, 1921). Proust was right: Blanche's statement has indeed been repeatedly and consistently misconstrued.

36. For further "evidence" of Albertine's masculinity, cf. Maar: "Proust . . . camouflaged the boys, dressing all the most desirable ones up as girls—a practice Gide reproached him for. . . . Proust's innocent blunders on the score can be as funny as they are moving, as when the Narrator's eye lights upon some 'fisher-girls'—as if fishing were such a female-dominated profession. Albertine's all-too-sturdy neck has become so familiar as to be almost wearisome. Less well known is the Narrator's recollection of the day Albertine allowed him to kiss her for the first time: he smiled, he remembers, with inward gratitude towards the unknown seducer 'who had wrought so profound a change in her and had so simplified my

task.' But what change could be so profound as a shift in sexual inclination? An Albert who had already succumbed to another man's embraces seems the only plausible explanation for Marcel's gratitude. The same goes for the crude phrase Albertine lets slip: *me faire casser . . . le pot*—street slang for a practice more usually attributed to the inhabitants of Sodom than to those of Gomorrah" (2001: 135–36). Maar may have a point about "casser le pot," but surely a loss of virginity is a profound enough shift to alter a young woman's attitude toward sexuality. And then, what are we to make of this "all-too-sturdy neck"? Interestingly, Justin O'Brien—who is, as we have seen, the transposition theory's strongest proponent—nonetheless attributes Albertine's neck, in a footnote, to Louisa de Mornand (1949: 940n10).

37. Marcel is fully aware of Albertine's "masculine" characteristics, and at one point explains them as deriving from the fact that she is a man in a woman's body, just as Charlus is a woman in a man's body: "It was perhaps, I told myself, Albertine's vice itself . . . that had produced in her that honest, frank manner, creating the illusion that one enjoyed with her the same loyal and unqualified comradeship as with a man, just as a parallel vice had produced in M. de Charlus a feminine delicacy of sensibility and mind" (F 826).

38. Charlus is so incensed by the list of lovers Morel reels off during a meeting in 1916 that he swears revenge (TR 130–31), and indeed plans at a later date to kill Morel (TR 167–68). But "it was of men alone that M. de Charlus was capable of feeling any jealousy so far as Morel was concerned. Women inspired in him none whatever" (C 283). Indeed, "since he admired everything about Morel, the latter's successes with women, causing him no offence, gave him the same joy as his successes on the concert platform or at cards" (C 284). And hence, in the end, "nothing could have pleased the Baron more than the idea of this marriage [between Morel and Jupien's niece]" (C 55)—even though Morel is actually in *love* with his fiancée, or at least thinks he is (C 59). Derwent May makes the same argument (41), adding that Proust's own life showed a pattern similar to that of Charlus: Alfred Agostinelli was married, and Proust was on excellent terms with the wife.

Charlus's indifference may have to do with the fact that he himself has had affairs with women (C 274), including Odette (C 401–2). A homosexual male, Proust implies, can imagine his partner having sex with another man, and can—at least in principle—even imagine him having sex with a woman. A heterosexual male, by contrast, can imagine his partner having sex with another man, but cannot imagine her having sex with a woman.

39. SG 709; my emphasis; cf. C 412, C 519, Ladenson 16, and Webb. Compare also Bersani: "Albertine's love for other women is a relation of sameness that Marcel, as a man who desires women, is condemned to see as an irreducibly unknowable otherness. . . . Marcel Proust the homosexual had to submit to the torture of being heterosexual for the sake of his art. Gide . . . failed to see this" (1989: 865).

40. For the idea that only art can communicate the essence of an individual, see also GW 540, GW 573–74, C 343. For the fundamental unknowability of other people in general, represented by the case of Albertine, see C 73–74, 520, 527–28.

41. For Elisabeth Ladenson, Marcel's fascination with lesbianism is indeed the best possible evidence that Marcel is not identical with Proust. "What I would suggest . . . is that Gomorrah be read as the signpost of fictionality in the *Recherche*. It is his lesbophilia that sets Proust's narrator apart from the author, that marks the novel as a novel rather than a perverse exercise in selective autobiography" (133).

Even Michael Maar, who believes that Proust's intention is to slip his homosexuality past the censor by means of "camouflage" (1997: 166), acknowledges that fictionalized humans take on a literary life of their own, escaping their narrowly allegorical function. Thus Maar finds at least "plausible" the jealousy of a heterosexual character for a bisexual woman engaging in "inconceivably alien [*unbegreiflich fremden*]" sexual acts (1997: 170).

42. The "Aveu" section of *Jean Santeuil* (1895–96), in which the eponymous hero coaxes an admission of bisexuality out of his lover, is a direct ancestor of Swann's confrontation with Odette at S 514–16, a confrontation which in turn prefigures the scene of revelation on the Balbec train (SG 701–4). See also Painter 2:208–9.

43. Gide would appear to be one critic who believes that Proust, as a homosexual author, should make his narrator homosexual too. As for the other group of uncharitable readers, namely those who do not believe a homosexual author *capable* of (or perhaps sufficiently interested in) fashioning heterosexual characters, Proust has—as so often—anticipated their response. He has Albertine make the absurd suggestion that Dostoevsky must have committed a murder, since so many of his characters are assassins, and Marcel dryly reply, "'It's possible that creative writers are tempted by certain forms of life of which they have no personal experience'" (C 510–11).

For a recent attempt to prove Proust's narrator homosexual, see Lavagetto (1996: 120); for an explanation of why this attempt also fails, see Compagnon 1997: 143–45.

44. TR 225. This famously unconventional sentence can only belong to the author, not the narrator, for reasons I discuss below.

45. Corr. 19:580. Compare Proust's remark to Mme de Pierrebourg: "*You are a novelist!* If I could create characters and situations like you do, how happy I would be!" (Corr. 8:250).

46. See Suzuki 74, Muller 165, Tadié 1971: 30n3. The "Mon Marcel" case, which I am about to discuss in the main text, is a particularly fascinating one (see III:1718). At first, there was no mention of the protagonist's name. Later, however, Proust added the phrase "on waking she had said to me: 'My Marcel,' 'My darling Marcel'" above the relevant line of his manuscript (*Cahier* VIII: 39 recto; my translation). And then, when the manuscript, complete with additions, had been typed up, Proust inserted by hand the final, crucial qualification: "she would find her tongue and say 'My—' or 'My darling—' followed by my Christian name, which, *if we give the narrator the same name as the author of this book, would be* 'My Marcel' or 'My darling Marcel.'" Clearly Proust wanted *both* the name *and* the disclaimer.

47. Drawing on de Manian deconstruction, David Ellison declares that the "darling Marcel" sentence is either "unreadable" or an indication that Proust's character shares his name: "the name of the protagonist and narrator is Marcel . . . , or at least it seems to be if the short passage in *La Prisonnière* . . . is itself readable" (139). These, however, are *not* the two choices. The sentence does not claim that the narrator's name *is* Marcel, but merely that one *could make it* Marcel—a crucial distinction, preserving the gap between author and narrator. Not unreadable, just (in this instance) unread.

48. It is true that there is an occasion on which the narrator is straightforwardly called "Marcel," without any qualifications (see C 202–3). But this comes after the "my darling Marcel" passage, and it is quite likely that we are simply meant to carry over the initial caveat, to take the word "Marcel" here as if it were in quotation marks or square brackets, a convenient placeholder inserted where the narrator wishes to use a proper noun. We should certainly not conclude, as Leo Spitzer does, that "the narrating I is identical to Proust himself, as we can tell from the opening words of a letter from Albertine, '*Mon pauvre Marcel*'" (427n30; my translation).

49. Compare Proust's inscription on Marie Scheikévitch's copy of *Du côté de chez Swann* (EA 257): describing future developments in the plot, he writes (among many other non-autobiographical things) that "you will see the terrible night I then spend, at the end of which I come crying to my mother to ask her permission for an engagement with Albertine." Surely even the most "rigid" biographical critic would stop short of taking the use of the first person as evidence that a tearful Proust asked his mother's permission to marry . . . Alfred Agostinelli.

50. Other critics to note the divergence between Proust and Marcel include Pierre-Quint (the first to do so), Brée 1951, Waters, and Deleuze (122). Proust himself tended to be delighted when readers made the distinction: see his letter to Paul Souday mentioning "the narrator whom you have with so much subtlety distinguished from me" (Corr. 19:38; qtd. in Muller 160).

When I say that Marcel is "not always" Proust, I mean that the novel is (a) not an autobiography, for all the elements borrowed (lazily) from Proust's own experience, and (b) not a treatise, for all the philosophical statements Proust himself endorses. I suggest below that Proust derives powerful effects from the mixture of reliable and unreliable assertions; similar arguments for the mixture of biographical, semi-biographical, and fictional elements could perhaps be imagined, though I do not yet know of any.

51. Marie Bénardaky, the primary "source" for Gilberte, had black hair (Painter 1:44).

52. The *Carnet de 1908* shows that Proust initially had in mind a division of the geography into "Le côté de Villebon et le côté de Méséglise" (56) before amending the former to "le côté de Guermantes" (94); even then, he was still toying with the idea of having a Duchesse d'Ermantes (116). There is clearly nothing fixed, let alone magical, about the name "Guermantes" as far as Proust is concerned.

Proustian biography is, however, a strange world indeed, and one can, if one looks hard enough, find within it the claim that Proust heard of the Guermantes as a young child, in a song his nursemaid sang to him (Hayman 284). Hayman's source is one P.-L. Larcher, author of *Le parfum de Combray: Pèlerinage proustien à Illiers*, a book whose content can readily be imagined. Yet when we look at the relevant page (46) of Larcher, we see nothing whatsoever about the Guermantes, nursemaids, or songs. Indeed, Larcher himself believes—quite incompatibly with the idea that the word "Guermantes" stuck in Proust's enchanted memory—that Proust derives it from Saint-Eman, name of an aristocratic family local to Illiers ("the fact that 'Guermantes' takes only the 'old-gold sonority' of its central syllable from [the name] Saint-Eman . . .: all that is the music of multiple assonances . . . destined to make us penetrate all the more deeply into the marvelous Proustian charm" [19–20; my translation]). Quite frankly, it feels at times as though one will never emerge from the forest of myth into the clearing of biographical fact.

53. Gérard Genette suggests (1969: 238) that Marcel's system may be based on a propinquity of sound: "Guermantes" rhymes with "amarante," and is also quite close to "orange," the first syllable ending in [R], the second having the nasal [ã] as its vowel. This idea receives some support from Marcel's impression of Brabant as a golden name, and Champi a purplish one (S 10, 56). The very fact that Proust appears to hesitate between orange/gold and purple/amaranthine—not identical colors by any means—may be further confirmation that he is inventing an association for his protagonist, rather than reproducing one of his own.

54. Cf. Dorrit Cohn: "If we understand the *Recherche* as a novel, we can no longer assume . . . that the ideological views it expresses are necessarily and invariably Proust's own" (72). Cohn's chapter is the most thorough and effective *mise au point* of the genre question to date; I depart from it only in the direction of still greater exhaustiveness and, more importantly, in attempting to provide a rationale for the mixture of reliable and unreliable narration.

55. "What are all the love stories in Proust but enormous amplifications of these aphorisms? Proust is La Rochefoucauld magnified ten thousand times" (O'Brien 1948a: 53).

56. The case of Martha Nussbaum is slightly more complicated, but ultimately analogous. Like Chessick, she believes that Marcel's epistemological skepticism is driven merely by personal hang-ups, not by philosophical commitments: "It is because he wishes not to be tormented by the ungovernable inner life of the other that he adopts a position that allows him to conclude that the other's inner life is nothing more than the constructive workings of his own mind" (1990: 271). And although at times she distinguishes narrator from author, she nonetheless concludes that the position stated in the text is "the final Proustian view" (1990: 280). Now the fact is that Marcel never claims other minds do not *exist*, but merely that their inner recesses cannot (directly) be *known*. Quite the contrary, Marcel is painfully aware of the separateness of Albertine's desires and perceptions; his desperate quest to understand them, particularly after her death, testifies both to the existence and to the remoteness of her interiority.

57. "The case of an affected old woman like M. de Charlus, who, as a result of seeing in his mind's eye only a handsome young man, thinks he himself has become a handsome young man . . . —such a case falls under a law which applies far more widely than to the Charluses alone, a law so generalised that not even love itself exhausts it entirely; we do not see our bodies . . . and we 'follow' our thoughts, the object that is in front of us, invisible to others" (C 464); "the case of M. de Charlus . . . on the whole, with slight discrepancies due to the identity of sex, accords very well with the general laws of love" (TR 188). Cf. also SG 431.

To this extent, Sartre's criticism—that "Proust thought he could draw on his homosexual experience when he set out to depict the love of Swann for Odette. . . . clearly, then, he must believe in the existence of universal passions whose mechanism does not vary appreciably when one modifies the sexual orientation, social condition, nationality, and historical situation of the individuals feeling them," with the result that "his novel contributes to the spread of the myth of human nature" (1948: 20; my translation)—is somewhat justified; but only somewhat. As I am about to show, passions are not entirely "universal" in Proust, even if they are indeed unaffected by history, geography, and class.

58. Morris Weitz notes (84) that there are other cases of happy love, including that of Norpois and Mme de Villeparisis. Weitz may, however, go too far in his conclusion. Like his fellow Untenables, he takes the existence of one or two failed maxims to vitiate the entire system: "Proust's treatment of love is the best example of the dissolution of essences in the search for them. His probing exhibition of love's great variety reveals an inexhaustible set of properties, no one of which is necessary, no collection of which is sufficient" (99); "although Proust may seek these laws or essences, he does not find them. Instead he discovers that our basic experiences do not have defining properties, that the undeniable, inexhaustible richness and complexity of these experiences preclude such essentialist definitions" (87).

59. "I saw the man of the slaughter-houses enter the room; he was indeed a little like Maurice, but—and this was odder—they both had in them something of a type *which I had never myself consciously observed in Morel's face* but which I now clearly saw to exist there; they bore a resemblance, if not to Morel as I had seen him, at least to a certain countenance which *eyes seeing Morel otherwise than I did* might have constructed out of his features. No sooner had I, out of features borrowed from my recollections of Morel, privately made for myself this rough model of what he might represent to somebody else, than I realised that the two young men, one of whom was a jeweller's assistant while the other worked in a hotel, were in a vague way substitutes for Morel. Was I to conclude that M. de Charlus, at least in a certain aspect of his loves, *was always faithful to a particular type* and that the desire which had made him select these two young men one after the other was the identical desire which had made him accost Morel on the platform at Doncières station; that all three resembled a little the ephebe whose form, engraved in the sapphire-like eyes of M. de Charlus, gave to his glance that strange quality which had alarmed me the first day at Balbec?" (TR 185; my

emphasis). Note that the ephebe in Charlus's eye is *formally* analogous to the "Venetian beauty" (TR 439) in Elstir's mind (and, presumably, to the *être de fuite* in Marcel's), but so different in *content* as to be difficult to imagine a priori.

60. My translation for Spitzer, Rousset, and Genette.

61. Marcel returns repeatedly to the idea that Albertine's kiss replaces that of his mother: see SG 312, 715, 720; C 2, 93, 108, 141–42; F 676.

62. "If we are to understand the love-objects chosen by our type as being above all mother-surrogates, then the formation of a series of them, which seems so flatly to contradict the condition of being faithful to one, can now also be understood . . . for the reason that every surrogate nevertheless fails to provide the desired satisfaction" (Freud 1957 [1914]: 169).

63. "I remember the hot weather that we had then, when from the foreheads of the farm labourers toiling in the sun drops of sweat would fall . . . ; they have remained to this day, together with that mystery of a woman's secret, the most enduring element in every love that offers itself to me. For a woman who is mentioned to me and to whom ordinarily I would not give a moment's thought, I will upset all my week's engagements to make her acquaintance, if it is a week of similar weather, and if I am to meet her in some isolated farm-house. Even if I am aware that this kind of weather, this kind of assignation, have nothing to do with her, they are still the bait which, however familiar, I allow myself to be tempted by" (SG 320); "Associated now with the memory of my love, Albertine's physical and social attributes, in spite of which I had loved her, oriented my desire on the contrary towards what at one time it would least readily have chosen: dark-haired girls of the lower middle class" (F 745).

64. Proust may have found a similar idea in Thomas Hardy's *The Well-Beloved* (Chessick 30).

65. "I knew that . . . the Duc and Duchesse de Guermantes . . . were real personages who did actually exist, but whenever I thought about them I pictured them either in tapestry, like the Comtesse de Guermantes in the 'Coronation of Esther' which hung in our church, or else in iridescent colours, like Gilbert the Bad in the stained-glass window . . . , or again impalpable, like the image of Geneviève de Brabant, ancestress of the Guermantes family, which the magic lantern sent wandering over the curtains of my room or flung aloft upon the ceiling—in short, invariably wrapped in the mystery of the Merovingian age" (S 241–42; cf. TR 240–41, 282).

· Perhaps it is in part because he has always before his mind, when he thinks of the name "Guermantes," the image of a magic lantern slide with a gold-colored castle (S 10) that he thinks of the name as orange-tinted. See, e.g., GW 2: "the atmosphere in which Mme de Guermantes existed in me, after having been for years no more than the reflexion of *a magic lantern slide* and of a stained-glass window, began to lose its *colours*" (my emphasis). This would constitute a different explanation from Genette's, cited earlier.

66. For Albertine, see GW 480, 496; for the *petite bande*, see BG 563; for Mlle de Stermaria, see BG 364; for the Roussainville peasant girls, see S 220–21;

for Gilberte, see TR 443. Gilberte is in fact connected to two places, the Ile-de-France, where Marcel has first imagined her, and Tansonville, where he has first seen her. "First she rose, each one of these women . . . , in the midst of one of those landscapes of my dreams . . . , the landscape to which my imagination had sought to attach her; then later I saw her from the angle of memory, surrounded by the places in which I had known her and which, remaining attached to them, she recalled to me. . . . So that the shadow of, for instance, Gilberte lay not merely outside a church in the Ile-de-France where I had imagined her [cf. S 138], but also upon a gravelled path in a park on the Méséglise way [cf. S 197–99]" (TR 441–42).

Gilles Deleuze recognizes the connection between women and their local landscapes, but he believes that it can be explained by Marcel's desire to know the women: the landscapes are, on Deleuze's interpretation, tools for understanding their inhabitants (7–8). It seems to me that Deleuze has the picture upside down here.

67. "Had I not loved Gilberte herself principally because she had appeared to me haloed with that aureole of being the friend of Bergotte, of going to look at cathedrals with him?" (BG 513; cf. S 138–39, S 582, BG 163, TR 443). René Girard is quite right to speak of "external mediation" in the *Recherche* (35, 200). For if Marcel's love objects often draw their fascination from the involvement of third parties, these third parties are not always *rivals* (Bergotte is not competing with Marcel for Gilberte but merely lending her some of his aura), not even always other *males* (they include Geneviève de Brabant), and not, for that matter, always *humans*. Instead they are mythical and pseudomythical entities like Gilbert le Mauvais, Charles Swann, and Bergotte the author (as opposed to Bergotte the dinner companion). One might perhaps quibble with Girard on the grounds that in Proust, mediation is necessary only in the case of people like Marcel, not in that of humanity at large.

68. Swann, of course, has this in common with Marcel. For him too, women gain in prestige by being associated with artworks—Vinteuil's sonata again (S 335–36), but also Botticelli's *Life of Moses* and *Jethro's Daughter*. "The vague feeling of sympathy which attracts one to a work of art . . . became a desire which more than compensated, thenceforward, for the desire which Odette's physical charms had at first failed to inspire in him" (S 318). I would claim that the "vague feeling of sympathy" here is a particular type of fellow-feeling directed toward the *painter*.

69. Nietzsche appears to feel the same way: some laws, like that of perspectivism, apply to all human beings, whereas others are merely "my truths" (BGE 231). (A full discussion of the paradox of perspectivism is, however, beyond the scope of this study; I would refer the interested reader to Anderson 1998 and 2002, Nehamas 1985 [chap. 2], and Poellner 1995 and 2001.) As in Proust, so in Nietzsche the personal truths are not useful as problem-solving tools but instead as beacons shining light on our own nature; as for Proust, so for Nietzsche it is a matter of making the Copernican turn from an attempt at objective judgment to

the investigation of the very subjectivity that makes such judgment precarious. "At times," he writes, "we find certain solutions of problems that inspire strong faith in *us*; some call them henceforth *their* 'convictions.' Later—we see them only as steps to self-knowledge, sign-posts to the problem we *are*" (BGE 231).

70. Leo Bersani phrases this point particularly succinctly: "The general laws . . . are mainly the laws of Marcel's responses to life. . . . What is general in the general laws—the narrator's claims to universal truths notwithstanding—is Marcel's unique point of view on the world" (1965: 237). "The narrator exposes his early illusions about the external world," Bersani continues, "but his present point of view seems almost more naive than the young Marcel's; he now finds, for example, a universally valid definition of love in his own peculiar experience of it" (238).

71. One example among many: "the disastrous way in which the psychopathological universe is constructed has decreed that the clumsy act, the act which we ought most sedulously to avoid, is precisely the act that will calm us" (F 616).

72. At times, exceptions follow hard on the heels of the ostensibly universal laws. One example: "every death is for others a simplification of life, it spares them the necessity of showing gratitude, the obligation of paying calls. And yet this was not the manner in which Elstir had received the news of the death of M. Verdurin" (TR 425). Marcel might simply have written, in the La Rochefoucauldian manner, "*often* a death"; the emphatic "every" serves as an ironic signal. (See also BG 174: "However characteristic it may be, the sound that escapes from a person's lips is fugitive and does not survive him. But it was not so with the pronunciation of the Bergotte family.")

73. Cf. "'I've been dreaming, the matter is quite simple. I am an indecisive young man, and it is a case of one of those marriages as to which it takes time to find out whether they will happen or not. There is nothing in this peculiar to Albertine.' *This thought brought me immense . . . relief*" (C 490; my emphasis).

74. Often, the refinement follows what one might loosely call a dialectical pattern, with Marcel swinging from extreme position *p* to extreme position *q*, its diametric antithesis, only to conclude that *p* is right but in a *q* kind of way. The Guermantes, for example, are neither supernatural nor entirely ordinary, but distinguished by virtue of earthly superiorities: "in the same way as Balbec or Florence, the Guermantes, after first disappointing the imagination because they resembled their fellow-men rather more than their name, could subsequently, though to a lesser degree, hold out to one's intelligence certain distinctive characteristics. . . . if people spoke of the Guermantes complexion, the Guermantes hair, they spoke also of the Guermantes wit" (GW 600; cf. 780). And music, more crucially, does not communicate an independently existing "divine world" which composers visit from time to time (S 498), but neither is it merely an elegant ornamental design (C 206–7, 259): instead design, in music as in art more generally, serves to convey an *immanent* world which is the soul of the individual artist (C 339–40, 508; cf. EA 365).

The most dramatic case of dialectical elaboration is, however, the one that will form the basis of chapter 3. Thesis: The problems of selfhood are solved, thanks to the discovery of an atemporal "true Self" (*adoration perpétuelle*). Antithesis: Personal identity is impossible, because people change so radically over time (*bal de têtes*). Synthesis: Unified selfhood is possible, but must incorporate the diachronic selves; the "true Self" must be supplemented by a "total Self" (*finale*). (Compare Jauss 259 and 277 on the movement from *temps retrouvé* through *temps écoulé* to *temps incorporé*.)

75. "I feel that there is much to be said for the Celtic belief that the souls of those whom we have lost are held captive in some inferior being, in an animal, in a plant, in some inanimate object" (S 59). Certain critics take this as Proust's own view—Gilles Deleuze, for example, writes that "Proust favors 'the Celtic belief that the souls of those we have lost are imprisoned in some inferior being, in an animal, a plant, an inanimate thing'" (89)—but it does not even appear to be the last statement of *Marcel* on the subject, let alone that of Proust. Only two pages further on, Marcel realizes that "the truth I am seeking lies not in the cup but in myself" (S 61); and his later lament that "eternal duration is promised no more to men's works than to men" (TR 524; cf. C 240) seems to undermine the metaphysical foundation on which the "Celtic belief" is built. Surely the last mentioned is, as Shattuck (145–46) and Curtius (38) have speculated, no more than a figure of speech.

76. This, for Vincent Descombes, is the implicit principle accounting for Proust's selection of genre. Descombes's truly ingenious idea is that there must be a specifically novelistic philosophy, a philosophy that would require (or at least justify) the use of a narrative form for its transmission (13, 78). In general, "The *philosophy of the novel* is that thought . . . is clearer . . . if it is converted into a relationship among characters" (272); in particular, the philosophy of *Proust's* novel is the additional idea that knowledge is acquired gradually, "beginning with illusions, with beliefs that are rectified little by little" (80). "The novelist shows that life is an apprenticeship" (246), because no knowledge can be had without preliminary error (cf. 241, 267). Space prevents me from going into the powerful argument in any detail.

77. "From the standpoint of natural history . . . everything about it seemed to me imbued with beauty" (SG 38). (The English has "instinct" here for "empreint," but this must be a typographical error.)

78. An example of an idea that "carries in itself its possible refutation" is given to us by Swann: "it struck him that if, like so many other men, he had been poor, humble, deprived, forced to accept any work that might be offered to him, or tied down by parents or by a wife, he might have been obliged to part from Odette . . . and he said to himself: 'People don't know when they're happy. One is never as unhappy as one thinks.' But he reflected that . . . he would sacrifice his work, his pleasures, his friends, in fact the whole of his life to the daily expectation of a meeting which, if it occurred, could bring him no happiness . . . and he said to himself that people did not know when they were unhappy, that one is never as happy as one thinks" (S 504).

79. I am indebted to Erin Carlston for this insight.

80. On Tadié's view, "every generality . . . is subjective, fictional" (1971: 423; my translation). Cf. Nicola Luckhurst, who characterizes all of the novel's maxims as "provisional" (22). Other critics feel that "almost any theory can be set up by careful . . . choice of quotations" (Brée 1951: 67), that "one can demonstrate almost anything by quoting from the *Search*" (Shattuck 124). I do not share these sentiments.

81. As Cohn puts it (78), it is hard to imagine an author constructing such an elaborate philosophical system for a fictional character without having *any* investment in it him- or herself.

82. In order for a "reliability gap" to open up between author and narrator, explains Tamar Yacobi, "the reader must encounter some incongruity" (346). Absent such infelicities, readers positing unreliability would surely lay themselves open to charges of arbitrariness, if not willfulness.

83. Roger Shattuck reads at least the *Captive* section ironically (103); similarly, Gilles Deleuze refuses to take seriously the idea of individuation by perspective, with the result that he is forced into rather byzantine strategies for the reintegration of a disintegrated world (148–50). As for Martha Nussbaum, she simply omits the theories on art altogether from her discussion of selfhood in Proust, a discussion which suffers considerably as a result, becoming far gloomier than it need be (1990: 271–74). And Vincent Descombes, finally, believes he can find counterevidence within the *Recherche* itself (209). I respond to this last claim in chapter 1.

84. Howard Moss offers the most concise statement of the view: "We have just read, of course, the very work Marcel is about to undertake. Like *Finnegans Wake*, *Remembrance of Things Past* is its own self-sealing device. Circular in structure, its end leads us back to its beginning" (109).

85. Bales believes that "these principles which the Narrator proposes to adopt in his forthcoming venture have been the selfsame ones which have underpinned the novel we have just read, that is Proust's" (17). For reasons I am about to spell out, this does not seem convincing to me.

86. See also Bersani 1965: 244, Descombes 5, Gross 379, Blanchot 23. My translation for Rousset and Warning.

87. Given its position almost at the incipit of Marcel's writing life, it is tempting to understand the importance of *Un amour de Swann* not in terms of its content—that is, not because the events of Swann's life prefigure certain events in Marcel's—but in terms of its form: Marcel writes it as a warm-up, so to speak, for his own autobiography.

88. On this very complicated issue, there are two schools of thought. One, espoused by Gareth Steel in his indispensable *Chronology and Time in "A la recherche du temps perdu"* (4, 166, 171), holds that the text we have before us has (fictionally) taken time to write, and that its narrator has evolved in the course of writing it. This is also my own position. (Brée seems to believe something similar: see 1969: 19.)

The alternative theory is that the time of narration is a single "instant intemporel" (Tadié 1971: 32; cf. Bersani 1965: 244), and that there is only one, stable, unchanging narrator responsible for the entirety of the tale we have before us. The Bois episode may *in reality* have been written in 1913, says Gérard Genette, but *within the fiction* it is supposed to coincide with the post-matinée moment: "this passage, written in 1913[, is] fictively (diegetically) contemporaneous with the final narrating, and therefore later than the war" (1980: 69n87). According to Genette, the Bois scene would simply be another instance of the narrator hiding behind the voice of the character. Just as the narrator brazenly informs us that Albertine's mole is on her chin (BG 578) even though he knows it is really on her upper lip (BG 624–65), so too he presents as objective fact what is merely the point of view of his former self on the Bois de Boulogne and the irrevocable passage of time: "Proust was anxious to tune the narrator's discourse to the hero's 'errors'" (1980: 223–24). But Genette's account is scarcely plausible. For in the mole instance, narrator and character are separated by decades; in the Bois, by contrast, the distance is at most two months (since the visit took place "this November," all we have—if that—is the space between November 1 and December 31). The narrator cannot be "tuning his discourse" to that of the protagonist, because he *is* the protagonist.

As a result, I do not believe Genette can be right that readers are supposed to consider the concluding pages of the first volume contemporaneous with the concluding pages of the last volume, to imagine that the "tableau of the Bois de Boulogne 'today' . . . is obviously very close to the moment of narrating" (1980: 69). However strongly Duncan Large may concur (244), the "today" of the Bois de Boulogne is not the moment closest in time to Marcel's entry into his vocation as a writer. That "aujourd'hui" (cf. I:414) clearly predates the "aujourd'hui même" (IV:622) of the Guermantes library, which itself predates the actual commencement of writing (TR 518).

89. The madeleine episode takes place late in Marcel's life—"for a long time I used to go to bed early" is *not* a reference to his childhood—but considerably in advance of the *matinée Guermantes*, the latter's revelations emerging "much later on" ("bien plus tard," I:47). Exactly where it falls within the novel's internal chronology is, however, an extremely complicated question, and I address it further in chapter 3. (For Marcel's protracted stays in two separate *maisons de santé*, see TR 47 and 238.)

90. The early-to-bed Marcel and the post-madeleine Marcel are Muller's "intermediate subjects" (see Muller 19, 36–37; Genette cites Muller at 1980: 44, 156).

91. "Something not unlike my grandmother's illness itself happened to me shortly afterwards [i.e., after the *matinée*], *when I had still not started to work on my book*" (TR 518; my emphasis).

92. Compare Steel 166, 175. Two of the most important prolepses run as follows: "if, in the course of time, I did discover the kind of pleasure and disquiet which I had just felt once again, and if one evening—too late, but then for all time—I fastened myself to it, of those trees [at Hudimesnil] themselves I was never to know what they had been trying to give me" (BG 407); "I felt . . . an en-

thusiasm which might have borne fruit had I remained alone and would thus have saved me the detour of many wasted years through which I was yet to pass before the invisible vocation of which this book is the history declared itself" (GW 544).

Intriguingly, Genette does not notice the second prolepsis. "It is . . . with respect to the experience of involuntary memory, and the literary vocation connected to it[,] that Proust was most careful in handling the focalization, forbidding himself to give any premature sign," he writes (1980: 200); "the suspense has been built up for a long time by a focalization that on this point was very rigorous." Even more fascinatingly, Proust himself seems to overlook it: "the only thing I do not say of the narrator-protagonist is that he becomes a writer in the end" (Corr. 19:647).

93. TR 382, 167. Cf. Tadié 1971: 376, Genette 1980: 68.

94. "Certes, il est bien d'autres erreurs de nos sens, on a vu que divers épisodes de ce récit me l'avaient prouvé, qui faussent pour nous l'aspect réel de ce monde. Mais enfin je pourrais à la rigueur, dans la transcription plus exacte que je m'efforcerais de donner, ne pas changer la place des sons, m'abstenir de les détacher de leur cause à côté de laquelle l'intelligence les situe après coup, bien que faire chanter doucement la pluie au milieu de la chambre et tomber en déluge dans la cour l'ébullition de notre tisane ne dût pas être en somme plus déconcertant que ce qu'ont fait si souvent les peintres quand ils peignent, très près ou très loin de nous, selon que les lois de la perspective . . . et la première illusion du regard nous les font apparaitre, une voile ou un pic que le raisonnement déplacera ensuite de distances quelquefois énormes" (IV:622).

The key sentence is admittedly somewhat opaque. While it insists that Marcel's novel will resist the temptation to impressionism and seek to offer a "transcription plus exacte" of "l'aspect réel de ce monde," diligently steering clear of at least some of the errors we are always likely to make in daily life ("je m'*efforcerais*"), it also goes on to defend impressionist novelistic practices in general. For my part, however, I am unable (after innumerable rereadings) to see the concessive as trumping the main clause.

95. The *récit*-narrator's unshakeable confidence: "At a much later point in this story, we shall have occasion to see this kind of contradiction expressed in clearer terms" (BG 708; cf. BG 278 and elsewhere). The *oeuvre*-inventor's relentless hesitancy: "was there still time and was I still in a fit condition to undertake the task?" (TR 511); "How could I not be anxious, seeing that nothing was yet begun and that . . . my hour might . . . strike almost at once?" (TR 512); "should I have time to exploit [the treasures of my mind]?" (TR 514); "Supposing that I were preserved from all accidents of an external kind, might I not nevertheless be robbed of the fruits of this good fortune by some accident occurring within myself . . .?" (TR 516, a fear strengthened by the fact that he does indeed suffer a stroke before beginning to write); "I was embarking upon my labour of construction almost at the point of death. . . . I felt that I no longer possessed the strength to carry out . . . my work" (TR 521); "And I should live in the anxiety of not knowing whether the

master of my destiny might not prove less indulgent than the Sultan Shahriyar, whether in the morning, when I broke off my story, he would consent to a further reprieve and permit me to resume my narrative the following evening" (TR 524); "for me was there still time? Was it not too late? And I had to ask myself not only: 'Is there still time?' but also: 'Am I well enough?'" (TR 525). The *Recherche* ends with a sentence that redeems its beginning ("Longtemps"/"dans le Temps"), promises a future masterpiece, and yet also warns us, at the same time, that the masterpiece may never appear: "So, *if I were given long enough to accomplish my work*, I should not fail . . . to describe men as occupying so considerable a place . . . in Time" (TR 531–32; my emphasis).

The narrator's anxiety may easily be understood, when we consider that he is starting out on a literary career as an "old man" (TR 350; cf. Shattuck 151). Proust, by contrast, had already published a volume of poetry and short stories, *Les plaisirs et les jours*, at the age of twenty-five (in 1896)—Marcel's comparable manuscript, which he refers to as mere *pages de collégien* (IV:618), never sees the light of day—and had outlined the *Recherche* in his thirty-seventh year (1908); he had, in fact, completed a full draft of the opening and conclusion, right down to the remarks about the fear of death (MPG 237–39), not long after his fortieth birthday. He clearly wishes Marcel's life to be neatly divided into a portion spent almost entirely on worldly activity and a portion, after the epiphanies of *Le temps retrouvé*, spent almost entirely on writing. Whereas Proust continued to go into society during the writing of the *Recherche* (Hayman 421, Shattuck 8), even when so ill that he nearly fell down the stairs, Marcel has a fall *before* he puts pen to paper (TR 518), and thereafter, we presume, steers clear of the *monde* (see SG 518, F 772, TR 435–36). As on other occasions, then, Proust borrows from his own experience to feed the story of Marcel, but makes significant changes.

96. Jauss, for one, does not seem to notice that Marcel has made a start on his *livre à venir* (279). Genette, by contrast, makes the appropriate distinction: "the book Marcel then begins to write *in the story* cannot legitimately be identified with the one Marcel has then almost finished writing *as narrative*—and which is the *Recherche* itself" (1980: 224). (As we saw, however, Genette believes that the future work, when it is completed, will turn out to be identical to the *Recherche*.)

97. Duncan Large (244) agrees that the novel is not "recursive" like *Finnegans Wake*, but his reasons are very different from mine. For Large as for Muller, the problem is that there is no solution of continuity between Marcel character and Marcel narrator—the one never quite reaches the other, so that the character can at no time actually become a narrator, and Marcel can never write his memoir (which Large unquestioningly equates with the future *oeuvre*). As his sole evidence for the "asymptotic" relationship between character and narrator, Muller adduces the fact that "the verbs from the conclusion of *Le temps retrouvé* are all in the past tense" (49–50; my translation): if the character really did turn into the narrator, so the theory runs, he would at that point presumably avail himself of the present tense. Muller's argument, which Large lifts directly, is frankly rather

mystifying. Those who keep journals typically describe their life in the past tense, albeit referring to events only hours old (this is precisely the situation at the end of the first volume and the end of the last volume, when Marcel refers back to extremely recent occurrences). And even those who fashion autobiographies occasionally decide to include, toward the end, the moment at which they started writing (in Sartre's *Nausea*, Roquentin unstartlingly concludes one of his entries by noting "I wrote" [193]). Are we really to say of these people that they never become narrators? There seems to be a confusion here between an event and its description, between the act of becoming a narrator and the act of *mentioning* becoming a narrator.

98. More dramatically (and perhaps less controversially), *The Magic Lantern* will also excise all the aesthetic meditations which *My Life* is happy to retain: "I should not have to trouble myself with the various literary theories which had at moments perplexed me. . . . Authentic art has no use for proclamations of this kind, it accomplishes its work in silence. . . . A work in which there are theories is like an object which still has its price-tag on it" (TR 278-79). As might be expected, most scholars have read these statements as something of an embarrassment for Proust. There is, however, no need to do so, as long as we remember that they are promises of a future project (Marcel's *Magic Lantern*) and not descriptions of a completed project (Proust's *Recherche*).

99. To use Arthur Danto's term, *My Life* and the *Recherche* are "indiscernibles," rather like a pile of bricks in a museum and a similar pile of bricks on a building site. See Danto 1981, chaps. 1 and 2. I am grateful to Alexander Nehamas for drawing my attention to Danto's argument.

100. Cf. Derwent May: "in no way does [Marcel], as a character in the novel, *create* those other people. Proust creates them; that is the difference" (68). "When 'I'—Marcel the narrator—pretends to remember, it is the author imagining," as Louis Martin-Chauffier puts it (62; my translation). See also Roland Barthes on the names of characters and places, "coded" by the author, "decoded" by the hero (1972: 128). Interestingly, Marcel shows (in another context) that he is aware of the distinction: "my mind would have been capable of creating the most difficult names. Unfortunately, it was not called upon to create but to reproduce" (SG 67–68).

101. Many have, indeed, attempted to explain Proust's selection of the madeleine. Ronald Hayman lists a few of them, apparently in order of increasing outlandishness: "the word 'madeleine' has religious associations, while his description . . . suggests the female orifice, and, for Serge Doubrovsky, Proust's emphasis on the 'little drop' of limeflower scent . . . insistently recalls the drop of sperm mentioned in the earlier account of masturbation, which is associated with repressed desire for the mother" (300). My own view is that the madeleine, with its "religious folds" (S 63), reinforces the idea of a secular communion, tea and cake replacing wine and wafer, involuntary memory replacing religious epiphany, presence to self replacing presence to the divine.

102. This sentence is extraordinary, for a number of reasons. It appears to consist in a narrator pronouncing himself, and his entire world (give or take one family), imaginary. (I explain below how we can resolve this paradox.) To make matters worse, however, *part* of that world—and the most insignificant part, a set of characters who are mentioned once and then forgotten—nonetheless escapes intact. What are we to make of the statement that "only the millionaire cousins of Françoise . . . are real people who exist"? How can real people be cousins of a fictional entity? Finally, it cannot even be true that the Larivières are the only imports from the actual world, since, to take one example, Proust uses the well-known Dr. Dieulafoy as a character in the novel.

103. Spitzer (437) and Deleuze (130) take these to be Proust's own sentiments, rather than those of his narrator. Picon goes even further (203), stating that the central contribution of Proust is a tradition of creation-free novels. He does not, however, discuss the fact that the *Recherche* is itself, in good measure, a work of imagination. For an argument similar to mine, by contrast, see the "Notice" of Rey and Rogers (IV:1174–5).

104. In Proust, the term *septuor* does not appear to mean a piece for seven players—a septet—but rather a piece whose primary theme has seven *notes*. Thus Vinteuil's masterwork can be a "septuor," even though it is a "pièce pour *dix* instruments" (III:767; my emphasis), because it is "a song on seven notes" (C 333).

105. Derwent May also points out that Marcel's aesthetics do not allow for novelistic production; yet he ends up, puzzlingly enough, deciding that "'Marcel's art' is in no way to be set against Proust's art" (68, 69, 75).

106. My view here departs (for once) from that of Leo Bersani, who writes that "the ambiguity in his contradictory statements that he is writing about his own life and that he has invented everything in his work is not satisfactorily resolved by attributing the first statement to Marcel and the second to Proust" (1965: 248).

107. See, e.g., Warning 16. Cf. Ellison, who considers the *Recherche* a form of therapy for a sick Proust who "does not wish to know or understand consciously" what he is doing (166). Paul de Man's position is complicated; I discuss it in chapter 1.

108. My translation of Genette. Cf. Bersani: "The narrator's theories have not really caught up with his practice. . . . some of the theoretical positions that inspired the narrator's work are made obsolete by the work itself" (1965: 10, 18). Similarly, Duncan Large feels "that in general the sophistication of Proust's novel surpasses the relatively traditional philosophical statements it contains—in other words, that he himself underestimated his achievement" (62). Yet as we saw above, Large also feels that Proust *overestimated* his own achievement, so there is some ambiguity here, just as there is in de Man.

109. Cf. the 1895 essay "Chardin et Rembrandt": "if Chardin did do everything I have said, he never intended it, and it is even highly probable that he never realized it" (EA 78).

110. The last paragraph—last on Bernard de Fallois's reconstruction, at any rate—hints at a future composition, but says nothing of the narrator deciding to write it, let alone of him having set to work. Indeed, it is cast in the plural and in the hypothetical mode, referring to "the fine things *we* shall write *if* we have talent enough" (BSB 201; my emphasis).

111. According to Large, Proust wrote the *Recherche* in order to fashion himself through writing, just as Nietzsche wrote *Ecce Homo* in order to give unity and justification to his own personality. Both attempts ended in failure, since each succeeded only in forging a fictional character, not an actual person: "the unified 'Nietzsche' who has become what he is in *Ecce homo* is just as much a textual construct as is Proust's narrator, and their . . . dreams of giving birth to themselves remain fantasies of control" (209). Large's accusation stands in strange tension with his claim, a mere two pages earlier, that "*Ecce homo* is a testament to Nietzsche's own ability . . . 'to transform every "It was" into an "I wanted it thus!"'" (207); it also overlooks the difference in genre between autobiography (the "I" in *Ecce Homo* belongs to Nietzsche) and fiction (the "I" in Proust belongs to Marcel).

112. We saw above that this is also Proust's own view. Note that the artworks we produce should, of course, not resemble the *Recherche* in terms of their *content*. Proust wishes to be what Nehamas calls a "second-order model" (1998: 124, 185–86): we are to be like him, as it were, by being different. In Marcel's words, "you can make a new version of what you love only by first renouncing it" (TR 525; cf. EA 335). I return to this point in chapter 3.

113. Drawing on Gilles Deleuze, Paul Ricoeur describes the *Recherche* as an "apprentissage de signes," i.e., a process by which Marcel learns to manipulate the signs (of nature, society, love, and art) that will ultimately allow him to "translate" his impressions into language and thus produce his *oeuvre*. (See Ricoeur 1992: 145, 150.) I would add that the *Recherche* is also, and perhaps more importantly, an apprenticeship in signs for its *readers*, allowing them to gain practical knowledge of how to read their own minds (TR 322) at the same time that they gain knowledge-by-acquaintance of the mind of Proust. And perhaps this is the only way to explain the necessity of the novel's length. Marcel does not require three thousand pages in order to *describe* his apprenticeship in signs, however long it may have *taken*; but it may be that *we* require them, and the patient attitude which they inspire, in order to complete *ours*.

For training, compare Descombes: "The philosophy of the novel is not to be sought in this or that thought content, but rather in the fact that the novel requires of the reader a *reformation of the understanding*. A novel, in order to be philosophical, does not need to communicate anything at all. What it does need is the philosophical power to exact *intellectual and moral work*" (35).

114. In mathematics, an infinite sequence is defined by two elements: (a) the first term in the series; (b) the rule for generating term $n+1$ from term n. Thus, for example, if we start from 1 and divide by two each time, we have the sequence 1, $1/2, 1/4 \ldots 1/2^{n-1}$, famous from Zeno's bisection paradox.

115. See Anderson and Landy, esp. 33–34.

Chapter 1

1. The Moncrieff/Kilmartin/Enright translation has "always." It also divides the single paragraph into two, for reasons that are not entirely clear.

2. Here, Marcel allows Mme de Villeparisis's carriage to carry the trees out of sight. At Martinville, by contrast, Marcel is captive on the front seat of the coach, unable to talk to his mother and father, who are sitting inside, or to the coachman, who is "little inclined for conversation." With nothing else to do, Marcel is "obliged . . . to attempt to recapture the vision of [his] steeples" (S 254–55), however tempted he is to shirk his duty ("I did not know the reason for the pleasure I had felt on seeing them upon the horizon, and the business of trying to discover that reason seemed to me irksome; I wanted to store away in my mind those shifting, sunlit planes and, for the time being, to think of them no more" [S 254]).

3. For a connection drawn between madeleine and steeples, see TR 255, TR 273; for "foundation-stones," see C 347 (cf. BG 404, GW 751, C 505, TR 509); and for the "invisible vocation," see GW 544. For the progress of the written account, see BG 35, GW 474, C 6, F 766, and F 788.

4. Thus Justin O'Brien (1948: 51), Ernst Curtius ("a little of the content they were hiding now appears in the light," 32), Luc Fraisse ("Behind that skin, what lay hidden was true reality, the essence of things," 43), and Chabot and Michaudon (35, 39) are all taken in by Marcel's claim to have extracted the essence of the steeples. (My translations for Curtius and Fraisse.) Other critics have, to be sure, noted the mysteriously underwhelming nature of the passage. Alexander Nehamas, for instance, writes that there is no depth, only surface, to be had (1987: 279–80); he goes on to claim that what is at stake is an imbrication of this surface within the narrative of a life—at which point my argument departs from his, as will shortly be apparent.

5. "My grandmother," writes Marcel, "loved grandeur, and . . . used to enjoy gazing at the steeple of Saint-Hilaire" (C 547; cf. TR 297–98); "she gazed up at . . . the worn old stones of which the setting sun now illumined no more than the topmost pinnacles and which, at the point where they entered that sunlit zone . . . , seemed to have mounted suddenly far higher, to have become truly remote" (S 87–88). Although the *Recherche* has her contemplating a single spire, in an earlier draft (BSB 184) she is looking at a *pair* of steeples, so that the link to Marcel at Martinville is even clearer.

6. SG 17–18. For Charlus's apparently inexplicable behavior, see S 199; BG 452–54, 462–66, 471–74; GW 386–402, 759–76.

7. This very fact—the juxtaposition, that is, of two stylistically heterogeneous treatments of the steeples episode—represents a crucial divergence from the "Impressions de route en automobile" that Proust published in the *Figaro* in November 1907 (the piece is reproduced in PM under the title "Journées en automobile"). Thanks to the reduplication, the *Recherche* version, unlike its precursor, hints at what exactly it is up to. Further, various distractions—an additional pair of churches, a set of maxims on time, and some similes other than those modify-

ing the steeples—have been removed, throwing the essential strategy of the passage into maximal relief.

8. Cf. Bersani: "the passage is, in fact, not very impressive, but it clearly suggests that the 'new truth' which brings Marcel such intense pleasure consists of metaphorical equivalents of the external scene. The steeples are compared to 'three birds perched upon the plain, motionless and conspicuous in the sunlight'; to 'three golden pivots.' . . . These images are what was hidden behind the steeples" (1965: 228). Similarly, Gaëtan Picon writes of the steeples passage that "nothing in it teaches us anything at all. . . . What grips the narrator are, instead, the metaphorical possibilities of these steeples: they are three birds, three golden pivots, three young girls of a legend. . . . nothing suggests that the value of the experience lies anywhere other than in this analogical . . . , 'relational' abundance" (165–66; my translation). Compare also Jean Milly (132–34) and perhaps Charles du Bos, though the latter's analysis is rather more cryptic: "what [the steeples] were hiding . . . is the call we transmit to our second self [*notre réalité seconde*]" (75).

9. S 253–54, 256; my emphasis. I have had to modify the English translation, since it unaccountably introduces the optical-illusion style here, entirely disdaining to translate "avaient l'air."

10. Fascinatingly, while the version Marcel publishes in the *Figaro* contains an explicit reference to the work of Elstir (F 788), what we are given to read in *Swann's Way*, after "a slight revision here and there" (S 255), says nothing about the painter: could it be that Marcel expunged all mention of his model under the pressure of an excessive anxiety of influence?

As for the article *Proust* published in the *Figaro*, it speaks of J. M. W. Turner (see PM 98). The Turner-Elstir connection makes at least local sense, given that Turner is famous for saying "my business is to draw what I see and not what I know is there" (cited by Proust at PM 178).

11. Cf. Bersani: "The primacy of impressions over objects is often rendered by sentence structure. The reader may, for example, be forced to experience the errors of perception before the rectifying but subjectively less interesting truths. . . . [And] certain syntactical habits . . . express more subtly Marcel's most profound intentions. There are numerous sentences in the novel in which pronouns, adjectives, or subordinate clauses precede their antecedents, or the words or clauses which they modify. We follow what is often a long development around an object of description before we know what the object is" (1965: 234).

12. "The hill which had been visible on the right of the Seine subsided [*s'abaissa*] by degrees" (*Sentimental Education* 2). With this novel, writes Proust, "the revolution is complete: what up until Flaubert had been action now becomes impression. Objects have as much life as people, for it is reasoning that later assigns external causes to every visual phenomenon" (EA 284–85).

Vincent Descombes notes the connection: "Marcel, in his inspired description of the steeples of Martinville, observes certain rules of style that Proust has identified in Flaubert, so that it is the steeples that change position, relative to one another, and not the observer who changes his point of view" (234). Descombes does so, however, in order to bolster his thesis that Marcel's claims about perspective should not be taken seriously. According to him, the only difference between the narrative and the prose poem is that the latter has added a little seasoning, in the form of mechanically applied literary forms borrowed from elsewhere; thus the style merely gives literary refinement to the initial version, rather than conveying any prelinguistic impression. Descombes's argument only holds up, of course, if one overlooks the series of *images* that also form part of the steeples composition. I shall turn to these in a moment.

13. Once again, I have amended the translation. The Modern Library version, "Elstir attempted to wrest from what he had just felt what he already knew," is ambiguous enough to lead some people to imagine that "wrest" connotes "salvage" rather than "extirpate," and that Elstir's aim is to reproduce the already known, rather than the newly felt. Thus Rawlinson (6): "Feeling must be transformed into thought, as 'Elstir attempted to wrest from what he had just felt what he already knew' . . . the particular impression must be 'translated' or 'converted' into the general law or form which it represents."

14. Chabot and Michaudon (36), like Brian Rogers (2001: 94), see the steeples' isolation as reflecting a sentiment peculiar to Marcel, namely the anticipatory anxiety he feels at the approach of a night that may or may not include a goodnight kiss (S 257–58). The loneliness of the spires would, on this view (which is not mine), be comparable to the clearly projected sadness of Golo: "Golo stopped for a moment and listened *sadly* to the accompanying patter read aloud by my great-aunt" (S 10; my emphasis).

15. Optical illusions are shared distortions, like historical watersheds: people go around saying that everything has changed since World War I, for example, when this is not really the case (TR 53, TR 139). Metaphors, by contrast, are idiosyncratic distortions, like *personal* watersheds: what marks a major turning point for Marcel—the moment of falling out of love with the Duchess—means nothing at all to anyone else, including her. See TR 469–73.

16. Céline's Ferdinand Bardamu: "From there you can see the whole valley, and in the distance a village in its hollow, huddled round a church tower planted like a nail in the reddening sky" (351).

17. Leo Bersani and Vincent Descombes are notable exceptions. Thus Bersani: "one person's 'optical illusions' cannot consistently be the same as someone else's. These errors of perception . . . reveal the existence of a particular point of view on the world. They are also metaphors" (1965: 207).

Bersani's view is, if anything, even rarer outside of Proust criticism. For in the extensive literature on metaphor, whose surface I can barely begin to scratch here, much is said about the vehicle shedding light on the tenor (Moran 110), or, more generally, betraying something about the workings of language (de Man) and the structure of thought (Lakoff and Johnson). (I borrow the terms *tenor* and *vehicle* from Richards 96.) Relatively little, by contrast, is said about idiosyncratic coinages that have no ambition of becoming standard.

18. Cf. Anderson 1998: 6: "A perspective painting works by representing the relations among objects. . . . Similarly, our cognitive perspectives determine only relations among the objects they posit, and not the properties of mutually independent things in themselves."

19. When the *Recherche* refers to Kant, it tends to invoke the second *Critique*, whether the categorical imperative (C 376) or the distinction between free and unfree worlds (GW 654, BG 107). But Proust's article on Flaubert alludes to the Kant of the first *Critique*, "with his Categories [and] his theories of Knowledge and of the Reality of the external world" (EA 282), and there is at least one statement in the novel that carries a similar epistemological flavor: "it is not only the physical world that differs from the aspect in which we see it; . . . all reality is perhaps equally dissimilar from what we believe ourselves to be directly perceiving . . . , just as the trees, the sun and the sky would not be the same as what we see if they were apprehended by creatures having eyes differently constituted from ours" (GW 81).

For "creatures having eyes differently constituted from ours," compare section A 42/B 59 of the first *Critique*. "What may be the case with objects in themselves," Kant writes here, "remains entirely unknown to us. We are acquainted with nothing except our way of perceiving them, which is peculiar to us, and which therefore does not necessarily pertain to every being, though to be sure it pertains to every human being." (A nonhuman type of being he often has in mind is God: see B 135, B 138–39, and B 145.)

20. This is Bersani's point: "metaphorical connections among apparently dissimilar incidents provide a literary documentation of the unity of personality. . . . To describe Franco-German relations in terms of his [Marcel's] relation with Albertine, and vice versa, is essentially to reveal the persistent concerns he brings to both types of experience" (1965: 122, 237). (For one example of Franco-German relations being linked to relations of love—both hetero- and homosexual—and even to snobbery, see the passage from TR 188–89 cited in my introduction.) Perhaps it is too strong to say that "in the comparisons he makes the narrator reduces the world to illustrations and repetitions of his own needs" (Bersani 1965: 237), since interests and values are also involved, and since the metaphors are as much an enrichment as an impoverishment of experience, but in its main lines my analysis parallels that of Bersani.

The Proustian view of the literary image bears certain similarities to that of the surrealists, who may, in turn, be drawing on Freud's account of "condensation" [*Verdichtung*] in dreams. (See Breton 31 and 49, and Freud 1983 [1900]: 218–27 for a classic example of "dream-work.") As Freud elsewhere explains (1953 [1900–1901]: 651), the "products of dream-condensation . . . are emphasizing in an effectively abbreviated form some common characteristic of the objects which they are thus combining. The content of the dream merely says as it were: 'All these things have an element x in common.'"

21. GM III:12, TI VI:5, 7. Nietzsche, confirms Arthur Danto (1965: 40), "does not contend, as Kant seemingly does, that a certain determined set of con-

cepts lies inherent in the human mind and is invariant as to differences between human beings. Rather, Nietzsche sees conceptual schemes as varying from society to society and possibly . . . from person to person." Cf. Anderson 1998 on Nietzsche, and de Lattre 2:175–76 on Proust.

22. In his essay on Flaubert, Proust makes it clear that artistic craft is a matter of turning an unconscious "vision" into conscious style: "Given that these grammatical singularities translate a new vision [of the world], how much effort must have been required to fix that vision properly, to move it *out of the unconscious and into the conscious . . .*!" (EA 288; my emphasis). Cf. BG 588: "the artist has gradually evolved [*dégagé*] the law, the formula of his unconscious gift."

23. This is perhaps what explains Marcel's tantalizing and perplexing hint that the inspiration behind the Martinville prose poem is just as musical as it is literary, that the poem is in a sense the verbal equivalent of a sonata. In the sentence that introduces it, Marcel explains that he wrote it in language because the inspiration came to him "in the form of words which gave me pleasure," even though deep down "what lay hidden behind the steeples of Martinville must be something analogous to a pretty phrase" (S 255). Later, he connects it to Vinteuil's *septuor*—"nothing resembled more closely than some such *phrase* of Vinteuil the peculiar pleasure which I had felt at certain moments in my life, when gazing, for instance, at the steeples of Martinville" (C 504–5; my emphasis; cf. TR 272, BSB 201)—confirming the fact that the "pretty phrase" of the first statement is a pretty *musical* phrase (after all, the steeples passage cannot be "analogous to" a *linguistic* phrase, since it already *is* one). What Marcel is saying is that the aesthetic stimulus produced by the steeples, though it "fram[es] itself in words in [his] head" (S 255), is at bottom more like a melody than a manuscript. For if aesthetic creation is a matter of accessing and giving form to the deepest realm of one's individual nature, if that realm is equivalent to one's perspective, and if perspective is crucially a matter of combinations, then a genre which is all combination and no semantic content is perhaps the aesthetic genre par excellence.

24. "These ambiguities, redundancies, and deficiencies recall those attributed by Dr. Franz Kuhn to a certain Chinese encyclopedia called the *Heavenly Emporium of Benevolent Knowledge*. In its distant pages it is written that animals are divided into (a) those that belong to the emperor; (b) embalmed ones; (c) those that are trained; (d) suckling pigs; (e) mermaids; (f) fabulous ones; (g) stray dogs; (h) those that are included in this classification; (i) those that tremble as if they were mad; (j) innumerable ones; (k) those drawn with a very fine camel's-hair brush; (l) etc.; (m) those that have just broken the flower vase; (n) those that at a distance resemble flies" (Borges 1999: 231). Borges's encyclopedia is probably best known via Michel Foucault, who alludes to it at the start of *Les mots et les choses*.

25. Descombes's argument runs as follows. It cannot be a question of translating a nonverbal feeling into language, he writes, since the feeling is in every case contained within an "inner book of unknown symbols" (TR 274), and books, of course, are already made up of words (222). So when it comes down to it, Marcel is not rendering impressions into expressions but merely one type of discourse,

i.e., conversation, into another, i.e., literature (230, 237–38). When Marcel makes his famous remark about "translation" (at TR 290–91), the examples he cites all involve casual responses, like "zut," which need to be refined into art.

· None of this, it seems to me, really counts as evidence. The "inner book" is just a metaphor, and not even an ideal one for Descombes's purposes, since one can hardly say that conversation is made up of "unknown symbols," of "hieroglyphs" difficult to decipher (TR 275). How could one translate an exclamation like "zut" into something more interesting if one did not possess additional information— information, that is, about the state of mind which provoked it? No, such remarks are no hieroglyphs. They may indeed require *rectification* (TR 291), but what is to be *translated* is the original impression, something that stands outside of language. Literary discourse is not a translation of conversational discourse; instead both are renditions, one adequate and the other inadequate, of the same extralinguistic impression. Thus writing, for Marcel, is "the rectification of an oblique interior discourse (*which deviates . . . from the first and central impression*) until it merges with the straight line which the impression ought to have produced" (TR 291; my emphasis).

26. Descombes distinguishes among "Marcel" (the character), "Proust the theorist" (the narrator), and "Proust the novelist" (the implied author). "Proust the novelist," on Descombes's view, produces a work that is far more sophisticated than the one proposed by "Proust the theorist." Thus Descombes is quite charitable: where there is a discrepancy between theory (Marcel's statements in *Time Regained*, for instance) and practice (Proust's novel), Descombes interprets it as the unerring instinct of a brilliant fiction writer, only betrayed by a limited intellectual understanding of his craft (21, 233). There are, however, plenty of indications that Proust is in control of the ironies in his text (and indeed Descombes cites some: see 28, 32, and 65). Proust may, as I argued in the introduction and will suggest again at the end of this chapter, be *consciously* constructing a novel that is smarter than its narrator, not just doing it by accident.

27. "If we believed in the perspectivism of Proust's own doctrine, we could look for as many perspectives as there are characters in the novel. There would be the narrator's point of view, the point of view of Charlus, the point of view of Mme Verdurin, and so on. And yet the perspectivism actually demonstrated in Proust's novel contains in fact only two perspectives: the perspective of the self . . . and the perspective of society" (Descombes 209).

To most readers of Proust, this will sound like a peculiar thesis. Not only do we receive a strong impression, in the case of characters like Albertine, of the existence of a powerful inner world shaping their experience, but we also have a triumvirate of artists who, as Marcel states and reiterates at some length, have the ability to make that inner world *known*.

Descombes's view obliges him to reject the various passages on art, and also to reduce all situations to that basic type, i.e., to the tension between an individual's deluded perception and the objective truth, "easily discovered by the outside observer" (200). Thus Marcel must be just as big a snob as Legrandin, his aesthetic reasons for enjoying salon life being so many pretexts and excuses (203–5); and Marcel must be just as wrong about Albertine as Swann is about Odette—that is to say, Albertine must be entirely "innocent" (217), running away not in order to indulge in lesbianism but merely (214) in order to finesse a marriage proposal out of Marcel! Descombes's interpretation is, as Marcel would say, "trop simple": "'I was engaged once. But I couldn't quite make up my mind to marry the girl—and anyhow she thought better of it herself, because of my undecided and cantankerous character.' This was, in fact, the *excessively simple* light in which I regarded my adventure with Albertine, now that I saw it only from outside" (TR 23; my emphasis).

28. Contrast the case of Robert with that of Elstir, who has found in a woman the very incarnation of patterns he carries around eternally as "the most intimate part of himself" (BG 586–87, cited in full in the introduction). A mysterious love like Elstir's requires art for its expression (F 593); an infatuation like Robert's, presumably, does not.

29. It is true that at one point Marcel refers to his way of thinking about Rachel as the simple truth: "I had seen stretched to its maximum the distance between objective reality and love (in Rachel, for instance, as she appeared to Saint-Loup and to me, in Albertine as she appeared to me and to Saint-Loup . . .)" (TR 324). But the passage from GW 214 cited above, with its important qualification— "if it can be said that Rachel the tart was more real than the other"—strongly suggests that "objective reality" here should be considered a shorthand, and not taken at face value.

30. It could be objected that imagery in the *Recherche* conveys only the protagonist's perspective, not that of the author. This is quite correct, "but after all metaphor is not the whole of style" (EA 283). I shall return in the coda to the question of Proust's own vision of the world and how the structure of his novel serves to communicate it.

31. I have rendered "instruits" as "trained" rather than "taught."

32. For Descombes, this is a *reductio* of Marcel's perspectivist view: "an understanding of Elstir's manner of seeing is possible only on condition that one *become Elstir.* . . . To see Elstir's canvases is to see the world through Elstir's eyes. But to see the world through Elstir's eyes is to have become Elstir"—which is, of course, impossible (45, 48). Again, Descombes seems to be taking figurative language rather too literally.

33. Even trying on Robert's viewpoint—which is not equivalent to his perspective—requires a "mental effort" on Marcel's part (F 593). While he can picture to himself *intellectually* how Robert sees Rachel, he cannot *experience* the emotion involved; he does not, in fact, fully share Robert's delusion, does not suddenly find Rachel desirable, any more than he finds certain men attractive once he has worked out why they are of interest to the Baron de Charlus (TR 185). Conversely, when Marcel learns how Albertine looks to Robert—which is to say, like the very ordinary person that she is—this does not alter his own sentiments in the slightest, any more than the discovery of Rachel's sordid past would alter those of her admirer.

Thus Marcel on his own feelings: "I who had made a mental effort to add to Rachel all that Saint-Loup had added to her of himself, I now attempted to subtract the contribution of my heart and mind from the composition of Albertine and to picture her to myself as she must appear to Saint-Loup, as Rachel had appeared to me. But how much importance does all this have? Would we give credence to these differences, even if we could see them ourselves?" (F 593). And on those of Robert: "True, if he had now learned that [her favors] had been offered to all the world for a louis, he would have suffered terribly, but would still have given a million francs to keep them, for nothing that he might have learned could have diverted him . . . from the path he had taken and from which that face could appear to him only through the web of the dreams that he had already spun" (GW 211).

Similarly, having learned from Elstir how to perceive land and water as interchangeable, Marcel nonetheless continues to divide the world up into sea and terra firma. In his imagination, the Duchesse de Guermantes remains connected until the end (TR 240) to the "région fluviatile" of her ancestral domain (I:170/S 243), "that land of bubbling streams where the Duchess taught me to fish for trout" (CG 7); his idealized memory of Gilberte, on the other hand, stays forever tied to the Tansonville hawthorns (TR 443).

34. See Deleuze 3–23 et passim. Marcel himself understands his perennial tilting at transcendence, Martinville effort included, as betraying a "fundamental trait" of his character: "I remembered—with pleasure because it showed me that *already in those days I had been the same* and that this type of experience sprang from *a fundamental trait in my character*, but with sadness also when I thought that since that time I had never progressed—that already at Combray I used to fix before my mind for its attention some image which had compelled me to look at it, a cloud, a triangle, *a church spire*, a flower, a stone, because I had the feeling that perhaps beneath these *signs* there lay something of a quite different kind which I must try to discover, some thought which they translated after the fashion of those *hieroglyphic characters*" (TR 272–73; my emphasis).

35. For Brabant see S 10; for Champi, S 56; for Agrigente, CG 592; for La Raspelière, SG 466; for Saint-Euverte, TR 496; and for Guermantes, S 241–47, GW 6, GW 28–30, GW 67, GW 274, GW 514, GW 744–45, GW 779, F 773, TR 240–41, and TR 282, as well as BSB 155–56. For high-society salons, see, e.g., SG 190–91; for actors and actresses in general, S 100–102; for Odette S 104; and for La Berma S 135 and BG 16. For Bergotte, S 129–30; for Elstir, BG 564–613 and GW 573–78; and for Vinteuil, C 331–47. For hawthorns S 193–95 and BG 685; for Hudimesnil BG 404–8; and for pear trees GW 212. For Balbec S 546–50 and F 773; for Doncières GW 122; and for Venice S 556–59, C 531, and C 555–56. For milkmaids BG 319 and C 178–80; for women of the Bois de Boulogne S 593–94; for young girls around Méséglise S 219–22; for *passantes* at Balbec BG 396–97; and for fellow diners in Rivebelle BG 543. For the Putbus chambermaid SG 166, SG 206–8, C 106, and F 693; for "Mlle d'Eporcheville" F 758–65; for Gilberte S 138–39, S 197–200, S 560–86, BG 84–85, BG 90–91, and still at C 173; for the

agate marble S 572; for the Duchesse de Guermantes S 248–51, GW 71–74, and GW 533; for Mlle Stermaria BG 364–66 and GW 525–26; for Albertine BG 558, BG 680–91, GW 479–506, SG 177–82, and SG 267–68; for Andrée SG 699–700, C 15–16, and F 681; for Gisèle BG 637–39; for the *petite bande* BG 505, BG 676, and BG 713–16; and for the thirteen other Balbec women SG 256.

36. "This was the point to which I invariably had to return, to those *beliefs* which for most of the time occupy our souls unbeknown to us, but which for all that are of more importance to our happiness than is the person whom we see, for it is through them that we see [her]" (BG 720); "It is because I *believed* in things and in people while I walked along those paths that the things and the people they made known to me are the only ones that I still take seriously and that still bring me joy" (S 260); "I had no longer a *belief* to infuse into them to give them consistency, unity and life . . . They were just women, in whose elegance I had no *faith*" (S 603); "in moments of musing contemplation of nature . . . we *believe* with the profoundest *faith* in the originality, in the individual existence of the place in which we happen to be" (S 220–21); "my primary, my innermost impulse . . . was my *belief* in the philosophic richness and beauty of the book I was reading . . . , whatever the book might be" (S 115); "since my visits to Elstir, it was on to certain tapestries, certain modern paintings that I had transferred the inner *faith* I had once had in the acting, the tragic art of Berma" (GW 39). My emphasis throughout this note.

37. Thus, in general, "we are attracted by any life which represents for us something *unknown* and strange, by a last illusion still unshattered" (GW 778). More specifically, "the belief that a person has a share in an *unknown* life to which his or her love may win us admission is, of all the prerequisites of love, the one which it values most highly" (S 139). And more specifically still, Marcel sees "in everything that surrounded Gilberte an indefinable quality [*une qualité inconnue*]" (S 591), pertaining to "the *unknown* world of her existence into which I should never penetrate" (S 200; cf. S 577).

It is a similar feature that endows certain proper nouns with their factitious glamour: "I had difficulty in rediscovering in the handsome but too human face of Mme de Guermantes the enigma [*l'inconnu*] of her name" (GW 280). And when it comes to places, likewise, "I did not then represent to myself cities [or] landscapes . . . as more or less attractive pictures, cut out here and there of a substance that was common to them all, but looked on each of them as on an *unknown* thing, different in essence from all the rest, a thing for which my soul thirsted" (S 551). Of Doncières, for example, Marcel recalls feeling that "the life led by the inhabitants of this *unknown* world must, it seemed to me, be a thing of wonder" (GW 122). My emphasis throughout this note.

38. This is the point at which I depart slightly from both Leo Bersani and Gérard Genette, since I do not see Proust (through Marcel) advertising metaphor as an epistemological tool, a device that allows us to see something in the objects compared that had previously remained concealed beneath habitual concepts and names. Genette appears to fault Marcel's images for failing to deliver such

knowledge (1966: 53), while Bersani celebrates them for succeeding in doing so: "In analogies," he writes (1965: 206–7), "one thing tends to be reduced to what makes it similar to another; but the trait they have in common may be a part of the specificity of an object or a feeling which we would never have noticed if we had successfully identified it with . . . the correct name." (Compare also de Souza 153: "these connections serve to bring out the essential nature of the flower.") It seems to me that analogies, under Proust's description, are highly eloquent on the subject of their producer and more or less silent when it comes to the objects compared.

A critic at the opposite end of the spectrum from Genette and Bersani is Rainer Warning: he, for his part, sees the metaphors as illuminating neither the objects nor their perceiver, but instead only the subjectivity of the *reader* (20, 31). In Warning's words, "for Proust as much as for Elstir, metamorphosis means the dissolution of all objectivity into an interminable multiplicity . . . of perspectives" (23). This claim seems easily refuted by the Elstir section of *Within a Budding Grove*.

39. GW 51–52. For names, see S 553–54: "whatever it was that my imagination aspired to . . . I had committed to the safe custody of names."

40. For a more sympathetic approach to the "accumulated metaphors," see Wimmers 85–107.

41. It is as though Proust were here realizing an idea for literature his narrator had already floated in *Contre Sainte-Beuve*: "Imagine a writer nowadays who would have the idea of treating the same theme twenty times over in different lights, and who would feel that he was doing something as deep, as subtle, as powerful, overwhelming, original, and striking as Monet's fifty cathedrals or forty water-lilies" (BSB 138). To be more accurate, Proust had already realized the idea in the 1907 *Figaro* article, "Journées en automobile." The *Figaro* piece, in which the steeples are seen at different times on different days, rather than across the space of a single sunset, is if anything slightly closer to Monet than its progeny in the *Recherche*.

42. Again, as should be obvious, the "golden pivots" appear at a time when the sun is still up and the carriage is in particularly dramatic motion.

43. Cf. "Saint-Hilaire's steeple . . . let fall . . . flocks of jackdaws which would wheel noisily for a while, as though the ancient stones . . . had struck them and driven them out" (S 86). In the main text, emphasis mine on "myself," "itself," and "themselves."

44. Thus de Man: "it is not true that Proust's text can simply be reduced to the mystified assertion (the superiority of metaphor over metonymy) that our reading deconstructs. The reading is not 'our' reading, since it uses only the linguistic elements provided by the text itself . . . The deconstruction is not something we have added to the text but it constituted the text in the first place . . . by reading the text as we did we were only trying to come closer to being as rigorous a reader as the author had to be in order to write the sentence in the first place" (17). I am grateful to Michael Lucey and Debarati Sanyal for their helpful comments and questions on this section, concerning both de Man and Genette.

45. It is notoriously difficult to pin down de Man's actual view on the question of authorial control. On the one hand, as we have just seen, de Man gives Proust—just as he gives other French poets and novelists (6)—the credit for producing such a brilliantly self-deconstructive text. On the other hand, de Man claims that "the whole of literature would respond in similar fashion" (16), leaving one to wonder in what, exactly, Proust's uniqueness (or even that of the French) now consists. On the one hand, de Man rigorously marks the dividing line between mystified narrator and insightful author; on the other, he periodically slides into attributing the "seductive," "deceptive" metaphors not to Marcel but to Proust ("Proust can affect such confidence," he writes, "in the persuasive power of his metaphors" [60–61]).

46. Since Genette is aware of this (1972: 43), it is somewhat surprising that he continues, in "Proust palimpseste," to characterize the metaphors as a failure: are we supposed to imagine that Proust aims to do one thing, instead does another, and somehow accidentally has his narrator make it obvious?

47. De Man is here taking one of Marcel's claims—"if I always imagined the woman I loved in the setting I most longed at the time to visit . . . it was not by the mere hazard of a simple association of thoughts [*association de pensée*]" (S 119)—and refusing to accept it, arguing that it is "reduced to naught" by the preceding sentence ("things . . . are in reality devoid of the charm which they owed, in our minds, to the association of certain ideas [*voisinage de certaines idées*]"). Marcel is not, however, being so foolish as to say one thing in one sentence and then the opposite in the following sentence; instead he carefully marks a distinction between random "association de pensée" on the one hand and internally motivated "voisinage d'idées" on the other. I shall shortly explain how the identification of woman with setting falls under the second category.

48. Paul de Man wishes us to believe that his analysis, which is largely drawn from nine pages in the first volume, applies to the *Recherche* as a whole. "After the rhetorical reading of the Proust passage, we can no longer believe the assertion," he writes, and "not only can similar gestures [of reading] be repeated *throughout* the novel, at *all* the crucial articulations or *all* passages where large aesthetic and metaphysical claims are being made—the scenes of involuntary memory, the workshop of Elstir, the septette of Vinteuil, the convergence of author and narrator at the end of the novel—but a vast thematic and semiotic network is revealed that structures the *entire* narrative" (16; my emphasis). Even if a metonymy really did lurk around every single metaphorical corner, however, it would still remain far from clear that the images carry as much of the argumentative burden as de Man appears to assign to them. In reality, Marcel's account of (say) involuntary memory is independent of the specific figures of speech in which it chooses to couch itself.

Now involuntary memory is, as it happens, a particularly important case, since it combines metaphor and metonymy in an entirely stable way. As Genette points out (1972: 55–58, 62–63; cf. Deleuze 55), involuntary memory consists in a moment of connection by analogy ("madeleine A = madeleine B") followed by a phase of dilation by contiguity ("madeleine B was surrounded by the Combray of its era"). And even those who, like Genette, privilege the metonymic spread of the second phase over the metaphoric link of the first have to admit that the one would not be possible without the other: were it not for the genuine, noncontingent connection between two taste sensations, the horizontal expansion could never take place.

49. It is only as a young adult, riding in the automobile that "respects no mystery" (SG 548–49), that Marcel learns the truth: "Beaumont, suddenly linked with places from which I supposed it to be so distinct, lost its mystery and took its place in the district" (SG 549). In his *Arcades Project*, Walter Benjamin calls this the "decisive passage in Proust concerning the aura" (560).

50. In this, one might compare Proust's achievement to that of (say) Vladimir Nabokov, who puts such odious images as "the seaside of her schoolgirl thighs" into the mouth of his character Humbert Humbert (*Lolita* 42).

51. Bersani makes a comparable, but incompatible, suggestion: "The 'désir premier' that most profoundly characterizes the narrator is not to be found in the recurrence of favorite metaphors . . . but rather in the constant effort we recognize in his writing to make every aspect of his experience enter into a metaphorical relation with every other aspect. His ambition is to portray a world in which nothing resists the imagination" (1965: 248).

52. As Genette demonstrates (1969: 291), the deepest truths in Proust always emerge by indirection. Genette also confirms the persistence of conceptual schemes (*ibid.* 230–32): Cottard, he writes, may evolve from a bungling to a sophisticated user of language, but his *preoccupation* with idiomatic expressions remains constant.

53. The manuscript versions of this passage make it clear that this is only what he thinks *at the time*: "j'écrivis pour soulager ma conscience et ne plus penser aux clochers de Martinville, cette petite page que j'ai retrouvée depuis et dont certes *au moment* je n'eus pas l'idée qu'elle pourrait avoir aucun rapport avec cette littérature qui avait été mon ambition et à laquelle j'avais renoncée." ("I wrote, to assuage my conscience and to stop thinking about the steeples of Martinville, this little page which I have subsequently found again and which, admittedly, I did not *at that time* realize would have any connection to the literature which it had been my ambition to produce and on which I had given up.") My emphasis; Proust's grammar.

Note that there is another, shorter-range "feint" in the narrative version of the scene, when Marcel sees the steeples for the last time . . . and then almost immediately sees them again. "I resumed my seat, turning my head to look back once more at the steeples, of which, a little later, I caught a farewell glimpse [*j'aperçus une dernière fois*] at a turn in the road" (S 254); "then they came into view for the last time [*ils se montrèrent une dernière fois*], and finally I could see them no more" (S 255). Clearly the first statement merely registers the *belief* of the *character*, rather than what the narrator knows to be true.

54. "In the case of sounds, for instance, I should be able to refrain from altering their place of origin, from detaching them from their cause, beside which our

intelligence only succeeds in locating them *after* they have reached our ears—though to make the rain sing softly in the middle of one's room . . . should not really be more misleading than what is so often done by painters when they paint a sail or the peak of a mountain in such a way that, according to the laws of perspective, the intensity of the colours and the illusion of our *first* glance, they appear to us either very near or very far away, through an error which the reasoning mind *subsequently* corrects by, sometimes, a very large displacement" (TR 526–27; my emphasis). For "intelligence . . . like the sound of thunder travels less rapidly" (F 731). Compare BG 566 ("presently my reason would reestablish between the elements the distinction which my first impression had abolished"), BG 569, SG 32, EA 284–85, and Corr. 28:388.

55. "The qualities and defects which a person presents to us," notes Marcel, "rearrange themselves in a totally different order if we approach them from a new angle—just as, in a town, buildings that appear strung in extended order along a single line, from another viewpoint are disposed in depth and their relative heights altered" (BG 619).

56. I discussed this issue in the introduction, pointing out that while Marcel is *initially* attracted to Bergotte's subjective idealism, "the metaphysicians to whom I was actually to become attached . . . would resemble him in nothing" (S 134).

57. According to Alexander Nehamas, Nietzschean perspectivism works the same way: "Truth and falsity are not relative concepts for perspectivism," Nehamas writes (1998: 148); "What is relative . . . is value." When I claim, at various junctures in this book, that perspective obstructs our knowledge of the external world, its axiological dimension is primarily what I have in mind. Perspective enriches the world by attaching a set of relative values to its various objects, making some appear to be richer than others, their acquaintance as a result more desirable; even when intellect manages to set such things at their actual worth, perspective continues to overrate them in the background. It thus makes it difficult for us to perceive the world as it is, which is to say as a collection of indifferent material possessing, so to speak, only the value we lend it. (The case of human beings is more complicated, but since we cannot normally access their interiority, similar considerations often apply.) It also makes it less *desirable* to perceive the world as it is, for precisely the same reasons. Both factors underlie Marcel's eventual Copernican turn.

58. As Picon rightly notes, "the mind does not simply do whatever it wants with reality" (127; my translation).

59. Roger Shattuck writes that "nothing in this carefully composed sequence encourages the reader to regard Marcel's product as a work of art" (156). I hope to have shown that there are reasons for considering the prose poem as an aesthetic artifact, at least under Marcel's own definition. Certainly, Shattuck's main evidence—that Marcel goes on to say he "never thought again of this page" (S 256)—is quite suspect: there is no question that Marcel *does* think about the page again, since he has it printed in the *Figaro* and mentions it, as I pointed out earlier, in almost every volume.

Admittedly, the statement "I never thought again of this page" is highly confusing. We should probably understand it as meaning "I never thought again of this page *as a child*," i.e., before Marcel revises it for publication in the *Figaro* (we need not count the intervening occasion on which he shows it to Norpois, since Marcel here pays no attention to the writing itself, focusing only on Norpois's reaction). The hypothesis finds support in the fact that Marcel describes his piece as having been lost or forgotten in between times, so that it needs to be "unearthed [*retrouvée*]" before he can work on it again. Furthermore, an early draft of *Du côté de chez Swann* merely refers to "cette petite page à laquelle aussitôt je ne pensai *plus*" ("this little page which I immediately put from my mind"), rather than making the much stronger claim "Je ne repensai *jamais* à cette page": here at least the period of oblivion is left completely open.

60. It is sometimes said that the "full consciousness" idea and the "optical instrument" idea are mutually exclusive, and that the inclusion of both within the final volume testifies (yet again) to Proust's carelessness. Proust, however, had an explicit theory about the two conceptions of reading, arguing not only that they are compatible but that they work in concert: "There is no better way of coming to find out what we ourselves feel than by trying to recreate in ourselves what a master has felt. In this intense effort, what we bring to light is our own thinking, as well as his" (PM 205). As always in Proust, if the self is to find itself, it has to take a detour.

61. Thus Gilles Deleuze says of the epiphanies involving the madeleine, the Martinville steeples, the uneven paving stones, and the starched napkin that "their meaning . . . signifies Combray, young girls, Venice, or Balbec. It is not only their origin, it is their explanation . . . which remains material" (12; cf. 40, 52, 56). We know, however, that the true "meaning" of involuntary memories is not reducible to their material content: "the permanent and habitually concealed essence of things is liberated *and our true self . . . is awakened*" (TR 264), and it is surely the latter effect that appears to make "the vicissitudes of life indifferent to [us], its disasters innocuous, its brevity illusory" (S 60). As for sensory impressions (like the steeples), they are even less "material" than the memories (like the madeleine), and should be kept separate—although Deleuze, like many a Proust scholar, lumps the two series together.

62. Compare also TR 272: "certain obscure impressions, already even at Combray on the Guermantes way, had solicited my attention in a fashion somewhat similar to these reminiscences, except that they concealed within them *not a sensation dating from an earlier time*, but a new truth, a precious image." These two statements should surely seal the distinction between sensory impressions (of the Martinville type) and involuntary memories (of the madeleine variety). Yet critics, for some reason, have not always appreciated it. Thus, for example, Pauline Newman writes "the sight of a hawthorn branch or of apple trees in bloom is enough to unleash the spontaneous flow of memory" (105; cf. 38); and Luc Fraisse is similarly convinced that "the privileged impression (Martinville steeples, Hudimesnil trees) is a case of unrecognized involuntary memory" (80). Such critics are,

in fact, inverting the relationship between the two phenomena. For it is not impressions that contain memories, but vice versa: a memory, writes Marcel, is like "some forgotten scroll on which [a]re recorded impressions of other days" (GW 82). My emphasis for the primary text, and translation for the critics.

63. Again, a comparison could be made with Nietzsche, who decries "that intellectual stoicism which ultimately refuses not only to affirm but also to deny; that *desire* to halt before the factual, the *factum brutum* . . .; that general renunciation of all interpretation (of forcing, adjusting, abbreviating, omitting, padding, inventing, falsifying, and whatever else is of the *essence* of interpreting)" (GM III: 24). For Nietzsche, or at least for the Nietzsche of *The Genealogy of Morals*, facts do exist but are not what is interesting or important: "this fact has to be interpreted: *in itself* it just stands there, stupid to all eternity" (GM III:7).

64. S 254, 255, 257; translation modified.

65. Proust feels the same way. Chardin, he writes, "taught us that an ordinary piece of pottery is as beautiful as a precious stone. This painter proclaimed the divine equality of all things in the mind of whoever considers them. . . . With Rembrandt . . . , we shall learn that beauty does not reside in objects. . . . We shall see that objects in themselves are nothing" ("Chardin et Rembrandt" [EA 76]).

66. The continuation, which castigates the very same "materialism" as a defect of the aging painter, shows us that Marcel himself should know better: "He was nearing the age at which . . . mental fatigue, by inclining us towards materialism . . ., begin[s] to make us entertain the idea that there may indeed be certain bodies, certain callings, certain rhythms that are specially privileged, realising so naturally our ideal that even without genius, merely by copying the movement of a shoulder, the tension of a neck, we can achieve a masterpiece. . . . A day will come when, owing to the erosion of his brain, he will no longer have the strength, faced with those materials which his genius was wont to use, to make the intellectual effort which alone can produce his work, and yet will continue to seek them out, ... surrounding them besides with an aura of superstition as if they were superior to all things else, as if there dwelt in them already a great part of the work of art which they might be said to carry within them ready-made" (BG 587–89). (I have replaced "admit" with "entertain the idea" as a translation of *admettre*. "Admit" risks making it sound as though Marcel approves the idea.)

67. Intriguingly, in revising the early drafts for the Martinville section, Proust gradually made things worse for Marcel. The published version, which replaces "ce qui se cachait au-dessus d'elles" ("what lay hidden above them") with "ce qui se cachait *derrière* elles" ("what lay hidden behind them"), and "quelque chose qu'ils semblaient signifier" ("something they seemed to signify") with "quelque chose qu'ils semblaient *contenir*" ("something they seemed to contain"), emphasizes the idea that Marcel locates the impression within the steeples. And it concludes, as we just noted, with Marcel believing that his page has successfully delivered the hidden essence of the steeples ("elle m'avait . . . débarrassé de ces clochers et de ce qu'ils cachaient derrière eux"); the typescripts, for their part, state merely that the page is good enough to release him from the obligation to *seek*

what might be hidden behind them ("elle m'avait . . . débarrassé de ces clochers et de *chercher* ce qu'ils cachaient derrière eux").

68. See the introduction. As I explained there, the statement that "in this book . . . there is not a single incident which is not fictitious" (TR 225) must be attributed to Proust, and not to Marcel.

69. As Descombes points out (169, 253, 255), the masterwork will have a narrative component as well as a set of impressions. To put it another way, while trees no longer inspire Marcel, human beings do: "'Perhaps in the new . . . part of my life which is about to begin, human beings may yet inspire in me what nature can no longer say'" (TR 238).

70. Marcel makes two conflicting statements about the feeling produced in him by the prose poem. In *Swann's Way*, he speaks of triumph: "I was so filled with happiness, I felt that it had so entirely relieved my mind of the steeples and the mystery which lay behind them" (S 253–57). In *The Fugitive*, by contrast, we hear of disappointment: "Those passages which, when I wrote them[,] were so colourless in comparison with my thought, so complicated and opaque in comparison with my harmonious and transparent vision, so full of gaps which I had not managed to fill, that the reading of them was a torture to me, had only accentuated in me the sense of my own impotence and my incurable lack of talent" (F 772). Perhaps we can account for the discrepancy by saying that the prose poem adequately captures an impression, and thus an extratemporal law of perspective, but fails to capture anything time-bound; the Marcel of *The Fugitive*, who has heard the *septuor* of Vinteuil and is now interested in the capacity of artworks to model diachronic structures (see C 336), perceives a "gap" he did not notice at the time—and projects it, erroneously, onto his earlier self.

Chapter 2

1. "I thought then of all that I had been told about Swann's love for Odette, of the way in which Swann had been tricked [*trompé*] all his life. Indeed, when I come to think of it, the hypothesis that made me gradually build up the whole of Albertine's character and give a painful interpretation to every moment of a life that I could not control in its entirety, was the memory, the rooted idea of Mme Swann's character, as it had been described to me. These accounts contributed towards the fact that, in the future, my imagination played with the idea that Albertine might, instead of being the good girl that she was, have had the same immorality, the same capacity for deceit as a former prostitute" (SG 275–76); "Being, in spite of myself, still pursued in my jealousy by the memory of Saint-Loup's relations with 'Rachel when from the Lord' and of Swann's with Odette, I was too inclined to believe that, once I was in love, I could not be loved in return. . . . No doubt it was foolish to judge Albertine by Odette and Rachel" (SG 714). See also SG 315–16.

2. It is for this reason, presumably, that Albertine's lesbian desires come to stand synecdochically for the terrifying inaccessibility of her inner world as a whole ("All that I had wanted to know about her life . . . merged into this one sole curiosity, to know in what manner Albertine experienced pleasure" [F 750]). Still, female bisexuality is not a necessary condition for male jealousy, as the case of Robert and Rachel makes clear. Hence Leo Bersani's careful and nuanced presentation of this point (in 1965 chap. 2) is ultimately more convincing than the extreme position occupied by Gilles Deleuze.

3. "'You remember my telling you about a friend, older than me, who had been a mother, a sister to me, with whom I spent the happiest years of my life. . . . Well, this friend (oh! not at all the type of woman you might suppose!) is the best friend of your Vinteuil's daughter, and I know Vinteuil's daughter almost as well as I know her'" (SG 701–2). "'I lied to you when I pretended that I had been more or less brought up by Mlle Vinteuil's friend. . . . I stupidly thought that I might make myself seem interesting to you by inventing the story that I had known the girls quite well'" (C 452).

4. Thus for example Marcel's intellect enables him to assimilate a complicated piece of music—"at the third or fourth repetition my intellect, having grasped . . . all the parts . . . , had spread them out in relation to one another and immobilised them on a uniform plane" (C 502; translation modified)—and to decipher an impressionist painting: "One's reason [L'intelligence] then set to work to make a single element of what was in one place black beneath a gathering storm, a little further all of one colour with the sky . . . , and elsewhere so bleached by sunshine, haze and foam . . . but which . . . you understood, identical in all these different aspects, to be still the sea" (BG 569). It also allows him to recognize people after a gap of many years. "In an old photograph of themselves, which they were one day to give me," he says in reference to the petite bande, "one cannot recognise them individually save by a process of reasoning" (BG 550–51); as for the Prince de Guermantes at the climactic matinée, "I recognised him only by a process of logical deduction [à l'aide d'un raisonnement], by inferring from the mere resemblance of certain features the identity of the figure before me" (TR 337).

5. "We understand the characters of people to whom we are indifferent, but how can we ever grasp that of a person who is an intimate part of our existence, whom after a while we no longer distinguish from ourselves, whose motives provide us with an inexhaustible source of anxious hypotheses, continually revised?" (BG 648).

6. "I pursued these reflexions basing myself on the assumption [hypothèse] that Andrée was truthful . . . and had been prompted to sincerity with me precisely because she had now had relations with me. . . . But the fact that Andrée no longer believed in the reality of Albertine might mean that she no longer feared . . . to concoct a lie which retrospectively slandered her alleged accomplice. Had this absence of fear permitted her to reveal the truth at last in telling me all that, or else to concoct a lie, if, for some reason, she . . . wished to cause me pain? Perhaps

she was irritated with me . . . because I had had relations with Albertine and she envied me" (F 815).

7. My reading, here, departs from that of Richard Terdiman (1976: 112) as well as from that of Malcolm Bowie (1987: 58), who writes that "jealousy in this view is the quest for knowledge in a terrifying pure form: a quest for knowledge untrammeled and unsupported by things actually known." As I shall shortly argue, however, a quest for knowledge untrammeled and unsupported by things actually known is in fact not a quest for knowledge at all, or at most only *incidentally* a quest for knowledge.

8. "'No, what Albertine wanted was . . . for me to make up my mind to marry her. . . . Yes, that's what she wanted, that was the purpose of her action,' my *compassionate reason* assured me; but I felt that, in doing so, *my reason was still basing itself on the same hypothesis which it had adopted from the start* [cf. C 488]. Whereas I was well aware that it was the other hypothesis which had invariably proved correct. . . . *This second hypothesis was not an intellectual one*" (F 567–69); "I thought it fitter that reality should finally turn out to accord with what my *instinct* had originally foreboded rather than with the wretched optimism to which I had later so cravenly surrendered. I preferred that life should remain on the same level as my *intuitions*" (F 824–25). My emphasis throughout this paragraph.

Marcel's two hypotheses about Albertine—of "licentiousness" and "*vertu absolue*"—date all the way back to the first summer in Balbec: "the supposition [*l'hypothèse*] that she was absolutely chaste (a supposition to which I had first of all attributed the violence with which Albertine had refused to let herself be taken in my arms and kissed . . .) . . . ran so entirely counter to the hypothesis which I had constructed that day when I saw Albertine for the first time" (BG 710; for the refused kiss and the first sighting, see BG 701–2 and BG 509, respectively).

For another treatment of the two hypotheses, see Luckhurst 101–6.

9. Compare Marcel's similar experiences from the era of Gilberte, about whom he entertains similar "hypotheses" (BG 260): "while my love," he writes, "unravelled every evening the ill-done work of the day, in some shadowed part of my being an unknown seamstress refused to abandon the discarded threads, but collected and rearranged them, without any thought of pleasing me or of toiling for my happiness, in the different order which she gave to all her handiwork" (S 583).

10. "My reason moreover asked nothing better than to prove to me that I had been mistaken as to her evil plans, as I had perhaps been mistaken as to her vicious instincts. . . . But in order to be really impartial and to have a chance of perceiving the truth, . . . ought I not to tell myself that if my reason, in seeking to bring about my cure, let itself be guided by my desire, on the other hand . . . my instinct, in trying to make me ill, might have allowed itself to be led astray by my jealousy?" (C 495). Cf. "Doubtless I had long been conditioned, . . . by the example of Swann, to believe in the truth of what I feared rather than of what I should have wished. . . . But I told myself that, if it was right to allow for the worst, . . . I must nevertheless not, out of cruelty to myself . . . , end up with the mistake of regard-

ing one supposition as more true than the rest simply because it was the most painful" (SG 315–16); cf. also "those lovers whom a . . . doubt leads alternately to found *unreasonable* hopes and *unjustified* suspicions on the fidelity of their mistresses" (GW 429; my emphasis). I will discuss the impact of the two-hypothesis problem on Proustian style in the coda.

11. On being too close to see, cf. "We imagine that we know exactly what things are and what people think, for the simple reason that we do not care about them. But as soon as we have a desire to know, as the jealous man has, then it becomes a dizzy kaleidoscope in which we can no longer distinguish anything" (F 699–700). And on not caring any more, vide Marcel's experience with Gilberte— "I did not think to ask her who the young man was with whom she had been walking along the Avenue des Champs-Elysées on the day when I had set out to call on her again [BG 272–73]. . . . I was no longer interested to know" (TR 6)—and Swann's with Odette: "Formerly, while his sufferings were still keen, he had vowed that, as soon as he had ceased to love Odette and was no longer afraid either of vexing her or of making her believe that he loved her too much, he would give himself the satisfaction of elucidating with her, simply from his love of truth and as a point of historical interest, whether or not Forcheville had been in bed with her that day when he had rung her bell and rapped on her window in vain. . . . But this so interesting problem, which he was only waiting for his jealousy to subside before clearing up, had precisely lost all interest in Swann's eyes when he had ceased to be jealous" (BG 131–32). Cf. also Large 151.

12. See F 815. And cf. TR 433: "Whether my alternative explanation was . . . true was a question that could be determined only by appeal to the testimony of the parties themselves, the sole recourse which is open in such a case—or would be if they were able to bring to their confidences both insight and sincerity. But the first of these is rare . . . and the second unknown."

13. Proust's typescript (BN manuscript NaF 16745, p. 125) reveals a few variants for the kimono passage: Marcel "took [*faisais*]" or "ventured [*hasardais*]" a step; Albertine throws her dressing gown across "my armchair [*mon fauteuil*]" or just "*the* armchair [*le fauteuil*]"; and she "*would* tell me nothing [*ne me dirait rien*]" or "*used to* tell me nothing [*ne me disait rien*]." In terms of the present discussion, however, none of these choices seems particularly significant.

14. Marcel's reluctance is all the more salient for readers who are familiar with Alfred de Musset, since the kimono incident appears to be a direct allusion to, and indeed reworking of, the latter's famous novel *La confession d'un enfant du siècle*. Musset's plot involves the hero, Octave de T***, harboring jealous suspicions concerning his lover Brigitte Pierson and her childhood friend, Henri Smith. In the climactic penultimate scene, Brigitte is asleep in bed (like Albertine), her dress (like Albertine's kimono) over a chair, and a love letter to Smith (like the putative letters of Albertine) in its pocket: "as I was leaving, a dress thrown over an armchair slipped to the ground beside me, and a folded piece of paper fell out of it. I picked it up: it was a letter, and I recognized Brigitte's handwriting. The envelope was not sealed; I opened it and read the following . . ." (302–3; my translation). In

this beautifully breathless sentence, all that stands between an open envelope and a perusal of its contents is a lonely semicolon. The contrast between Octave's frantic, instinctive gathering of evidence and Marcel's hypotactic, deliberative delay could not, I think, be greater.

15. "Then, feeling that the tide of her sleep was full . . . , I would climb deliberately and noiselessly on to the bed, lie down by her side, clasp her waist in one arm, and place my lips upon her cheek and my free hand on her heart and then on every part of her body in turn. . . . The sound of her breathing, which had grown louder, might have given the illusion of the panting of sexual pleasure, and when mine was at its climax, I could kiss her without having interrupted her sleep. I felt at such moments that I had possessed her more completely, like an unconscious and unresisting object of dumb nature" (C 88). It is hard to agree with Richard Bales (59–60) that "there is something close to the idyllic about some of the scenes in *La Prisonnière*, as when she [Albertine] is asleep"!

16. Marcel's first experience of spying—when he stumbles across Mlle Vinteuil's illicit rendezvous with her female friend at Montjouvain (S 224–33)—occurs quite by accident, and he seems to wish to excuse himself for his voyeurism by alleging that "if I had moved away I would have made a rustling sound" (224–25). Similarly, at the start of *Sodom and Gomorrah*, Marcel is merely on the lookout for insect pollination (SG 2–4) and has not the slightest intention or indeed anticipation of catching Charlus at a mating ritual with Jupien. But when Charlus accompanies Jupien to his shop, Marcel follows the couple without a second thought, basing his strategy (SG 10) on the Montjouvain incident, which, we may infer, has left no unsavory aftertaste in his mouth. When, finally, we come to the brothel scene, we find Marcel motivated only by his "curiosity" (TR 181) and perfectly willing to let Jupien hide him behind an air vent so that he can observe Charlus without himself being noticed (TR 193–94; cf. Tadié 1971: 44–5).

Marcel Muller (144–54) reads the three homosexual scenes observed by the narrator as transpositions of homosexual episodes *experienced* by the *author*, and views the various excuses Marcel offers for his timely presence in key locations as a way for Proust to imply that he only knows about such activities because he has witnessed them at second hand. This interpretation seems somewhat speculative, and leaves no room for the differences in attitude between one scene and the next.

17. Just so, when she pretends not to be Swann's daughter (and hence not Jewish), Gilberte "doubtless knew that many people must be whispering: 'That's Swann's daughter.' But she knew it only with that . . . vague and remote knowledge for which we are at no pains to substitute a more precise knowledge based on direct observation" (F 792–93).

As for Marcel, he continues to keep himself in a relatively comfortable zone of ambivalence even after he has received enough evidence to persuade him of Albertine's bisexuality. For although he is thoroughly convinced of her "guilt" at an unconscious level, his conscious mind tells him he is not sure either way—just as it did when he was convinced of her "innocence." Full awareness of his own attitude only dawns at the time of writing: "*I realise now* that during this period . . .

I underwent the martyrdom of living in the constant company of an idea quite as novel as the idea that Albertine was dead . . . : the idea that she was guilty. When I thought I was doubting her, I was on the contrary believing in her; similarly I took as the starting point of my other ideas the certainty . . . of her guilt, while continuing to imagine that I still felt doubts" (F 721–22; my emphasis).

18. La Rochefoucauld agrees, although he seems to think decapitation preferable: "The cure for jealousy is certain knowledge of what we were afraid of, for it puts an end to life or love. It is a cruel remedy, but kinder than doubt and suspicions" (*Posthumous Maxims* 514). In Proust, by contrast, there is no dishonor in delusion as long as it fosters happiness. Marcel feels nothing but tender indulgence, for example, toward his parents, whose happy marriage (one of the very few in the novel) is sustained in part by voluntary obliviousness; "my mother," he writes, "looked at [my father] with tender respect, but not too hard, not wishing to penetrate the mysteries of his superior mind" (S 12). As Rosemary Lloyd puts it, in Proust "love's ignorance is preferable to love's knowledge" (61).

19. Thus Gilles Deleuze, who thinks that "the Search for lost time is in fact a search for truth" (15; cf. 159), and, following him, Georges Poulet (1968: 333). Thus also Louis Martin-Chauffier (60) and Justin O'Brien, according to whom "Marcel Proust's chief preoccupation is to seize and reproduce the truth" (1948: 51). And thus, finally, Gérard Genette, who claims that "every truth, even the most 'devastating,' is good to learn" (1969: 249; my translation) and even (246) that Marcel *enjoys* having place-names disenchanted through etymology. This last claim is patently false: "in a name that was at first sight as individual as the place itself, like the name Pennedepie," laments Marcel, "I was *disappointed* to find the Gallic *pen* which means mountain" (SG 679; my emphasis). Malcolm Bowie— who refuses to dismiss volumes IV and V in the usual way (1987: 47), and who discusses the dangers involved in the quest for knowledge (*ibid.* 58)—forms a rare exception to the mathecentric rule. Roland Barthes (1986: 272) forms a second.

20. It is of course possible that the "today" of the SG passage predates the final phase of Marcel's life (in the introduction, I explained that Marcel must have written his memoir over a long period of time, changing his views as he did so). The TR passage is less susceptible, however, to such an objection.

21. "I was but imperfectly aware of the nature which guided my actions; today, I have a clear conception of its *subjective truth*. As for its *objective truth*, that is to say whether the intuitions of that nature grasped more exactly than my reason Albertine's true intentions, . . . that I find difficult to say" (C 468; my emphasis). Given these two types of standard, it is even possible, on Marcel's account, to lie (to oneself) while telling the truth (to someone else). Thus, when he feels as though he has slept until five in the afternoon, he is "lying to [him]self" when he "brazenly" tells Françoise that "it must be at least ten o'clock!" (C 154).

22. Once we understand this, we can continue to learn from love without suffering from it, or at least while suffering less than we have before. "At the time of life . . . which Swann was approaching," writes Marcel, "a man can content himself with being in love for the pleasure of loving without expecting too much in

return" (S 277); "as life goes on, we acquire such adroitness in the cultivation of our pleasures, that we content ourselves with the pleasure we derive from thinking of a woman . . . without troubling ourselves to ascertain whether the image corresponds to the reality" (S 569). These statements offset the famous remark that "a woman is of greater utility to our life if, instead of being an element of happiness in it, she is an instrument of suffering, and there is not a woman in the world the possession of whom is as precious as that of the truths which she reveals to us by causing us to suffer" (F 669; cf. TR 316).

23. The phrase "to stand perfectly still and watch someone sleeping becomes tiring after a while" is a deliberately awkward one. First of all, the claim itself is somewhat absurd: no one is likely to believe that foot fatigue is the crucial factor driving Marcel's movement toward the kimono. And second, it takes the form of a maxim. Rather than saying that his own legs were troubling him, that is, Marcel universalizes the complaint, as though all of us were given to standing still and watching others sleep. Of course, Marcel makes vast numbers of sweeping statements; barely a page goes by without him offering pearls of wisdom on society, love, art, time, and countless other topics. Yet usually the aim is (apparently) to enlighten the reader. Here, by contrast, it merely enables Marcel to take refuge behind a generalized mass of sleep-watchers, and thus to find a convenient excuse for his inaction.

For some reason, the Modern Library translation does not render the phrase ("regarder dormir sans bouger finit par devenir fatigant") as a maxim. It has, instead, "perhaps I took this step forward also because to stand perfectly still and watch *her* sleeping *became* tiring after a while" (my emphasis), presumably on the basis of a decision that "finit" is a past historic rather than a present-tense verb. This seems unlikely, given that most of the other indicative verbs—including the main verb of the sentence in question—are, as is quite common in Proust, in the imperfect and pluperfect, and that the only exception is a short series of perfects ("jamais je n'ai touché au kimono, mis ma main dans la poche, regardé les lettres").

24. Thus Nicolas Grimaldi: "When once its mechanism has been set in gear, the imagination can no longer be checked" (51; my translation). Grimaldi's reading seems to me, however, to beg the question of *why* things should be so—and, of course, how things can sometimes be otherwise, as they clearly are in the kimono scene.

25. Hence Swann's feeling that there are (at least) three beings within him, the indifferent man he was to begin with, the "amorous personality" (BG 132) who simply took pleasure in Odette's presence, and finally the "new person" (S 323) who jealously seeks to wrest her from all other men (S 432). Marcel similarly separates himself from his fact-hungry jealousy: "all these details . . . Was it not I . . . who had desired them, or rather my famished grief, longing to feed and to wax fat upon them?" (F 639).

So autonomous is the jealousy mechanism, in fact, that it derives an "intellectual pleasure" (S 388) from the very news that causes us—the nonintellectual part of us, anyway—the greatest pain. "The most terrible reality brings us, at the same time as suffering, the joy of a great discovery," notes Marcel (SG 703). Again, compare Nietzsche: "The attraction of everything problematic, the delight in an *x*, however, is so great in such more spiritual, more spiritualized men that this delight flares up again and again . . . even over the jealousy of the lover. We know a new happiness" (GS second preface 4).

26. Once jealousy has set in, the lover may indeed be forced to content himself with reassurances that his beloved is faithful—with the mere removal of pain, rather than any positive pleasure—but this is not at all how things were at the outset, or how they were bound to become. "The pleasure which at the beginning he had hoped to obtain from caresses, he receives later *not in its natural form* but instead from friendly words, from mere promises of the loved woman's presence, which . . . bring with them a delicious relief from tension" (TR 187; my emphasis).

For the claim that jealousy is indispensable to love, see Bales 56; Bersani 1965: 43, 63, 77; and Maurois 213.

27. It is true that the very fact of the driver coming forward of his own accord seems to exclude the possibility of collusion with Albertine. Still, it might—as Marcel briefly realizes (C 169)—simply point to a moment of dissension between the pair of conspirators. Indeed, the driver amends his story only two days later to include the claim that he followed Albertine constantly at a discreet distance, a fact which at the very least proves him to have been lying on one occasion or the other. Having attributed the initial confession to a *brouille*, Marcel must surely suspect the subsequent partial retraction of following a *rapprochement*, whatever he later says (C 171). Thus he cannot, deep down, entirely trust the chauffeur, any more than he can Andrée or even—as it turns out (F 714)—Aimé, one of his most resourceful operatives.

28. "To all the evidence that corroborated my original version, I had stupidly preferred mere assertions by Albertine" (F 824). Thus for example at SG 314–15: "Albertine merely gave me her word, a categorical word unsupported by proof. But this was precisely what was best calculated to calm me. . . . It is moreover the property of love to make us at once more distrustful and more credulous, to make us suspect the loved one, more readily than we should suspect anyone else, and be convinced more easily by her denials" (Marcel is here reversing the 348th of La Rochefoucauld's maxims, namely, "When in love, we often doubt what we most believe"). Even when Albertine is dead, nothing changes: "When Aimé had gone, I thought how much [better] it would have been if I could now interrogate Albertine herself" (F 664–65). For want of being able to hear her lies, Marcel begins to speak them for her—"just as we have the faculty of making up stories to soothe our anguish" (F 626)—imagining an entire scene between himself and a penitent beloved (F 715–16).

29. Swann behaves in exactly the same way toward Odette: "One day he was trying—without hurting Odette—to discover from her whether she had ever had any dealings with procuresses. He was, as a matter of fact, convinced that she had

not . . . and Swann, wishing to be rid of the purely material but none the less burdensome presence of the suspicions, hoped that Odette would now extirpate it for ever" (S 525).

30. Marcel is equally shocked on hearing from Aimé of evidence that seems to incriminate Albertine: "My happiness, my life required that Albertine should be virtuous; they had laid it down once and for all that she was. . . . This explains why, *believing mistakenly that I was uncertain* whether Albertine did or did not love women, and believing in consequence that a proof of Albertine's guilt would not tell me anything that I had not often envisaged, I experienced, in the face of the images . . . which Aimé's letter evoked for me, an unexpected anguish, the most painful that I had ever yet felt" (F 694; my emphasis).

31. "I did not look at Albertine as I said this, so that I did not see her expression, which would have been her sole reply, for she said nothing" (C 140).

32. "It did not occur to me that the apathy reflected in my thus delegating to Andrée or the chauffeur the task of soothing my agitation, by leaving them to keep watch on Albertine, was paralysing and deadening in me all those imaginative impulses of the mind, all those inspirations of the will, which enable us to guess and to forestall what a person is going to do" (C 21).

33. Cf. "It is true that we are unaware of the particular sensibility of each of our fellow-creatures, but as a rule we do not even know that we are unaware of it" (F 735).

Martha Nussbaum phrases the point about self-deception particularly effectively, defining rationalization as "an activity of self-explication engaged in at a superficial and intellectual level which, by giving us the confidence that we have accomplished a scientific analysis and arrived at exact truth, deters us from a deeper or fuller inquiry" (1990: 254). "The very feeling that he is being subtle and profound, that he is 'leaving nothing out of account, like a rigorous analyst,'" she adds, "leads Marcel into complacency, deterring him from a richer or deeper inquiry" (1990: 264; cf. 1983: 155).

From the fact that the intellect breeds blissful ignorance, however, Nussbaum rather rashly concludes that intuition and pain are, on Marcel's view, absolute guarantors of accurate knowledge (1990: 266–67). Claiming that love not only involves pain but is nothing but pain through and through—"love is not a structure in the heart waiting to be discovered; it is . . . made up out of experiences of suffering. It is 'produced' in Marcel's heart by Françoise's words" (1990: 267–68; cf. 1983: 156)—Nussbaum then infers that "the cataleptic impressions of love are . . . the unchallenged foundations of all knowledge" (1990: 273). Now even if we charitably took the last statement to refer only to the foundations of all *self*-knowledge, we would still have to recognize that other, and indeed more solid, foundations exist for that, most notably those of involuntary memory and art. Nor, in any event, are love and suffering strictly interchangeable. It surely cannot be the case that Marcel's love for Albertine is produced by Françoise's chilling words at the end of *The Captive*, since he has already described himself as in love with, or at least having been in love with, Albertine on several occasions over the course of their five-year acquaintance (BG 581, GW 487, C 17). Pain is not equivalent to love; love is not equivalent to knowledge; and rationalization may well be more acceptable in Proust's world, perhaps even more essential, than Nussbaum is prepared to admit.

34. "The child cannot possibly have felt his mother's departure as something agreeable or even indifferent. How then does his repetition of this distressing experience as a game fit in with the pleasure principle? ... At the outset he was in a *passive* situation—he was overpowered by the experience; but, by repeating it, unpleasurable though it was, as a game, he took on an *active* part" (Freud 1961 [1920]: 15). For further instances of repetition compulsion in Proust, see F 635 and S 522.

35. We have already seen that self-deception is "a by-product of the instinct of self-preservation" (C 105). It is strong enough even to withstand powerful opposing evidence, since "the facts of life do not penetrate to the sphere in which our beliefs are cherished; they did not engender those beliefs, and they are powerless to destroy them; they can inflict on them continual blows of contradiction and disproof without weakening them" (S 209). For a similar reflex in Saint-Loup, "an instinctive desire to preserve his love [*l'instinct de conservation de son amour*] that was perhaps more clear-sighted than he was himself," see BG 497; for the same reflex operating in nonromantic circumstances, see S 251.

36. The German term *Wissenschaft* denotes both scholarship at large and science in particular. In the present context, it seems reasonable to assume that Nietzsche is thinking of academia (as the quest for knowledge) in general, even though nineteenth-century scientists may perhaps be the most obvious examples of the tendency he is describing.

37. This goes against the claim, advanced by some readers, that Nietzsche subscribes to a "pragmatist" theory of truth, "refus[ing] to admit the notion of a truth disconnected from interests and needs" (Rorty 1991: 2; cf. 1982: 150; 1991a: 61; 1998: 3) and holding that "*p* is true and *q* is false if *p* works and *q* does not" (Danto 1965: 72). If Nietzsche were indeed a pragmatist about truth, then there would be no room in his philosophy for pernicious knowledge: harmful beliefs would be false *by definition*, just as correct beliefs would be beneficial by definition. What we find, however, is that while beliefs *may* be both true and useful (HI 3; GS 110, 344), truths can also be "deadly" (HI 9, 10; GS 107, 381; BGE 39; TI I:5; NW 14: 368–72) and falsehoods indispensable: "untruth is the condition of life" (NW 12: 48; cf. BT 18, GS 121, BGE 4, ASC 5, WP 853). Illusions are crucial not only to thought (NW 12:23, WP 48) but also to action. "In order to act we require the veil of illusion; such is Hamlet's doctrine" (BT 7; cf. HI 1, 7; NW 12:224; NW 14: 87; WP 492; EH II:4). As though trying to erase any remaining doubt, Nietzsche directly confronts and rejects the pragmatist line at *Beyond Good and Evil* 39. "Nobody is very likely to consider a doctrine true merely because it makes people happy or virtuous," he contends here. "Something might be true while being harmful and dangerous in the highest degree. Indeed, it might be a basic characteristic of existence that those who would know it completely would perish."

In short, Nietzsche clearly demarcates between truth and utility throughout his career, implying that it *is* possible to determine the truth-value of a claim independently of the extent to which it "works" and of the "interests" of all human beings. Nietzsche may well be pragmatically spirited when he places human needs above the truth, but he does not, for all that, give the latter a pragmatist definition: truth, for him, remains what it is independently of those needs. (For a similar dismissal of Nietzsche's purported pragmatism, see Nehamas 1985: 54.)

38. "The will to truth . . . is merely a form of the will to illusion" (NW 14: 369). For the primogeniture of will to faith in Proust, see S 518, where Marcel describes Swann's more credulous aspects—those, that is, which believe in Odette's love for him, as opposed to those which suspect perfidiousness on her part—as "these older, more autochthonous inhabitants of his soul."

39. Edgar Allan Poe, in his own (and most famous) narrative of epistolary theft, to which Proust alludes at SG 528, would appear to agree with Nietzsche's (and Pascal's) assessment. His professional epistemologist, the flat-footed Prefect of Police G—, is the *esprit de géométrie* incarnate, an adept of nineteenth-century science who can see little further than the end of his microscope. It is of course not he but Arsène Dupin, the one for whom knowledge is a sport rather than an ultimate desideratum, who is able to solve the mystery; and when Dupin magically produces the letter that had seemed impossible to find, the Prefect, in the most astonishing episode of the story, runs off without stopping to ask how he has managed it (338). For G— and his ilk are only able, as Dupin makes plain, to "extend or exaggerate their old modes of *practice*, without touching their principles" (341): they are capable, that is, of attending to the *whats*, *whens*, and (in the present case) *wheres* of criminal behavior, but extremely reluctant to raise any questions concerning the *hows* (still less *whys*) of their own activity.

Chapter 3

1. Throughout this chapter I capitalize the word *Self* when referring to the overall structure of an individual consciousness, as distinct from the individual incarnations (lowercase *selves*) that populate it. In Proust these are "*le* moi" (or "moi-même") and "*les* moi" respectively (see, e.g., BG 255, which speaks of the "slow and painful suicide of that self which loved Gilberte [*du moi qui en moi-même aimait Gilberte*]").

2. When Marcel writes that "habit gives to the mere association of ideas between two phenomena, according to a certain school of philosophy, the illusory force and necessity of a law of causation" (F 679–80), the philosopher he has most prominently in mind is clearly Hume. Cf. Jones 165n1.

3. See Bersani 1965, Dancy, and Muller, respectively.

4. Thus Roger Shattuck is confident (a) that the crucial division lies in the faculties, (b) that it consists in two main parts of the soul (intelligence and intuition), and (c) that these two may be brought into alignment in the manner advocated

by the ancient Greeks (127)—all of which seem to be somewhat problematic assumptions, as will become clear in what follows. Malcolm Bowie (1998: 20) does reproduce a crucial line from Proust, indicating the existence of diachronic selves ("what we suppose to be our love or our jealousy . . . is composed of an infinity of successive loves"), but he nevertheless speaks of the multiple self in its synchronic dimension alone (see e.g. 5, 10). Indeed he would like, if at all possible, to diminish it still further, to a dimensionless void, "a vacancy awaiting substance and structure" (10). When he also cites Proust's protagonist as claiming that an artwork conveys the essence of its creator (19), he leaves one wondering what kind of essence a "vacancy" could possess.

The vacancy model is one Leo Bersani explicitly rejects as an early, discarded hypothesis on the part of Proust's narrator: "the self so meticulously analyzed in the narrative of *A la Recherche* is anything but an 'empty apparatus'" (1965: 107). Bersani's brilliant and painstaking analysis, which overlaps at many junctures with my own, nevertheless reduces the synchronic division to mere "emotional background"—i.e., causal explanation—for the diachronic (see esp. 52). This cannot be correct, since Marcel clearly views the two as entirely separate phenomena. "I had always considered each one of us to be a sort of multiple organism," he writes, "*not only* at a given moment of time . . . *but also* . . . as a sequence of juxtaposed but distinct 'I's which would die one after the other" (TR 352; my emphasis). Other critics to downplay the synchronic division have included Genette 1966, Picon, Poulet 1963, Dancy, and May.

5. "Proust thought that if memory could retrieve what created us, that retrieval itself would be tantamount to becoming what one was" (Rorty 1989: 118). It is far from clear what Rorty understands by "what one [is]," since he also thinks that Proust "rid himself of the fear that there was an antecedent truth about himself, a real essence" (103). I will argue that there *is*, on Proust's view, an innate essence to each individual; but that this essence does not by any means constitute a truth about the *whole* Self.

6. As far as Bowie is concerned, the problems of selfhood "can have and need have no solutions" (1998: 5, 2). Richard Terdiman, having first written off "the self which Proust defines as highest" as "a false self" and Proust's proposed resolution as, in consequence, "a false resolution" (1976: 246–47), later goes on to reject involuntary memory for good measure: "I am convinced that large numbers of Proust's readers have never truly believed that the phenomena [*sic*] Proust described was real enough to occupy the conceptual space he attributes to it" (1993: 237). And Gilles Deleuze, whose complex analysis incorporates both the synchronic and the diachronic aspects of self-division (see esp. 119, 165), nonetheless seems to underestimate Proust's response to both. For him, Proust's world is a world in fragments. The two *côtés*, he claims, are not *really* connected, just linked by "transversals" (149); even travel does not unite disparate sites but "affirms only their difference" (113). Now while this may apply to train travel, the very opposite is true of automobile rides, as Marcel makes quite explicit (SG 549–50; the same amendment would also apply to Poulet 1963: 93). Similarly, it is on foot that Mar-

cel discovers the geographical continuity of Méséglise and Guermantes (TR 3–4), after having witnessed their *social* interpermeability in the Cambremer-d'Oloron marriage (F 913). When, at last, Mlle de Saint-Loup offers living proof that the two *côtés* are not as distinct as Marcel once thought, the evidence comes first and foremost in the form of "high roads," and only *secondarily* as "transversals" (TR 502). For these and other reasons, it is difficult to accept Deleuze's final verdict.

7. See, e.g., Parfit 305. For his part, Jonathan Dancy phrases the question extremely succinctly, at least in its diachronic aspect (20). He appears, however, not quite to understand the answer Proust offers, since he takes him to be claiming that involuntary memory makes us taste today's tea and madeleine also in the past (rather than, as seems more reasonable, making us taste *yesterday's* tea and madeleine also in the *present*, alongside the analogous set of sensations generated by an immediate physical cause). Indeed, he takes Proust to be arguing that we can never have the same experience twice, that "we can no longer see things the way they then seemed to us" (21). This is surely the exact *opposite* of what involuntary memory shows us, on Proust's view (that it is Proust's, as well as Marcel's, can be seen at EA 253–55). For if the phenomenon indicates anything, it is that we *can* see, feel, and taste things again in exactly the same way, even after decades of life have gone by.

8. For the narcissistic superego, see Freud 1957 [1914]: 93–99. Freud is not yet using the term *superego* here, but the "special psychical agency" he mentions, that agency which "constantly watches the actual ego," measuring it by its own ideal standards and thus ensuring a yield of narcissistic satisfaction (95), is surely the same component under a different name.

9. A word is in order here on the subject of Derek Parfit's hugely influential study *Reasons and Persons*, since Parfit mentions Proust—and more specifically the "death" of selves—in the course of his meditation on personal identity (305). Like Proust, Parfit believes that "there are two unities to be explained; the unity of consciousness at any time, and the unity of a whole life" (217). Unlike Proust, however, Parfit does not spend much time investigating how such unity may be secured. He is more concerned with proving that as long as we have such unity, it should not matter to us where it came from: an artificial replica of a unified consciousness is, he claims, just as good as the real thing.

While Parfit believes that a great deal rides on this second question, it is far from evident what one really stands to gain from contemplating a choice between artificial and natural brains. Furthermore, almost all of his arguments on the subject rely on "evidence" from science-fiction thought experiments, many of which are not only fanciful but also intrinsically vitiated. Thus for example a set of claims is "supported" (251) by an imaginary case in which I am capable of dividing my mind, then reuniting it, at will, and in which one half of my mind can "look and see" what is going on in the other half (247). Yet the very definition of the split-brain condition is that one half of one's mind *cannot* "look" at the other, cannot be aware even that there *is* a split, let alone (in the imaginary scenario) decide to bring it to an end.

10. "Each of these Albertines was different, as is each appearance of the dancer whose colours, form, [and] character, are transmuted according to the endlessly varied play of a spotlight. . . . For this was the point to which I invariably had to return, to those beliefs which for most of the time occupy our souls unbeknown to us, but which for all that are of more importance to our happiness than is the person whom we see, for it is through them that we see him [or her], it is they that impart his [or her] momentary grandeur to the person seen" (BG 719–20). On this point, cf. Deleuze 67–68; on the implicit theory of knowledge underpinning the *Recherche*, see chapter 1 here.

11. This is what is meant by "le temps incorporé" (IV:623/TR 529): time is, as it were, held within the body under the guise of memory traces, sediments of former selves. See also Jauss 259.

12. Though he may at times believe otherwise, he never fully loses this original cathexis (C 173); while he may feel indifferent to a much older (and, in his mind, radically different) Gilberte (TR 438, 443), he still retains a fondness for the "true" Gilberte. "Time which changes human beings does not alter the image which we have preserved of them" (TR 438).

The same goes for Albertine. Marcel may protest (too much?) that he "never thought of her now" (TR 58) and that her memory is entirely "*indifférente*" to him (IV:589/TR 475), but his grief gives him away: "Ah! if Albertine had been alive, how delightful it would have been, on the evenings when I had dined out, to arrange to meet her out of doors, under the arcades! . . . But alas, I was alone" (TR 64–65).

13. The analogy between personal and political constitutions is of course as old as Plato's *Republic*. Hobbes famously picks it up in his *Leviathan* as, subsequently, does Hume in his *Treatise of Human Nature*: "I cannot compare the soul more properly to any thing than to a republic or commonwealth, in which the several members are united by the reciprocal ties of government and subordination" (261). It is from here, most likely, that the metaphor passes to Nietzsche—"what happens here is what happens in every well-constructed and happy commonwealth [*Gemeinwesen*]; namely, the governing class identifies itself with the successes of the commonwealth. In all willing it is absolutely a question of commanding and obeying, on the basis . . . of a social structure composed of many 'souls'" (BGE 19)—and thence, in somewhat modified form, to Freud: "the ego's position is like that of a constitutional monarch, without whose sanction no law can be passed but who hesitates long before imposing his veto on any measure put forward by Parliament" (1989 [1923]: 57).

14. Similarly, Jupien's niece manages to "forget"—though forgetting in Proust only ever designates a shift in the hierarchy—Morel's many charms: "in the fullness of time these stony fragments end by slipping into a place where they cause no undue laceration, from which they never stir again; their presence is no longer felt: the pain has been forgotten, or is remembered with indifference" (C 259).

15. Cf. "only imagination and belief can differentiate from the rest certain objects, certain people" (GW 32).

16. "Our ego [*notre moi*] is composed of the superimposition of our successive states" (F 733).

17. The point comes out even more clearly in the early manuscripts: "this intermittently acknowledged self perceives these affinities between two ideas. . . . He, and no other, should write my books" (BSB 193–94). It is sometimes assumed (e.g., by Rousset [143]) that the involuntary memories of *Le temps retrouvé* provide Marcel with the material for his *récit*; this seems, however, somewhat unlikely, especially given the chronology of the latter's genesis (for which, see my introduction).

18. "And these moments of the past do not remain still; they retain in our memory *the motion which drew them towards the future* . . . drawing us along in their train" (F 659); "The taste of our breakfast coffee brings with it that vague *hope* of fine weather which so often long ago . . . suddenly smiled upon us in the pale uncertainty of the dawn. An hour is not merely an hour, it is a vase full of scents and sounds and *projects* and climates" (TR 289); "If, even in thought, I pick from the bookshelf *François le Champi*, immediately there rises within me a child who takes my place . . . and who reads it as he read it once before, with the same impression of what the weather was like then in the garden, the same dreams that were shaping themselves in his mind about the different countries and about life, the same *anguish about the next day*" (TR 285); "the stiffness of the napkin had . . . caressed my imagination not only with the sight of the sea as it had been that morning but with the smell of my room, the speed of the wind, the sensation of *looking forward* to lunch, of wondering which of the different walks I *should take*" (TR 269; my emphasis throughout this note). Cf. also C 25, F 733, and Poulet 1968: 326. We might refer to these recollected fears and desires as *past futures*. They are, perhaps, the obverse of the *future pasts* in which, as we shall see shortly, Proust takes an equal interest.

19. "Days in the past cover up little by little those that preceded them and are themselves buried beneath those that follow them. *But each past day has remained deposited in us*, as in a vast library where, even of the oldest books, there is a copy which doubtless nobody will ever ask to see. And yet should this day from the past . . . rise to the surface . . . , then for a moment names resume their former meaning, people their former aspect, [and] we ourselves our state of mind at the time" (F 733). Compare F 658: "We exist only by virtue of what we possess, and we possess only what is really present to us, and many of our memories, our moods, our ideas sail away. . . . Then we can no longer take them into account in the total which is our personality. *But they know of secret paths by which to return to us.*" And, finally, BSB 27: "My body . . . lay guessing at its surroundings. *All those which it had known* from childhood onward offered themselves in turn to its groping memory, reassembling round it every place I had ever slept in, *even those which for years I had not called to mind* and might never have called to mind till my dying day." My emphasis throughout this note.

20. "No doubt we ourselves may change our social habitat and our manner of life and yet our memory, clinging still to the thread of our personal identity, will

continue to attach to itself at successive epochs the recollection of the various societies in which . . . we have lived" (TR 403). On this point, cf. Everett Knight: "the significance of Marcel's mystical experiences is precisely that they prove the *continuity of the Self*" (111).

Involuntary memory also allows us to seize the passage of time, something we cannot normally do. As we vacillate (TR 267–68) between the self of today and the self of yesteryear, experiencing each directly and from within, we are able to measure all that has changed (our beliefs, our projects) *against the yardstick of that which has remained the same* (the sound of a name, the taste of tea). "Should a sensation from a bygone year . . . enable our memory to make us hear that name with the particular ring with which it then sounded in our ears, we feel at once . . . the distance that separates the dreams which at different times its same syllables have meant to us" (GW 4; cf. Poulet 1963: 66). In order to perceive "a fragment of time in the pure state," then, we need to situate ourselves (momentarily) "outside time"; the two concepts—pure time and timelessness—are thus distinct (contra Rousset 142) but in no way contradictory (as has been claimed, for some reason, by Genette 1980: 160, Champigny 132, and Blanchot 20).

21. Note that Proust himself, in the 1912 letter to Bibesco and the 1913 interview in *Le temps*, speaks of involuntary memory delivering the essence of a *sensation* (which is of course in part subjective), not the essence of a *thing* (*Letters* 227, EA 255). Proust's approach is far more plausible than Marcel's. Involuntary memory cannot reveal *both* the essence of an object *and* the essence of the self perceiving it, since the essence of the self is precisely to be inferred from the way in which it *distorts* the perception in a similar way on each occasion. Marcel's claim here may be yet another instance of his enduring tendency, analyzed in chapter 1, to mistake his own projections for features of external objects.

22. Marcel's account thus provides, among other benefits, an entirely new way of understanding *nostalgia*. If we enjoy memories of times past, he implies, it is not because those times themselves were enjoyable, nor simply because our imagination flatters us that they were. After all, it is a general principle in Proust that nothing possesses value in and of itself, not names (GW 4), days (BG 81), places (F 884), people (BG 513), objects (EA 76), or landscapes (S 606), and certainly not memories (GW 756). Proust is, in fact, at pains to make sure Marcel remembers not just the happy times but also mundane and even traumatic moments: Marcel's boot reminds him of his grandmother's death (SG 210–13), the clinking spoon brings back a moment of abject creative impotence (TR 257–58; cf. Bales 16), and the madeleine itself summons up nothing more than Aunt Léonie's room on a Sunday morning, a scene laid out in all its tedious and bathetic detail over six long pages prefaced by the broad disclaimer "to live in, Combray was a trifle depressing" (S 65).

While the memory may be unappealing, however, the *act of recollection* always carries its share of pleasure. (Genette [1972: 95] and Parfit [514n42] acknowledge this fact; Deleuze [20] and Terdiman [1993: 198] do not. In the case of Deleuze, the explanation may be that he rather improbably considers the "meaning" of each privileged moment to be a material object or place, as we saw above.) Memory warms the heart not for what it gives us of the objects recalled but for what it gives us of ourselves: "I remembered—with pleasure because it showed me that already in those days I had been the same and that this type of experience sprang from a fundamental trait in my character" (TR 272–73; cf. C 513, BSB 23). As a result, even the most painful memory of all, that of the grandmother, is something Marcel clings to "with all [his] strength" (SG 214–15).

23. For a description of how this works, as well as a discussion of the difference between Kant's uniform set of necessary "categories" and Nietzsche's variable "perspectives," see Anderson 1998. See also Anderson 1999, which provides an extremely useful working definition of perspective in the Nietzschean (and Kantian) mode. "Nietzsche," writes Anderson here, "understands perspectives along loosely Kantian lines: perspectives include schemes of concepts which organize the data of our experience and thereby give the world a certain 'look' for us" (49).

24. "The universe is true for us all and dissimilar to each one of us. . . . it is not one universe, but millions, almost as many as the number of human eyes and brains in existence, that awake every morning" (C 250). Compare Nietzsche: "There are many kinds of eyes . . . and consequently there are many kinds of 'truths'" (WP 540).

25. Here one should compare Locke's *Essay Concerning Human Understanding* (1689): "as far as any intelligent being can repeat the idea of any past action *with the same consciousness it had of it at first*, and with the same consciousness it has of any present action; so far it is the same personal self" (303; my emphasis).

26. Compare also Marcel's reference to "that environment which itself is invisible but through the translucent and changing medium of which we [look]— that is to say those beliefs which we do not perceive" (C 191).

27. At what exact point in the story does Marcel eat his madeleine? This is an immensely difficult question. From *Noms de pays: Le nom* onward, Marcel narrates a good part of his life (years 1892 to 1916) in chronological order, but in all these pages he never so much as mentions the madeleine episode, notwithstanding the profound impact he claims it had on him (Genette 1980: 45). Some critics, like Moss (99), are so baffled that they end up believing the episode to have taken place very early in Marcel's life, before the involuntary memory of Adolphe's room experienced on the Champs-Elysées (BG 91), that of Gilberte experienced in Balbec (BG 299–301), and all the rest. At the other extreme, Hans Robert Jauss situates the madeleine "am schluß der Erzählung" (281). This cannot be right, however, since the madeleine revelation is incomplete, so that the "early bedtimes" have yet to turn into long nights spent writing. ("For a long time I would go to bed early" [S 1]; "If I worked, it would be only at night" [TR 524]).

Clearly, the madeleine epiphany must strike fairly late in the narrator's career, "many years" after his childhood sojourns in Combray (S 60), and yet before his vocation finally declares itself. But when? Unfortunately, the clues are contradictory. On the one hand, we know that the madeleine follows hard on the heels of a period during which Marcel recalls various rooms, those of Combray, Balbec, Paris, Doncières, Venice, and Tansonville. Thus it must postdate the visit to Gilberte, now Mme de Saint-Loup, described at the start of the final volume. On the other hand, the madeleine must *predate* the performance of Vinteuil's *septuor*, long before Tansonville, since that performance reminds Marcel of the feelings the madeleine generated (C 513; cf. GW 756, TR 255). To resolve the conflict, Gareth Steel suggests (58) that Marcel eats his madeleine shortly before hearing the *septuor*, but that the madeleine does not stop him lying awake every night remembering various rooms (S 262), so that even rooms he inhabits in subsequent years (Venice, Tansonville) can be added to the list.

The problem with Steel's view is that the *septuor* epoch is one in which Marcel is living alone with Albertine (C 6), whereas the madeleine moment takes place in the absence of love (S 4) and the presence of Maman (S 60). I myself would place the madeleine during the "many years" spent in sanatoria (TR 238), during a brief stay at home (cf. Muller 43–44, Genette 1980: 44). Proust originally saw the *septuor* sequence coming close to the end of the novel, and it is quite possible that the stray pluperfect tense at III:883 (C 513) is a relic of that structure, one which would have been amended had he only lived long enough.

28. One example of Marcel working back from effect to cause, analyzing his own actions as though they were those of a stranger: "the memory of Mme de Guermantes at the Opéra . . . *must have been* charming . . . , *since* it was always to it . . . that my ideas of love returned; . . . in my dreams I *no doubt* distorted it completely, *for* whenever I saw Mme de Guermantes I realised the disparity . . . between what I had imagined and what I saw" (GW 72–73; my emphasis).

29. Art alone, we recall, "expresses for others *and renders visible to ourselves* that life of ours which cannot effectually observe itself" (TR 300; my emphasis). Cf. Bersani 1965: 227.

30. A point with faintly Kantian echoes. Cf. *Critique of Pure Reason*: "We can cognize of things *a priori* only what we ourselves have put into them" (B xviii).

31. Proust himself appears to have learned, in exactly that way, from his own writing: "just as, while reading Stendhal, Thomas Hardy, or Balzac, I have picked up on deep features of their instinct," he tells Jacques Copeau, "so, while reading myself, I have elicited post hoc some constitutive features of my unconscious" (Corr. 12:180). (For the "phrases-types" of Hardy and company, see III:877–80/ C 506–9.)

32. Thus friendship, according to Marcel, causes us to "sacrifice the only part of ourselves that is real and incommunicable (otherwise than by means of art) to a superficial self" (GW 540). Compare *Gay Science* 354: "Man, like every living being, thinks continually without knowing it; the thinking that rises to *consciousness* is only the smallest part of all this—the most superficial and worst part—for only this conscious thinking *takes the form of words*. . . . [Now] consciousness does not really belong to man's individual existence but rather to his social or herd nature. . . . Consequently, given the best will in the world . . . to 'know ourselves,' each of us will always succeed in becoming conscious only of what is not individ-

ual but 'average.'. . . . Fundamentally, all our actions are altogether incomparably personal, unique, and infinitely individual; there is no doubt of that. But as soon as we translate them into consciousness *they no longer seem to be*." And compare also S 309: "in the letters written to us by a woman we love, we find fault with . . . the words of the message, because they are not fashioned exclusively from the essence . . . of a particular person."

33. In Proust, whatever Gilles Deleuze may claim (123), a character's sexual preference does not constitute the deepest truth of his or her nature. Marcel speaks, quite the reverse, of the "tiny original personality of the individual"—our unique essence—being hijacked by "some *generic* defect or malady" (TR 107; my emphasis). Thus when Charlus is at his most overtly homosexual, he has not become who he is but, on the contrary, "travelled as far as was possible from himself," and is now "masked by what he had become, by what belonged not to him alone but to many other inverts" (*ibid.*). (Marcel's critique is leveled, of course, at Charlus's decreasing distinctness, not at his homosexuality.)

34. Compare, in *Contre Sainte-Beuve*, "the family face, that face which the personality of each wearer had changed and adapted to its own requirements, intellectualised by some, coarsened by others, like the room in a castle which has been, according to the inheritor's taste, now a study, now a gymnasium" (BSB 160); and compare Marcel himself, who "was beginning to resemble all my relations: [including] my father who—*in a very different fashion from myself, no doubt . . .*—took so keen an interest in the weather" (C 95; my emphasis).

35. This approach to style, as ultimate expression of character, is often assumed to have been invented by the romantics (see pages 751–52 in Gumbrecht, arguably the definitive history of the concept). Still, Erasmus, in 1516, holds strikingly similar views: "As each individual has his own appearance, his own voice, his own character and disposition, so each has his own style of writing . . . style is at once an imaging of the mind in its every facet" (76–79). (For further reflections on style and personality, see Robinson; see also Cohen.)

36. It is true that our personality comes through even in our *spoken* language—in the latter's *style*, at least: "our intonation embodies our philosophy of life, what a person invariably says to himself about things" (BG 667); "what interested me [in people's stories] was not what they were trying to say but the manner in which they said it and the way in which this manner revealed their character" (TR 39); even "Bergotte's way of speaking . . . was attached to the thought of Bergotte . . . by vital links" (BG 171). Still, although "human speech *reflects* the human soul," it is "without *expressing* it as does literary style" (BG 169; my emphasis). Perhaps the idea is simply that the ratio of idiosyncratic to generic forms is higher in artistic production. Crafting a personal style is not, on this view, a matter of free invention, but instead a matter of allowing already existing tendencies to dictate choices in more and more areas. Conversation leaves little time for such a discipline, and the pressures of direct communication tend to go against it.

37. For a fuller discussion, see my introduction.

38. Although it incorporates several discrete elements and involves subtle shifts in tone and emphasis, Proust's style—unlike Nietzsche's famously "multifarious" *set* of styles, none of which is peculiarly his own—presents itself as largely uniform and distinct. It is extremely difficult to separate out the three components that are probably lodged within it, namely (1) a reflection of Proust's perspective, (2) a reflection of Marcel's perspective, and (3) a reflection of or recipe for a universally applicable notion of subjectivity. I shall make some suggestions, however, at the end of this book.

39. Already in *Jean Santeuil* (118), "this was *his* life, this was the flavour which things have only for each one of us, and for us alone have kept it."

40. Proust's new infinite is remarkably similar to Nietzsche's: "the world has become 'infinite' for us all over again, inasmuch as we cannot reject the possibility that it may include infinite interpretations" (GS 374).

41. More famously but analogously, Swann views Odette as though she were a Botticelli, seeing her no longer as a perfect specimen of an Odette de Crécy but as a failed attempt at an ideal that surpasses her. The Odette-Botticelli juxtaposition allows Swann to reinterpret what he considers defects, like Odette's over-large eyes ("her eyes were beautiful, but so large they seemed to droop beneath their own weight, strained the rest of her face" [S 276]), as positive features, somehow justified within a different overall context: "she stared at him fixedly, with that languishing and solemn air which marks the women of the Florentine master in whose faces he had found a resemblance with hers; swimming at the brink of the eyelids, her brilliant eyes, wide and slender like theirs, seemed on the verge of welling out like two great tears" (S 330). Similar miracles transform Elstir's wife, in Marcel's eyes, from a "heavy" human being into a painted portrait (BG 588) and the Princesse de Guermantes, flawed incarnation of her own special brand of beauty, from a set of "unfinished" line segments into "an ideal figure" (GW 46).

42. Cf. "such were the quintessentially aristocratic qualities that shone through the husk of this body . . . *as, through a work of art, the industrious, energetic force which has created it*" (GW 567; my emphasis).

43. Surprising as it may sound, there are things Marcel omits even from the staggeringly thorough *récit* of his life we are given to read. Of Albertine, for example, he writes that "the prospect of her continued society was painful to me in another way which I cannot explain in this narrative" (C 236).

44. Alasdair MacIntyre would agree with Nietzsche that it takes narrative to unify a life. But for MacIntyre, that narrative—like all narrative—is fundamentally *moral* in character: "narrative," he writes, "requires an evaluative framework in which good or bad character helps to produce unfortunate or happy outcomes" (1980: 57). Even if (as is unlikely) this is not a chiasmus, and MacIntyre is archly acknowledging that virtue is often punished and vice rewarded, the generalization is hard to accept. For important events, such as the earthquake at Lisbon, have a way of affecting individuals independently of their (and others') virtuous planning or vicious scheming, and we have no need to believe otherwise in order to understand, say, *Candide*, *The Trial*, or the Book of Job.

45. Given this statement, it is rather surprising to find Gilles Deleuze claiming that "one would look in vain in Proust for platitudes about the work of art as organic totality in which each part predetermines the whole, and in which the whole determines the part" (102). "Even the painting by Vermeer," Deleuze continues, "is not valid as a Whole but because of the patch of yellow wall planted there as a fragment of still another world. In the same way, the little phrase of Vinteuil, 'interspersed, episodic,' about which Odette says to Swann: 'Why do you need the rest? Just that is *our* piece.'" (Cf. Descombes 108: "Marcel learns that when an authentic aesthetic prize is grasped, the event involves accentuation of a *part* at the expense of the *whole*.")

Odette, one might counter, is hardly the best judge of the sonata's aesthetic qualities; surely Marcel, who praises the complex structure that ends up incorporating it (C 346), is a more reliable source. And when it comes to *The View of Delft*, it is only Bergotte—on the point of death, and quite likely falling into a similar "materialism" to that of the aging Elstir (BG 587)—who considers its "little patch of yellow wall" detachable from the overall context. As Nehamas notes (1985: 229), Marcel would almost certainly disagree with Bergotte, and so a fortiori would Proust, that obsessive planner and painstaking "architect" of a labyrinthine masterwork. For Proust, as is widely known (Rousset 138, Muller 55–56, Schmid 64, Shattuck 127 . . .), wrote the novel's conclusion (*adoration perpétuelle* and *bal de têtes*) at the same time as its opening, and frequently informed correspondents of where the narrative was headed. (See, e.g., the letter to Rivière, cited in an epigraph to my introduction; and see MPG 114–240 for an early version of the finale.) It is odd, then, that Deleuze should wish to deny "that Proust had the notion—even vague or confused—of the antecedent unity of the Search" (103).

46. All necessity, in Proust, is relative and retrospective. First of all, any given element within my life could have been otherwise (i.e., is otherwise in one or more possible worlds) and remains therefore, from an objective point of view, thoroughly contingent; when I forge a beautiful whole of which it becomes the indispensable part, the type of "necessity" I give it is only ever internal to the composition. Second, its place within the artwork is always determined *après coup*, and is, indeed, liable to *change* as fresh events cast their different light back upon it. One might think here of "Wagner, retrieving some exquisite fragment from a drawer of his writing-table to introduce it, as a *retrospectively necessary* theme, into a work he had not even thought of at the time he composed it" (C 208; my emphasis). And compare Rorty: "Proust's novel is a network of small, interanimating contingencies. . . . Such contingencies make sense only in retrospect—and they make a different sense every time redescription occurs" (1989: 100–101).

47. In fact, one could argue that Augustine's *Confessions* already *do* look rather more like those of Teresa than the former might have wanted. While Augustine does make grand claims for the power of conversion—"it was as though the light of confidence flooded into my heart and *all* the darkness of doubt was dispelled" (8.12, 178; my emphasis); "we are made as one and regain that unity of self which we lost by falling apart in the search for a variety of pleasures" (10.29, 233)—still,

the tenth book shows him continuing to doubt and continuing to fall apart ("I have become a problem to myself" [10.16, 223]). Though conversion is billed, in book 8, as the definitive solution to our woes, in book 10 Augustine ends up conceding that "no one should be confident that although he has been able to pass from a worse state to a better, he may not also pass from a better state to a worse" (10.32, 238). In my own view (although I recognize it is not universally shared), Augustine's decision to continue his narrative beyond the moment of conversion throws a new, and uncertain, light upon the conversion itself—a conversion that no longer seems as total as it otherwise would have seemed.

48. "Jealousy is thus endless, for even if the beloved, by dying for instance, can no longer provoke it by her actions, it may happen that memories subsequent to any event suddenly materialise and behave in our minds as though they too were events, memories which hitherto we had never explored, which had seemed to us unimportant, and to which our own reflexion upon them is sufficient, without any external factors, to give a new and terrible meaning . . . the past . . . often comes to life for us only when the future has come and gone—and not only the past which we discover after the event but [even] the past which we have long kept stored within ourselves and suddenly learn how to interpret" (C 107). Cf. C 205: "sometimes our attention throws a different light upon things which we have known for a long time and we remark in them what we have never seen before."

49. "In real life, novels do not end" (*Carnet de 1908* [92]); cf. "the life of the writer does not come to an end with this particular work" (TR 311). It is true that there is an Augustinian atmosphere in the final pages of the *Recherche*, Marcel's epiphanic experience being followed by a (relative) removal from life (cf. SG 518, GW 428). Nonetheless, there also seems to be an awareness that the time of ultimate clarity never arrives, life being nothing but a sequence of errors (F 775).

50. For MacIntyre, each life allows for one and only one valid account—"what is better or worse for X depends on the character of *that intelligible narrative* which provides X's life with its unity" (1981: 209; my emphasis)—and hence, as he sees it, for a single (albeit complex) moral framework. While MacIntyre acknowledges that our lives may change dramatically (200), he does not draw what would seem to be an inevitable conclusion, namely that our *stories* may change too, and that the meaning of the individual actions they contain is not fixed for all time (by being defined, say, as the hierarchy of intentions responsible for each [193]) but is, on the contrary, liable to vary from one version to the next. There are, in fact, no a priori grounds for ascribing a set value to a particular course of behavior; *one can never know in advance what the significance of any given event will have been.*

Richard Shusterman articulates a critique similar to mine. "For any open series of narrative events," he writes, "given an indeterminate future in terms of which these events can be interpreted and also given the future revisability of past narrative interpretations, there will always be more than one narrative that can fit the facts of the individual" (184). And "if the self is constituted by narrative and there is no one true narrative, then there is no one true self" (185). (Needless to say, "true self" does not mean the same thing in Shusterman as in Proust.)

51. Cf. Shattuck 164–65. As Shattuck points out (152–60), Proust ultimately presents life as being in the service of art, rather than the other way around (for all that his narrator may reduce his own body, at TR 304, to the "seed" out of whose husk the masterwork will spring).

52. See Alexander Nehamas's *Nietzsche: Life as Literature* (esp. chap. 6, "How One Becomes What One Is"). Judging by Nehamas's account, Proust parallels Nietzsche in his analysis of the processes of self-discovery and self-creation, except that Proust would not grant the newly forged Self any measure of truth (174), whether or not it is acknowledged by outside observers (188). One finds a slightly different account of self-fashioning, though of equally Nietzschean inspiration, in Michel Foucault's *The Care of the Self.* In the case of Foucault, however, the turn to "the care of the self" marks a serious (and ultimately unaccounted-for) departure from earlier, strenuously anti-Sartrean denials of individual autonomy. It is thus not always clear what to make of the later works of Foucault in the context of his oeuvre as a whole (see Nehamas 1998: 157–88 for a critical but ultimately charitable reading).

53. "It was for herself that she obeyed these canons in accordance with which she dressed, as though yielding to a superior wisdom of which she herself was the high priestess" (BG 293).

54. Almost exactly, but not quite: Odette is, in the end, a failure, and Marcel's ultimate judgment on her (TR 488) is appropriately negative. Odette fails by giving style only to her *body*, not to her *character.* And Charlus fails, analogously, by focusing on his true Self (his inimitable, inextinguishable wit) to the exclusion of his total Self (if his identity disintegrates so spectacularly toward the end of the novel, this inattention may be partly to blame—though see Robert Pippin's "On 'Becoming Who One Is'" for an ingenious alternative explanation). Neither he nor Odette undertakes a project that could, if completed, give retrospective meaning to their existence; as I am about to suggest, and as Anderson argues in "Nietzsche on Truth, Illusion, and Redemption," such a project is indispensable to self-fashioning.

55. Marcel agrees entirely: "The link may be uninteresting, the objects trivial, the style bad, but unless this process has taken place the description is worthless [*tant qu'il n'y a pas eu cela, il n'y a rien*]" (TR 290).

Notice that Nietzsche speaks here of the "constraint of a single taste": contrary to what is often said in Nietzsche's name, and to what Nietzsche himself sometimes gives us to believe, there is room for a consistent ("essential") feature of personality, a motionless denizen of the mental deep, within his philosophy. "Learning changes us," he writes at BGE 231, "but at the bottom of us, really 'deep down,' there is, of course, something unteachable, some granite of spiritual *fatum,* of predetermined decision and answer to predetermined selected questions. Whenever a cardinal problem is at stake, there speaks an unchangeable 'this is I.'" Thus in the case of human individuals at least, a thing is *not* just the sum of its effects.

Similarly, Nietzsche may write, in an unpublished note, that "facts are what there are not" (WP 481), but *The Genealogy of Morals* (for one) relies heavily on a

distinction between facts and interpretations: "man's 'sinfulness' is . . . the interpretation of a fact, namely [the fact] of physiological depression" (GM III:17,129;
cf. III:7,107 and III:24,151). Facts, that is, are what there *are* in Nietzsche's of-
ficial philosophy. Since Duncan Large—who draws repeatedly on WP 481 (128,
175)—does not believe that either Proust or Nietzsche ultimately has room for
facts and essences of any kind (see e.g. 169), I must depart from his conclusions,
while concurring with his elegant statement of the problem (170).

56. The ideal of unity amid diversity is one to which Nietzsche strongly
subscribes—"this shall be called *greatness*: being capable of being as manifold as
whole, as ample as full" (BGE 212)—but one which, as Anderson has pointed out
(1998: 18), is by no means unique to him, being widely held by philosophers in
the German classicist tradition. Compare for example Leibniz's *Monadology* §58:
"Through this means has been obtained the greatest possible variety, together
with the greatest order that may be; that is to say, through this means has been obtained the greatest possible perfection."

57. On the future perfect in Proust, compare Robert Pippin: "with Proust, life
seems led in perpetual future perfect tenses and subjunctive moods. . . . Not, my
motive for X-ing now is M, given my current understanding of situation S. But, I
will have meant to X, because of what will have been M should the situation have
turned out S" (2000: 73). Duncan Large (chap. 5) presents a thorough discussion
of the future perfect in both Proust and Nietzsche, but here as elsewhere he takes
both to believe, rather recklessly, in the truth of their own projections.

58. "It seemed to me that in years to come, when we had forgotten one another
[*après que nous nous serions oubliés l'un l'autre*], when I should be able to look back
and tell her that this letter which I was now in the course of writing to her had not
been for one moment sincere, she would answer: 'What, you really did love me,
did you?'" (BG 260); "It was the reposeful tranquillity of such *forgetfulness* that
in anticipation I preferred" (BG 270). Cf. "I had sold a Chinese porcelain bowl in
order to buy her flowers. It had indeed, during the gloomy period that followed,
been my sole consolation to think that one day I should be able with impunity to
tell her of so tender an intention" (TR 7). Compare also Marcel's ruminations on
wartime *mores*: "our own age no doubt, when its history is read two thousand years
hence, *will seem . . . to have bathed* men of pure and tender conscience in a vital element which will strike the future reader as monstrously pernicious" (TR 213). My
emphasis throughout this note.

59. Other instances of *illusion volontaire* (II:681) dot the novel at regular intervals. In order to make it easier to forget about Gilberte, for instance, Marcel
pretends—without fully crediting it himself—that his withdrawal is temporary.
"I said to myself: 'This is the last time that I shall refuse an invitation to meet her;
I shall accept the next one.' To make our separation less difficult to realise, I did
not picture it to myself as final. But I knew very well that it would be" (BG 251).
Conversely, in order to maintain a feeling of control over his relationship with
Albertine, he tricks himself into believing that he can end it whenever he likes, in
spite of the fact that he knows, deep down, that he cannot: "in my heart of hearts,

when I said to myself: 'I shall leave her soon,' I knew that I would never leave her" (F 640).

And we have already seen, in chapter 2, how Marcel's two "hypotheses" allow him to enjoy, and yet also to distrust, the fantasy that Albertine's departure is merely a ruse designed to force a marriage. "'Yes, that's what she wanted, that was the purpose of her action,' my compassionate reason assured me; but I felt that, in doing so, my reason was still basing itself on the same hypothesis which it had adopted from the start. Whereas I was well aware [*je sentais bien*] that it was the other hypothesis which had invariably proved correct" (F 568).

60. In Proust, the second function is largely performed by intellect, the third by will and intuition. Thus the fact that (for instance) we are able to believe we desire a separation while also realizing we do not indicates, in Marcel's view, a discrepancy between the more sagacious *volonté* and the ever-hopeful *intelligence*. "It is true," he tells us (BG 596), "that something in me was aware of this role that beliefs play: namely, my will; but its knowledge is vain if one's intelligence and one's sensibility continue in ignorance; these last are sincere when they believe that we are anxious to forsake a mistress to whom our will alone knows that we are still attached." And a similar mechanism allows Marcel, or at least the part of him that thinks in language, to imagine that he can be a writer and also remain in society, in spite of the fact that a preverbal aspect of him recognizes the conflict: "I *told* myself this, but I was well aware [*je sentais bien*] that it was not true" (F 772).

More recent, "modular" approaches to brain functioning could equally be employed to account for the phenomenon of lucid self-delusion, as indeed could Freud's more rudimentary tripartite model. In Freud, the Ego is the part of the mind that tends to believe it speaks for the self as a whole; Id leads Ego astray on a regular basis; and as Freud suggests in his 1928 essay on "Humour," the Superego can at times occupy the position of passive, faintly amused spectator. When individuals do not achieve their desires, argues Freud, they simply laugh at them, compensating a blow to the narcissism of Ego with a triumph for that of Superego: "the humorous attitude" thus "consists in the subject's removing the accent from his own ego and transferring it onto his super-ego. To the super-ego . . . the ego can appear tiny and all its interests trivial" (218–19). Or as Nietzsche puts it at BGE 78, "whoever despises himself still respects himself as one who despises."

61. This is confirmed by the fact that the *oeuvre* already starts to change Marcel's life, dramatically restructuring his scale of values, *before he has recorded a single word of it*. Just as for Bergotte (BG 182) and Ruskin (BA 11), so too for Marcel writing immediately becomes a duty to which all others must be sacrificed (TR 436), being the very activity that makes his life worthwhile. His book itself is thus, in a certain sense, secondary to his self-understanding as a writer. It is a fortiori less important that the book be autobiographical: fiction (à la Bergotte) or even still-life painting (à la Elstir) would be just as effective, and would serve just as well (if not better) the subsidiary aim of communicating perspective.

62. While Elstir's "manner" changes, going through mythological, Japanese-influenced, realist, and impressionist phases (BG 565–66, GW 575–77), his pro-

ductions still continue to express a fundamental, unchanging personality. Thus for example a relatively lifelike painting of a waterside carnival and an impressionist painting of a hospital and a church both convey the same unconscious—indeed consciously *denied*—presupposition on Elstir's part that value is "all in the painter's eye" (GW 576). So too with Odette, "a vestimentiary personality peculiar to this woman . . . gave to the most dissimilar of her costumes a distinct family likeness" (BG 267); and so again Marcel's *tone* may vary across his memoir, as we shall see in the coda, but his *style* bespeaks a solid bedrock of immutable character. Like tone, perhaps, "manner" may map to one of many diachronic selves, while style always maps to the single true Self. (Alternatively, changes in manner may simply indicate a movement on the artist's part toward his "inner homeland [*patrie*]": see C 342.)

Coda

1. "La lecture n'est pas soutenable au-delà de cinq ou six pages"; "On peut mettre en fait qu'il ne se trouvera pas un lecteur assez robuste pour suivre un quart d'heure, d'autant [plus] que l'auteur n'y aide pas"; "Au bout des sept cent douze pages de ce manuscrit . . . après d'infinies désolations d'être noyé dans d'insondables développements et de crispantes impatiences de ne pouvoir jamais remonter à la surface—on n'a aucune, aucune notion de ce dont il s'agit. Qu'est-ce que tout cela vient faire? Qu'est-ce que tout cela signifie? Où tout cela veut-il mener?—Impossible d'en rien savoir! Impossible d'en pouvoir rien dire!" Normand wrote the review under his pseudonym, Jacques Madeleine.

2. One could, after all, allege that Odette is no more decorous when married than she was when single: consider the fact that Bloch brags of having savored the "delights of Eros" with her at BG 489 (cf. BG 52, and Steel 50).

3. "I remembered only long afterwards that it was upon that same sofa that, many years before, I had tasted for the first time the delights of love with one of my girl cousins" (BG 208).

4. "Paralipsis" is Genette's term (1980: 52, 205). The opening of *Le côté de Guermantes* provides a clear example: "The twittering of the birds at daybreak sounded insipid to Françoise. Every word uttered by the maids upstairs made her jump; disturbed by all their running about, she kept asking herself what they could be doing. *In other words, we had moved*" (GW 1; my emphasis). Compare S 215—"I formed the habit of going out by myself on such days, and walking towards Méséglise-la-Vineuse, during that autumn when we had to come to Combray to settle my aunt Léonie's estate; *for she had died at last*" (my emphasis)—and BG 728. See also Houston 38.

5. "It was not on that evening, however, that my cruel mistrust began to take solid form. No, *to reveal it here and now, although the incident did not occur until some weeks later*, it arose out of a remark made by Cottard" (SG 262; my emphasis).

6. The division of life into discrete phases (for which cf. Genette 1980: 142, 156) is palpable in the very first sentence, with its famous *passé composé*: "Long-

temps je *me suis couché* de bonne heure." Right from the start, that is, Proust's narrator presents his life as riven into at least two periods, one of early bedtimes (which must now be finished, given the verb tense) and one of late nights (which must still be ongoing).

7. "The first of these [snowy] days . . . marked a stage in the progress of my love, for it was like a first sorrow that we shared together" (S 566–67); "And there was another day when she said to me: 'You know, you may call me Gilberte.' In any case, I'm going to call you by your first name. It's too silly not to'" (S 573).

Colin Moore has suggested (pers. comm.) that the iterative scenes also reconfirm what, in the introduction, I referred to as Marcel's rage for generalization—his overwhelming tendency, that is, to take a single phenomenon as synecdochically representing an overall state of affairs, whether or not it actually does so. The periodic relapses into "singulative" style would, on this reading, serve the function of giving the game away.

8. "At the third or fourth repetition my intellect, having grasped . . . all the parts . . . , [had] projected and immobilised them on a uniform plane" (C 502; cf. S 295–96). Compare BSB 181: "Time has assumed a dimension of space."

For the simultaneous availability of memories, see Poulet 1963: 117–35, Genette 1980: 78, Bowie 1998: 63, and Terdiman 1976: 171. Terdiman may go a little far, however, in suggesting that information is similarly available to the *reader* all at once, so that there are no surprises in the novel. Thus, for example, he claims that in the early parts of the *Recherche* "everything is already present: the problem, the false solutions, the promise of a solution, the meaning of the solution" (124); yet the meaning of the solution is precisely what is missing from the madeleine episode, and what needs to be filled in at the *matinée Guermantes*. (Proust deliberately *removed* it, in fact, from early drafts of the madeleine episode: see I:700–701 for a crucial pair of clarifications, now to be found at TR 260 and 264–65.) Similarly, one might take issue with the claim that the "dramatic energy" of Charlus's expulsion from the Verdurin salon has been "systematically drained away" (104), since the single most important detail—whether or not Charlus will survive the plot against him—remains unknown to us.

9. "It is only for narrative convenience that I have frequently in these pages confronted one of Albertine's false statements with her previous assertion on the same subject. This previous assertion, as often as not, . . . had slipped past unperceived" (C 198). The prolepsis example comes from BG 579.

10. "If I were to write a novel," declares Proust in 1913, "I would try to capture the changing music of successive days [*différencier les musiques successives des jours*]" (*Chroniques* 107); of his own future novel, which I have been calling *The Magic Lantern*, Marcel notes, "I should have to execute the successive parts of my work in a succession of different materials" (TR 261; cf. GW 545).

11. "I have suggested hitherto the different aspects that the social world assumes in the eyes of a single person only by supposing that it does not change," writes Marcel at SG 192, "but there is more to it than that . . . even salons cannot be portrayed in a static immobility which has been conventionally employed up to

this point for the study of characters, though these too must be carried along as it were in a quasi-historical momentum." And "other people," he adds, "while they change in relation to ourselves, change also in themselves" (C 83).

12. "I was now well awake . . . the good angel of certainty had made all the surrounding objects stand still" (S 9); "scarcely had daylight . . . traced across the darkness . . . its first white, correcting ray, than the window, with its curtains, would leave the frame of the doorway in which I had erroneously placed it, while, to make room for it, the writing-table, which my memory had clumsily installed where the window ought to be, would hurry off at full speed" (S 263–64).

13. The "stout lady" is a case of what, in chapter 1, I called "pre-predication." (Other examples may be found at S 493, BG 259, C 254, TR 106–7, and TR 391.) For his part, Marcel refers to the device—which he finds in Dostoevsky and Mme de Sévigné—as a literary analogue of impressionism: "Mme de Sévigné, like Elstir, like Dostoievsky, instead of presenting things in their logical sequence, that is to say beginning with the cause, shows us first of all the effect, the illusion that strikes us" (C 510; cf. BG 315). Proust himself finds it also in Flaubert (EA 284–85); Picon quite reasonably adds Stendhal to the list (64).

14. "And so it was that, for a long time afterwards, when I lay awake at night and revived old memories of Combray, I saw no more of it than this sort of luminous panel" (S 58); "Thus it is . . . that I still see her again today, silhouetted against the screen which the sea spreads out behind her, and separated from me by . . . the interval of time that has elapsed since then—the first impression, faint and tenuous in my memory, desired, pursued, then forgotten, then recaptured, of a face which I have many times since projected upon the cloud of the past in order to be able to say to myself, of a girl who was actually in my room: 'It is she!'" (BG 558–59). Cf. Muller 40.

15. SG 191; my emphasis. Cf. "Let us for the moment simply say, *while Albertine waits for me at Saint-Jean de la Haise*, that if there was one thing which Morel set above the nobility . . . it was his artistic reputation" (SG 557–58; my emphasis). See also SG 31, 585, 648; C 279; TR 145.

16. By SG 187, "Gilberte's book-cover and her agate marble . . . were [now] to me a book-cover and a marble like any others."

17. "Another pair of strollers, half-stopping in their walk, would say to each other: 'You know who that is? Mme Swann! That conveys nothing to you? Odette de Crécy, then?' 'Odette de Crécy! Why, I thought as much. . . . I remember I slept with her on the day MacMahon resigned. . . . How pretty she was! She lived in a very odd little house with a lot of Chinese stuff. I remember we were bothered all the time by the newsboys shouting outside; in the end she made me get up and go.' *Without hearing these reflections*, I could feel all about her the indistinct murmur of fame" (S 597–98; my emphasis).

18. "We, *mankind*, have created this entire world which is of any concern to us [*diese ganze Welt, die uns wirklich etwas angeht*]" (WP 552). Compare also WP 616 ("The world *with which we are concerned* [*Die Welt, die* uns etwas angeht] is false")

and 556 ("The question 'what is that?' . . . At the bottom of it there always lies 'what is that for *me*?'").

19. Walton (48) notes that comparisons tend not to be reversible: it would make little sense, for example, for Romeo to tell the world that "the sun is Juliet." (At best, reversal yields a counterpart with its own distinct set of resonances; thus while a Platonist would presumably be happy hearing that artists are liars, "liars are artists" would be more likely to please the ears of a Nietzschean.) But this nonreversibility only holds, it seems to me, in cases where the aim is to shed light on an object or concept. Here, where what is at stake is a subjective organization of experience, it does not apply. Not only are young girls compared to flowers—as, most prominently, in the title of the second volume—but flowers, such as the hawthorns, are compared to young girls (S 156, S 197, BG 685; cf. Poulet 1968: 385–6, Bersani 1965: 28). Similarly, while Marcel's sadness is like that of Swann (S 39–40), Swann's is also like that of Marcel (S 422); and while a piece of agate resembles the beloved's eyes (S 572), the beloved's eyes also resemble "an opalescent agate cut and polished in two places" (BG 719).

20. For expansion at the level of plot, see Shattuck 130, Terdiman 1976: 181, and Schmid 67, 72. (The most dramatic instance of incompletion at this level is of course the substantial hiatus between TR 237 and TR 238—neither at the start, then, nor quite at the end of the novel.) For expansion within sentences, see Milly 190–91. Unlike Milly (10, 164, 167), however, and unlike Genette (1966: 62), I do not believe Proust's world proliferates wildly in all directions; instead, like the Japanese flower, its expansion is always limited by a metaphorical teacup.

21. "Pour Albertine, [2] grâce à une vie toute différente ensemble [3] et où n'avait pu se glisser, dans un bloc de pensées où une douloureuse préoccupation maintenait une cohésion permanente, aucune fissure de distraction et d'oubli, son corps vivant n'avait point, [1] comme celui de Gilberte, cessé un jour d'être celui où je trouvais ce que je reconnaissais [6] après coup être [4] pour moi ([5] et qui n'eût pas été pour d'autres) les attraits féminins" (IV:84).

22. For Zenonian elements in Proust, see the illuminating chapter in Goodkin (chap. 3, esp. p. 87).

23. "But it is perhaps crediting Morel's brain with too much logic to attempt to disentangle all these contradictions. His nature was really like a sheet of paper that has been folded so often in every direction that it is impossible to straighten it out" (SG 588–89).

24. "Noiselessly I opened the window and sat down on the foot of my bed" (S 42).

25. "A single feeling is often made up of contrary elements" (BG 253; cf. Bersani 1965: 88, Curtius 74–75, Pierre-Quint 133, Bowie 1987: 54, Shattuck 24, 30). One example: "Greatly to our astonishment, when Brichot told her how sorry he was to learn that her dear friend [the Princess Sherbatoff] was so seriously ill, Mme Verdurin replied: 'You know, I'm bound to confess that I feel no regret at all. It's no use feigning emotions one doesn't feel . . .' No doubt she spoke thus [1] from want of energy, because she shrank from the idea of wearing a long face

throughout her reception; [2] from pride, in order not to appear to be seeking excuses for not having cancelled it; yet also [3] from fear of what people might think of her and [4] from social shrewdness, because [a] the absence of grief which she displayed was more honourable if it could be attributed to a particular antipathy, suddenly revealed, for the Princess, rather than to a general insensitivity, and because [b] her hearers could not fail to be disarmed by a sincerity as to which there could be no doubt" (C 317).

26. "We make little use of our experience, we leave unfulfilled on long summer evenings or premature winter nights the hours in which it had seemed to us that there might nevertheless be contained some element of peace or pleasure. But those hours are not altogether wasted [*perdues*]. When new moments of pleasure call to us in their turn, moments which would pass by in the same way, equally bare and one-dimensional, the others recur, bringing them the groundwork, the solid consistency of a rich orchestration" (GW 543).

27. Proust learns from Chardin the art of seeing everyday reality as a still life (EA 70); Marcel learns the same art from Elstir (see chapter 1 here), and a different one from Renoir (GW 445). Presumably, we ourselves are supposed, by the end of our reading experience, to be able to borrow Proust's perspective in a comparable way.

28. Brian Rogers belongs in the first category: "the passage from one association to another depends upon the *author's* individual personality. . . . This individual world is shown as it is remembered by the *narrator*, sensitive to the associations it had for him" (1965: 170–71; my emphasis). Vincent Descombes, as we saw in chapter 1, belongs in the second.

29. It is not sufficient simply to say that "Proust's text . . . states in its form exactly what it states in its paraphrasable philosophical content" (Nussbaum 1990: 7). To be sure, "form" does, at times, recapitulate "content" (one thinks of sentence structure); but style can itself be an autonomous conveyor of worldview (as is the case with Marcel's metaphors), and can—as I am about to show—serve purposes entirely unrelated to the transmission of ideas or attitudes.

30. The same goes, of course, for any number of other characters in the novel, each with his or her own idiosyncratic linguistic proclivity. (See the brilliant analysis throughout Genette 1969.) Vincent Descombes writes, we recall, that "If we believed in the perspectivism of Proust's own doctrine, we could look for as many perspectives as there are characters in the novel. There would be the narrator's point of view, the point of view of Charlus, the point of view of Mme Verdurin, and so on" (209). One can only respond that this is exactly what we *do* find.

31. Proust clearly believes in the existence of fictional-world-specific laws. If, in a painting by Gustave Moreau, a poet finds himself followed by a bird, that conjunction obeys "laws different from the laws of our world"; similarly, "this flower grows in this valley near this woman *because this woman is going to die*" (EA 365; my emphasis).

32. As we saw in the introduction, the principle of irony—the fact that any attempt to achieve a certain result will necessarily end up thwarting it, so that if

we do eventually reach our goal, it has ceased to be of interest to us—finds itself periodically suspended; this suspension, while temporarily cheering, is in the long run a source of even greater despair.

33. Certain critics (including Descombes 41–42, Raimond 336, and Weitz 86) take the omniscience of one narrator to be evidence that Proust does not really believe in the inaccessibility of other minds: while Proust *says* that we know nothing about our fellow humans, they argue, he *shows* us the precise workings of their thoughts, thus contradicting his stated belief. What Descombes and company overlook is the fact that they are reading a *fiction*, so that Proust is only demonstrating "access" to the thoughts of characters he has *invented*, rather than to real-life individuals of his acquaintance.

The objection might carry weight if Marcel, a character in the novel, were actually listening in on other characters' inner monologues: in that case Proust would, at least, be guilty of having created a fictional world in which person *A* can see into the soul of person *B*. But that is not what is going on. Instead the text performs startling gyrations to make it clear that the omniscient narrator is reporting information to which the character is not, and could never be, privy. ("Mlle Vinteuil *felt* the sting of her friend's sudden kiss. . . . And she murmured into Mlle Vinteuil's ear *something that I could not distinguish*" [S 228–30; my emphasis]). In fiction, the novel seems to suggest, we can enjoy the rare pleasure of (make-believedly) knowing other minds; in real life, we are thrown back on calculation, hearsay, and hypothesis.

34. EA 110. Proust is writing here from a reader's position, but the same would quite possibly go for the experience of *creating* a fictional world.

35. As I mentioned in the introduction, Vincent Descombes views the selection of the Bildungsroman genre as itself pregnant with philosophical implications, suggesting that in Proust's opinion knowledge is acquired gradually, "beginning with illusions, with beliefs that are rectified little by little" (80). Perhaps we, too, are meant to *work* for our enlightenment, rather than, as Baudelaire would say, carrying off heaven in one go.

36. "Composers were warned not to strain the attention of their audience, as though we had not at our disposal different degrees of attention, among which it rests precisely with the artist himself to arouse the highest" (SG 290). Compare the "different states and impressions which my consciousness would simultaneously unfold while I was reading" (S 115). On sentences requiring us to focus on various ideas at once, see Bowie 1998: 35; on the *dressage des facultés*, see Deleuze 129.

BIBLIOGRAPHY

Anderson, R. Lanier. 1998. "Truth and Objectivity in Perspectivism." *Synthèse* 115: 1–32.

———. 1999. "Nietzsche's Views on Truth and the Kantian Background of His Epistemology." In *Nietzsche, Epistemology, and Philosophy of Science.* Ed. Babette E. Babich. Vol. 2 of *Nietzsche and the Sciences.* London: Kluwer. 47–59.

———. 2002. "Sensualism and Unconscious Representations in Nietzsche's Account of Knowledge." *International Studies in Philosophy* 34: 95–117.

———. n.d. "Nietzsche on Truth, Illusion, and Redemption." Unpublished manuscript.

Anderson, R. Lanier, and Joshua Landy. 2001. "Philosophy as Self-Fashioning: Alexander Nehamas's 'Art of Living.'" *Diacritics* 31: 25–54.

Augustine. 1961. *Confessions.* Trans. R. S. Pine-Coffin. London: Penguin.

Bakhtin, M. M. 1981. *The Dialogic Imagination.* Trans. Caryl Emerson and Michael Holquist. Austin: U of Texas P.

Bales, Richard. 1995. *Proust: A la recherche du temps perdu.* London: Grant and Cutler.

Barthes, Roland. 1972. "Proust et les noms." In *Le degré zéro de l'écriture.* Paris: Seuil. 121–34.

———. 1986. "An Idea of Research." Trans. Richard Howard. In *The Rustle of Language.* New York: Hill and Wang. 271–76.

———. 1986a. "Longtemps, je me suis couché de bonne heure . . ." Trans. Richard Howard. In *The Rustle of Language.* New York: Hill and Wang. 277–90.

Beckett, Samuel. 1965. *Proust / Three Dialogues.* London: Calder.

Benjamin, Walter. 1968. "The Image of Proust." In *Illuminations.* Trans. Harry Zohn. New York: Schocken. 201–16.

———. 1999. *The Arcades Project.* Trans. Howard Eiland and Kevin McLaughlin. Cambridge: Harvard UP.

Bergson, Henri. 1944. *Creative Evolution.* Trans. Arthur Mitchell. New York: Modern Library.

Bersani, Leo. 1965. *Marcel Proust: The Fictions of Life and Art.* Oxford: Oxford UP.

———. 1989. "Death and Literary Authority." In *A New History of French Literature.* Ed. Denis Hollier. Cambridge: Harvard UP. 861–66.

Blanche, Jacques-Emile. 1921. *Propos de peintre, deuxième série: Dates.* Paris: Emile-Paul.

Blanchot, Maurice. 1959. *Le livre à venir.* Paris: Gallimard.

Borges, Jorge Luis. 1962. "Pierre Menard, Author of the *Quixote.*" Trans. Donald A. Yates and James E. Irby. In *Labyrinths: Selected Stories and Other Writings.* Ed. Donald A. Yates and James E. Irby. New York: New Directions. 36–44.

———. 1999. "John Wilkins' Analytical Language." Trans. Suzanne Jill Levine, Eliot Weinberger, and Esther Allen. In *Selected Non-Fictions.* Ed. Eliot Weinberger. New York: Penguin. 229–32.

Bowie, Malcolm. 1987. *Freud, Proust, and Lacan: Theory as Fiction.* Cambridge: Cambridge UP.

———. 1998. *Proust among the Stars.* London: Harper Collins.

Brée, Germaine. 1951. "New Trends in Proust Criticism." *Symposium* 5: 62–71.

———. 1969. *Du temps perdu au temps retrouvé: Introduction à l'oeuvre de Marcel Proust.* Paris: Belles Lettres.

Breton, André. 1985. *Manifestes du surréalisme.* Paris: Gallimard.

Carter, William. 2000. *Marcel Proust: A Life.* New Haven: Yale UP.

Céline, Louis-Ferdinand. 1983. *Journey to the End of the Night.* Trans. Ralph Manheim. New York: New Directions.

Cervantes Saavedra, Miguel de. 1885. *The Ingenious Gentleman Don Quixote of La Mancha.* Trans. John Ormsby. New York: Macmillan.

Chabot, J., and P. Michaudon. 1992. "Les clochers de Martinville." *L'information littéraire* 44.2: 32–39.

Champigny, Robert. 1958. "Temps et reconnaissance chez Proust et quelques philosophes." *PMLA* 73: 129–35.

Chessick, Richard. 1987. "The Search for the Authentic Self in Bergson and Proust." In *Psychoanalytic Approaches to Literature and Film.* Ed. Maurice Charney and Joseph Reppen. London: Associated UP. 19–36.

Cohen, Ted. 1998. "On Consistency in One's Personal Aesthetics." In *Aesthetics and Ethics: Essays at the Intersection.* Ed. Jerrold Levinson. Cambridge: Cambridge UP. 106–25.

Cohn, Dorrit. 1999. "Proust's Generic Ambiguity." In *The Distinction of Fiction.* Baltimore: Johns Hopkins UP. 58–78.

Compagnon, Antoine. 1989. *Proust entre deux siècles.* Paris: Seuil.

———. 1997. "La dernière victime du narrateur." *Critique* 598: 131–46.

Cooper, John. 1996. "Reason, Moral Virtue, and Moral Value." In *Rationality in Greek Thought.* Ed. Michael Frede and Gisela Striker. Oxford: Clarendon. 81–114.

Curtius, Ernst Robert. 1928 [1925]. *Marcel Proust.* Trans. Armand Pierhal. Paris: Revue nouvelle.

Dancy, Jonathan. 1995. "New Truths in Proust?" *Modern Language Review* 90: 18–28.

Danto, Arthur. 1965. *Nietzsche as Philosopher*. New York: Macmillan.

———. 1981. *The Transfiguration of the Commonplace*. Cambridge: Harvard UP.

de Botton, Alain. 1997. *How Proust Can Change Your Life*. New York: Vintage.

de Lattre, Alain. 1978–85. *La doctrine de la réalité chez Proust*. 3 vols. Paris: José Corti.

Deleuze, Gilles. 1972. *Proust and Signs*. Trans. Richard Howard. New York: George Braziller.

de Man, Paul. 1979. *Allegories of Reading: Figural Language in Rousseau, Nietzsche, Rilke, and Proust*. New Haven: Yale UP.

de Souza, Sybil. 1939. *La philosophie de Marcel Proust*. Paris: Rieder.

Descombes, Vincent. 1992. *Proust: Philosophy of the Novel*. Trans. Catherine Chance Macksey. Stanford: Stanford UP.

du Bos, Charles. 1922 [Jan.–Mar. 1921]. "Marcel Proust." In *Approximations*, vol. 1. Paris: Plon. 58–115.

Duchêne, Roger. 1994. *L'impossible Marcel Proust*. Paris: Laffont.

Ellison, David R. 1984. *The Reading of Proust*. Baltimore: Johns Hopkins UP.

Erasmus, Desiderius. 1992. *Collected Works of Erasmus*. Trans. James F. Brady and John C. Olin. Toronto: U of Toronto P.

Finch, Alison. 2001. "Love, Sexuality, and Friendship." In *Cambridge Companion to Proust*. Ed. Richard Bales. Cambridge: Cambridge UP. 168–82.

Flaubert, Gustave. 1922. *Sentimental Education: The Story of a Young Man*. Trans. Dora Knowles Ranous. New York: Brentano's.

Foucault, Michel. 1986. *The Care of the Self*. Trans. Robert Hurley. New York: Random House.

Fraisse, Luc. 1995. *L'esthétique de Marcel Proust*. Paris: SEDES.

Frank, Joseph. 1963. "Spatial Form in Modern Literature." *The Widening Gyre*. New Brunswick: Rutgers UP. 3–61.

Freud, Sigmund. 1953 [1900–1901]. "On Dreams." Trans. James Strachey. In *The Complete Psychological Works of Sigmund Freud*. Vol. 5. London: Hogarth. 633–86.

———. 1953 [1928]. "Humour." Trans. Joan Riviere. In *The Complete Psychological Works of Sigmund Freud*. Vol. 5. London: Hogarth. 215–21.

———. 1957 [1914]. "On Narcissism: An Introduction." Trans. C. M. Baines. In *The Complete Psychological Works of Sigmund Freud*. Vol. 14. London: Hogarth. 73–102.

———. 1961 [1920]. *Beyond the Pleasure Principle*. Trans. James Strachey. New York: Norton.

———. 1983 [1900]. *The Interpretation of Dreams*. Trans. James Strachey. London: Penguin.

———. 1989 [1923]. *The Ego and the Id*. Trans. Joan Riviere. New York: Norton.

Genette, Gérard. 1966. "Proust palimpseste." In *Figures*, vol. 1. Paris: Seuil. 39–67.

————. 1969. *Figures*, vol. 2. Paris: Seuil.

————. 1972. *Figures*, vol. 3. Paris: Seuil.

————. 1980. *Narrative Discourse: An Essay in Method*. Trans. Jane E. Lewin. Ithaca, NY: Cornell UP.

Gide, André. 1951. *Journal*. Paris: Gallimard.

Girard, René. 1965. *Deceit, Desire, and the Novel: Self and Other in Literary Structure*. Trans. Yvonne Freccero. Baltimore: Johns Hopkins UP.

Goodkin, Richard. 1991. *Around Proust*. Princeton, NJ: Princeton UP.

Grimaldi, Nicolas. 1993. *La jalousie: Etude sur l'imaginaire proustien*. Arles: Actes Sud.

Gross, David. 1985. "Bergson, Proust, and the Revaluation of Memory." *International Philosophical Quarterly* 25: 369–80.

Gumbrecht, Hans Ulrich. 1986. "Schwindende Stabilität der Wirklichkeit: Eine Geschichte des Stilbegriffs." *Stil: Geschichten und Funktionen eines Kulturwissenschaftlichen Diskurselements*. Ed. Hans Ulrich Gumbrecht and K. Ludwig Pfeiffer. Frankfurt: Suhrkamp.

Hayman, Ronald. 1990. *Proust: A Biography*. New York: Harper Collins.

Henry, Anne. 1981. *Marcel Proust: Théories pour une esthétique*. Paris: Klincksieck.

————. 1989. "Proust du côté de Schopenhauer." In *Schopenhauer et la création littéraire en Europe*. Ed. Anne Henry. Paris: Klincksieck. 149–64.

————. 2000. *La tentation de Marcel Proust*. Paris: PUF.

Homer. 1951. *The Iliad of Homer*. Trans. Richmond Lattimore. Chicago: U of Chicago P.

Houston, J. P. 1962. "Temporal Patterns in *A la recherche du temps perdu*." *French Studies* 16: 33–47.

Hume, David. 1960 [1740]. *A Treatise of Human Nature*. Oxford: Clarendon.

Jauss, Hans Robert. 1986. *Zeit und Erinnerung in Marcel Prousts "A la recherche du temps perdu."* Frankfurt: Suhrkamp.

Jones, Peter. 1975. *Philosophy and the Novel: Philosophical Aspects of "Middlemarch," "Anna Karenina," "The Brothers Karamazov," "A la recherche du temps perdu," and of the Methods of Criticism*. Oxford: Oxford UP.

Joyce, James. 1990. *Ulysses*. New York: Vintage.

Kant, Immanuel. 1997. *Critique of Pure Reason*. Trans. Paul Guyer and Allen W. Wood. Cambridge: Cambridge UP.

Knight, Everett W. 1962. *Literature Considered as Philosophy: The French Example*. New York: Collier.

Ladenson, Elisabeth. 1999. *Proust's Lesbianism*. Ithaca, NY: Cornell UP.

Lakoff, George, and Mark Johnson. 2003. *Metaphors We Live By*. Chicago: U of Chicago P.

Larcher, P.-L. 1971. *Le parfum de Combray: Pèlerinage proustien à Illiers*. Illiers: Illiers.

Large, Duncan. 2001. *Nietzsche and Proust: A Comparative Study*. Oxford: Oxford UP.

La Rochefoucauld, François duc de. 1959. *Maxims*. Trans. Leonard Tancock. London: Penguin.

Lavagetto, Mario. 1996. *Chambre 43: Un lapsus de Proust*. Trans. Adrien Pasquali. Paris: Belin.

Leibniz, Gottfried Wilhelm. 1992. *Discourse on Metaphysics and the Monadology*. Trans. George R. Montgomery. Buffalo: Prometheus.

Lejeune, Philippe. 1989. *On Autobiography*. Trans. Katherine Leary. Minneapolis: U of Minnesota P.

Levin, Harry. 1950. "Proust, Gide, and the Sexes." *PMLA* 65: 648–52.

Lloyd, Rosemary. 1995. *Closer and Closer Apart: Jealousy in Literature*. Ithaca, NY: Cornell UP.

Locke, John. 1997 [1690]. *An Essay Concerning Human Understanding*. London: Penguin.

Luckhurst, Nicola. 2000. *Science and Structure in Proust's "A la recherche du temps perdu."* Oxford: Oxford UP.

Maar, Michael. 1997. *Die Feuer- und die Wasserprobe: Essays zur Literatur*. Frankfurt: Suhrkamp.

———. 2001. "The Sins of Padua: Proust Meets Mme Putbus's Maid." *New Left Review* 10 (July–Aug.): 133–39.

MacIntyre, Alasdair. 1980. "Epistemological Crises, Dramatic Narrative, and the Philosophy of Science." In *Paradigms and Revolutions: Appraisals and Applications of Thomas Kuhn's Philosophy of Science*. Ed. Gary Gutting. Notre Dame, IN: U of Notre Dame P. 54–74.

———. 1981. *After Virtue: A Study in Moral Theory*. London: Duckworth.

Macksey, Richard. 1977. "The Architecture of Time: Dialectics and Structure." In *Proust: A Collection of Critical Essays*. Ed. René Girard. Westport, CT: Greenwood. 104–21.

Madeleine, Jacques [Jacques Normand]. 1971 [1912]. "En somme, qu'est-ce?" In *Les critiques de notre temps et Proust*. Ed. Jacques Bersani. Paris: Garnier. 13–20.

Martin-Chauffier, Louis. 1943. "Proust et le double 'je' de quatre personnes." *Confluences* 21: 55–69.

Maurois, André. 1949. *A la recherche de Marcel Proust*. Paris: Hachette.

May, Derwent. 1983. *Proust*. Oxford: Oxford UP.

Milly, Jean. 1975. *La phrase de Proust: Des phrases de Bergotte aux phrases de Vinteuil*. Paris: Larousse.

Moran, Richard. 1989. "Seeing and Believing: Metaphor, Image, and Force." *Critical Inquiry* 16: 87–112.

Moss, Howard. 1962. *The Magic Lantern of Marcel Proust*. New York: Macmillan.

Muller, Marcel. 1965. *Les voix narratives dans la "Recherche du temps perdu."* Geneva: Droz.

Musset, Alfred de. 1973 [1830]. *La confession d'un enfant du siècle*. Paris: Gallimard.

Nabokov, Vladimir. 1997. *Lolita*. New York: Vintage.

Nehamas, Alexander. 1981. "The Postulated Author: Critical Monism as a Regulative Ideal." *Critical Inquiry* 8: 133–49.

———. 1985. *Nietzsche: Life as Literature.* Cambridge: Harvard UP.

———. 1987. "Writer, Text, Work, Author." In *Literature and the Question of Philosophy.* Ed. Anthony J. Cascardi. Baltimore: Johns Hopkins UP. 265–91.

———. 1998. *The Art of Living: Socratic Reflections from Plato to Foucault.* Berkeley: U of California P.

Newman, Pauline. 1952. *Marcel Proust et l'existentialisme.* Paris: Nouvelles Editions Latines.

Nietzsche, Friedrich. 1903. *Nietzsche's Werke.* Leipzig: Naumann.

———. 1966 [1886]. *Beyond Good and Evil.* Trans. Walter Kaufmann. New York: Random House.

———. 1967. *The Birth of Tragedy.* Trans. Walter Kaufmann. New York: Vintage.

———. 1967a. *The Will to Power.* Trans. Walter Kaufmann and R. J. Hollingdale. New York: Random House.

———. 1969 [1888]. *The Genealogy of Morals / Ecce Homo.* Trans. Walter Kaufmann. New York: Random House.

———. 1974 [1882–87]. *The Gay Science.* Trans. Walter Kaufmann. New York: Random House.

———. 1979 [1872–73]. "On Truth and Lies in a Nonmoral Sense." Trans. Daniel Breazeale. In *Philosophy and Truth: Selections from Nietzsche's Notebooks of the Early 1870's.* Ed. Daniel Breazeale. Atlantic Highlands, NJ: Humanities. 79–97.

———. 1983 [1873]. "David Strauss, the Confessor and Writer." Trans. R. J. Hollingdale. In *Untimely Meditations.* Cambridge: Cambridge UP: 1–55.

———. 1983 [1874]. "On the Uses and Disadvantages of History for Life." In *Untimely Meditations.* Ed. R. J. Hollingdale. Cambridge: Cambridge UP: 57–123.

———. 1990 [1888]. *Twilight of the Idols / The Antichrist.* Trans. R. J. Hollingdale. London: Penguin.

Nussbaum, Martha C. 1983. "Fictions of the Soul." *Philosophy and Literature* 7: 145–61.

———. 1990. *Love's Knowledge: Essays on Philosophy and Literature.* Oxford: Oxford UP.

O'Brien, Justin. 1948. *The Maxims of Marcel Proust.* New York: Columbia UP.

———. 1948a. "Marcel Proust as a *Moraliste.*" *Romanic Review* 39: 50–69.

———. 1949. "Albertine the Ambiguous: Notes on Proust's Transposition of Sexes." *PMLA* 64: 933–52.

———. 1950. "Proust, Gide, and the Sexes." *PMLA* 65: 653.

Painter, George D. 1989 [1959]. *Marcel Proust: A Biography.* 2 vols. London: Chatto and Windus.

Parfit, Derek. 1984. *Reasons and Persons.* Oxford: Oxford UP.

Pascal, Blaise. 1964. *Pensées.* Paris: Garnier.

Picon, Gaëtan. 1995 [1963]. *Lecture de Proust*. Paris: Gallimard.

Pierre-Quint, Léon. 1925. *Marcel Proust: Sa vie, son oeuvre*. Paris: Kra.

Pippin, Robert B. 2000. *Henry James and Modern Moral Life*. Cambridge: Cambridge UP.

———. Forthcoming. "On 'Becoming Who One Is' (and Failing): Proust's Problematic Selves." In *Philosophical Romanticism*. Ed. Nikolas Kompridis. London: Routledge.

Plato. 1989. *Symposium*. Trans. Alexander Nehamas and Paul Woodruff. Indianapolis: Hackett.

———. 1995. *Phaedrus*. Trans. Alexander Nehamas and Paul Woodruff. Indianapolis: Hackett.

———. 1996. *Parmenides*. Trans. Mary Louise Gill and Paul Ryan. Indianapolis: Hackett.

Poe, Edgar Allan. 1956. *Selected Writings of Edgar Allan Poe*. Ed. Edward H. Davidson. Cambridge, MA: Riverside.

Poellner, Peter. 1995. *Nietzsche and Metaphysics*. Oxford: Oxford UP.

———. 2001. "Perspectival Truth." *Nietzsche*. Ed. John Richardson and Brian Leiter. Oxford: Oxford UP. 85–117.

Poulet, Georges. 1952. *Etudes sur le temps humain*, vol. 1. Paris: Plon.

———. 1963. *L'espace proustien*. Paris: Gallimard.

———. 1968. "Marcel Proust." In *Mesure de l'instant*, vol. 4 of *Etudes sur le temps humain*. Paris: Plon. 299–335.

Proust, Marcel. 1927. *Chroniques*. Paris: Nouvelle Revue Française.

———. 1947. "Introduction." John Ruskin. *La Bible d'Amiens*. Trans. Marcel Proust. Paris: Mercure de France. 9–95.

———. 1949. *Letters of Marcel Proust*. Ed. and trans. Mina Curtiss. New York: Random House.

———. 1955. *Jean Santeuil*. Trans. Gerard Hopkins. London: Weidenfeld and Nicolson.

———. 1970–93. *Correspondance*. Ed. Philip Kolb. 21 vols. Paris: Plon.

———. 1971. *Contre Sainte-Beuve*. Paris: Gallimard.

———. 1976. *Le carnet de 1908*. Paris: Gallimard.

———. 1982. *Matinée chez la Princesse de Guermantes: Cahiers du "Temps retrouvé."* Paris: Gallimard.

———. 1984. *By Way of Sainte-Beuve*. Trans. Sylvia Townsend Warner. London: Hogarth.

———. 1987–88. *A la recherche du temps perdu*. Paris: Gallimard.

———. 1992. *In Search of Lost Time*. Trans. C. K. Scott Moncrieff, Terence Kilmartin, and D. J. Enright. London: Chatto and Windus.

———. 1994. *Essais et articles*. Paris: Gallimard.

———. 1997. *Pastiches et mélanges*. Paris: Gallimard.

Raimond, Michel. 1966. *La crise du roman*. Paris: José Corti.

Rawlinson, Mary Crenshaw. 1982. "Art and Truth: Reading Proust." *Philosophy and Literature* 6: 1–16.

Richards, I. A. 1965. *The Philosophy of Rhetoric.* New York: Oxford UP.

Ricoeur, Paul. 1992. *Oneself as Another.* Trans. Kathleen Blamey. Chicago: U of Chicago P.

Robinson, Jenefer M. 1985. "Style and Personality in the Literary Work." *Philosophical Review* 44.2: 227–47.

Rogers, Brian. 1965. *Proust's Narrative Techniques.* Geneva: Droz.

———. 2001. "Proust's Narrator." In *Cambridge Companion to Proust.* Ed. Richard Bales. Cambridge: Cambridge UP. 85–99.

Rorty, Richard. 1982. *Consequences of Pragmatism.* Minneapolis: U of Minnesota P.

———. 1989. *Contingency, Irony, and Solidarity.* Cambridge: Cambridge UP.

———. 1991. *Essays on Heidegger and Others.* Vol. 2 of *Philosophical Papers.* Cambridge: Cambridge UP.

———. 1991a. "Nietzsche, Socrates, and Pragmatism." *South African Journal of Philosophy* 10.3: 61–63.

———. 1998. *Truth and Progress.* Vol. 3 of *Philosophical Papers.* Cambridge: Cambridge UP.

Rousset, Jean. 1995. *Forme et signification: Essai sur les structures littéraires de Corneille à Claudel.* Paris: José Corti.

Sartre, Jean-Paul. 1948. *Qu'est-ce que la littérature?* Vol. 2 of *Situations.* Paris: Gallimard.

———. 1965. *Nausea.* Trans. Robert Baldick. London: Penguin.

Schmid, Marion. 2001. "The Birth and Development of *A la recherche du temps perdu.*" *Cambridge Companion to Proust.* Ed. Richard Bales. Cambridge: Cambridge UP. 58–73.

Schopenhauer, Arthur. 1958. *The World as Will and Representation.* Trans. E. F. J. Payne. New York: Dover.

Sedgwick, Eve Kosofsky. 1990. *Epistemology of the Closet.* Berkeley: U of California P.

Shattuck, Roger. 1982. *Marcel Proust.* Princeton, NJ: Princeton UP.

Shusterman, Richard. 1997. *Practicing Philosophy: Pragmatism and the Philosophical Life.* New York: Routledge.

Spitzer, Leo. 1970. "Le style de Marcel Proust." Trans. Alain Coulon, Eliane Kaufholz, and Michel Foucault. In *Etudes de style.* Paris: Gallimard. 397–473.

Steel, Gareth H. 1979. *Chronology and Time in "A la recherche du temps perdu."* Geneva: Droz.

Suzuki, Michihiko. 1959. "Le 'je' proustien." *Bulletin de la Société des amis de Marcel Proust* 9: 69–82.

Tadié, Jean-Yves. 1971. *Proust et le roman.* Paris: Gallimard.

———. 1996. *Marcel Proust: Biographie.* Paris: Gallimard

Terdiman, Richard. 1976. *The Dialectics of Isolation: Self and Society in the French Novel from the Realists to Proust.* New Haven, CT: Yale UP.

———. 1993. *Present Past: Modernity and the Memory Crisis.* Ithaca, NY: Cornell UP.

Walton, Kendall L. 1993. "Metaphor and Prop Oriented Make-Believe." *European Journal of Philosophy* 1.1: 39–56.

Warning, Rainer. 1996. "Ecrire sans fin: La *Recherche* à la lumière de la critique textuelle." In *Proust: Ecrire sans fin*. Ed. Rainer Warning and Jean Milly. Paris: CNRS. 13–32.

Wassenaar, Ingrid. 2000. *Proustian Passions: The Uses of Self-Justification for "A la recherche du temps perdu."* Oxford: Oxford UP.

Waters, Harold A. 1960. "The Narrator, Not Marcel." *French Review* 33: 389–92.

Webb, Heather. "The Lesbian Lacuna in Proust's *A la recherche du temps perdu*." Unpublished manuscript.

Weitz, Morris. 1963. *Philosophy in Literature: Shakespeare, Voltaire, Tolstoy, and Proust*. Detroit: Wayne State UP.

White, Edmund. 1999. *Marcel Proust*. New York: Penguin.

Wimmers, Inge Karalus Crosman. 1978. *Metaphoric Narration: The Structure and Function of Metaphors in "A la recherche du temps perdu."* Chapel Hill: U of North Carolina P.

Wolitz, Seth L. 1971. *The Proustian Community*. New York: NYU P.

Yacobi, Tamar. 1987. "Narrative Structure and Fictional Mediation." *Poetics Today* 8: 335–72.

INDEX